Combat Operations
of the Korean War

ALSO BY PAUL M. EDWARDS

Small United States and United Nations
Warships in the Korean War
(McFarland, 2008)

The Hill Wars of the Korean Conflict: A Dictionary
of Hills, Outposts and Other Sites of Military Action
(McFarland, 2006)

Combat Operations of the Korean War

Ground, Air, Sea,
Special and Covert

PAUL M. EDWARDS

McFarland & Company, Inc., Publishers
Jefferson, North Carolina, and London

To Dr. E. Wayne Chandler,
long time friend and associate,
to whom much is owed

LIBRARY OF CONGRESS CATALOGUING-IN-PUBLICATION DATA

Edwards, Paul M.
Combat operations of the Korean War : ground, air, sea, special
and covert / Paul M. Edwards.
p.   cm.
Includes bibliographical references and index.

ISBN 978-0-7864-4436-6
softcover : 50# alkaline paper ∞

1. Korean War, 1950–1953 — Campaigns — Encyclopedias.   I. Title.
DS918.E354   2010   951.904′24 — dc22   2009038646

British Library cataloguing data are available

On the cover: Operation Highboy, set up for direct fire into enemy bunkers,
January, 1952; fire and smoke ©2009 Shutterstock

Manufactured in the United States of America

*McFarland & Company, Inc., Publishers
Box 611, Jefferson, North Carolina 28640
www.mcfarlandpub.com*

Table of Contents

Acknowledgments

Many persons are involved in the production of a book, not the least of which are the many who actually turn the manuscript into a finished product. These men and women in the editorial departments, proof readers, copy readers, as well as production workers, and the like, are highly significant and rarely recognized.

In terms of source materials, first thanks must go to the hundreds of historians who have written monographs dealing with many of these operations, and in doing so have collected materials, often difficult to locate, that allowed this compilation to be accomplished. There is also a large collection of highly useful but generally unknown information to be found among the personal memoirs published by individuals through independent presses. Unfortunately, these works rarely have wide distribution, though the memories reported are invaluable. The Center for the Study of the Korean War has collected a large number of these volumes, and I wish to express appreciation to the director, Gregg Edwards, and staff of the center, located on the Independence, Missouri campus of Graceland University. As well, credit must be given to other libraries and institutions that have been so helpful: the librarians at the Frederick Madison Smith Library, Graceland University, Independence Campus; the most helpful staff at the Modern Military History Headquarters Branch at the main building of the National Archives on Pennsylvania Avenue in Washington, D.C., and the National Records Center in the Federal Building on Suitland Road, Maryland; also, recognition is given to director Mike Divine and his staff at the Harry S Truman Museum and Library in Independence; the Central Plains Region National Archives and Records Administration; the Allied Forces Command and Staff College Library at Fort Leavenworth, Leavenworth, Kansas, and the very helpful staff at the Chester Nimitz Library at the Naval Academy in Annapolis, Maryland.

Several secondary works need to be mentioned, as they were invaluable: Gordon L. Rottman, *Korean War Order of Battle*, makes any research into the Korean War much easier; Lynn Montross, Hubard Kuokka, and Norman Hicks' five volume *U.S. Marine Operations in Korea;* Walter G. Hermes, *Truce Ten and Fighting Front;* Roy E. Appleman, *South to the Naktong, North to the Yalu* and *Escaping the Trap;* and Billy C. Mossman, *Ebb and Flow: November 1950–July 1951* are all highly significant. Also very helpful have been Donald Knox, *The Korean War: Uncertain Victory;* Lee Ballenger, *The Outpost War;* Charles Whiting, *Battleground Korea: The British in Korea;* Ted Barris, *Deadlock in Korea: Canadian at War 1950–1953;* T. R. Fehrenbach, *This Kind of War* (2000 edition); James I. Matray, *Historical Dictionary of the Korean War;* Paul M. Edwards, *Korean War Almanac;* James F. Schnabel and Robert J. Watson, *The History of the Joint Chiefs of Staff, The Joint Chiefs of*

Staff and National Policy, vol. 3, *The Korean War*, parts 1 and 2, 1978–79; and Edward Marolda (ed.), *The U.S. Navy in the Korean War*.

Special acknowledgment should be made to Paul Wolfgeher of Independence, Missouri. A Korean veteran assigned to the 1st Loud-speaker and Leaflet Company during the war, Wolfgeher owns the largest collection of Psy-War propaganda leaflets in the country, as well as being a compiler of vast amounts of war related information. Much of his material has been donated to the Center for the Study of the Korean War and has been a significant help in compiling this work.

Unfortunately, neither the Democratic People's Republic of Korea nor the People's Republic of China has allowed much access to their archives and we must acknowledge that if, and when, these facilities are opened, some of our understanding about these events will change dramatically. Acknowledgement must be made to the Woodrow Wilson Institute, and particularly the work of Kathryn Weathersby, whose translations of Soviet documents has been most significant in understanding a little of the Communist side of the story.

While this information is still limited, their preliminary insights have been most helpful.

The illustrations used are all from the collections at the Center for the Study of the Korean War and are used with their permission. Nevertheless, acknowledgement should be made, and appreciation offered, to those wonderful donors who over the years have placed these photographs with the center, thus making them available for uses such as this. While some photographs are released from the United States Army photographers, most used were taken in the field by the average GI with what was generally no more than a box camera.

In a more personal sense I wish to extend my thanks to Gregg Edwards, Paula Tennant, Greg Smith, Nancy Eisler, Tim Rives, Darian Cobb, Mark Corriston, and Cindy Easter for the contributions they have made. And to Graceland University for support in this effort. And, as always, to my wife, Carolynn Jean, my deepest appreciation for letting me go on (and on) and for providing love and comfort. And, of course, to Bailey asleep on the desk.

Abbreviations and Key Words

A	Airfields in proximity to U.S. Army installations
AAA	Antiaircraft artillery
aka	Also known as
AM	Fleet minesweeper
APA	Attack transport ship
BAR	Browning automatic rifle
BB	Battleship
BCFK	British Commonwealth Forces Korea
CA	Heavy cruiser
CCF	Chinese Communist Forces
CCRAK	Combined Command for Reconnaissance Activities, Korea
CIA	Central Intelligence Agency
CincFE	Commander in chief, Far East Command
CincPac	Commander in chief, Pacific
CincPacFleet	Commander in chief, Pacific Fleet
CincUNC	Commander in chief, United Nations Command
CL	Light cruiser
CNO	Chief of naval operations
ComNav FE	Commander of Naval Forces Far East
CPV	Chinese People's Volunteers
CV	Aircraft carrier
DD	Destroyer
Defilade	Protected by natural obstacles from enemy observation
DMZ	Demilitarized Zone
DSC	Distinguished Service Cross
DSO	Distinguished Service Order
DWC	Died while captured
EUSAK	Eighth U.S. Army in Korea
FA	Field artillery
FAFIK	Fifth Air Force in Korea
FEAF	Far East Air Force
FEC	Far East Command
GB	Great Britain
GPO	Government Printing Office
HMAS	His/Her Majesty's Australian Ships
HMCS	His/Her Majesty's Canadian Ships
HMNZS	His/Her Majesty's New Zealand Ships
HMR	Marine Corps Transport Helicopter Squadron
HMS	His/Her Majesty's Ships (Great Britain)
JACK	Joint Assistance Command, Korea
JCS	Joint Chiefs of Staff
JTF	Joint Task Force
K	Airfield designated as major installations
KATCOM	Korean Augmentation to the Commonwealth
KATUSA	Korean Augmentation to the U.S. Army
KIA	Killed in action
KMC	Korean Marine Corps
Knot	One nautical mile (6080.2 feet per hour)
KPA	Korean People's Army (North Korea)
KPN	Korean People's Navy (North Korea)

KSC	Korean Service Corps	RN	Royal Navy (British)
LSD	Landing Ship, Dock	RNZN	Royal New Zealand Navy
LSMR	Landing Ship, Medium Rocket	ROK	Republic of Korea
LST	Landing Ship, Tank	ROKA	Republic of Korea Army
LSU	Landing Ship, Utility	ROKAF	Republic of Korea Air Force
MAG	Marine Aircraft Group	ROKN	Republic of Korea Navy
MATS	Military Air Transport Service	Scajap	Shipping Control Administration Japan
MC	Military Cross		
MLR	Main line of resistance	SK	South Korea
MSR	Main supply route	SOD	Special operations
MSTS	Military Sea Transportation Service	TF	Task Force
		TG	Task Group
NAVFE	Naval Forces Far East (U.S.)	UK	United Kingdom
NK	North Korea	UN	United Nations
NKPA	North Korean People's Army	UNC	United Nations Command
OPLR	Outpost line of resistance	UNPFK	United Nations Partisan Forces, Korea
PLA	People's Liberation Army (Chinese)		
		UNPIK	United Nations Partisan Infantry, Korea
PLAAF	People's Liberation Army Air Force (Chinese)	USAF	United States Air Force
PLAN	People's Liberation Army Navy (Chinese)	USMC	United States Marine Corps
		USN	United States Navy
POW	Prisoner of war	USNS	United States Naval Ships
Psy-War	Psychological Warfare	USS	United States Ship
RAAF	Royal Australian Air Force	VT	Vicinity Time (Variable Time)
RAF	Royal Air Force	X	Airfield designated as auxiliary strip
RAN	Royal Australian Navy		
RCN	Royal Canadian Navy	ZI	Zone of Interior (meaning U.S.)
RCT	Regimental combat team		

Preface

It was a war that ended with a whimper not a bang.
John Toland

For the past several years, while working with Graceland University's Center for the Study of the Korean War in Independence, Missouri, I have had numerous occasions to talk with veterans who, lacking any major military event upon which to tie their service, recall their involvement in a specific operation. Sometimes the operation they remember was little more than the attack on an individual hill or the bombardment of a single bridge; other times it would mean the occupation or destruction of a fortification. The operation of which they speak might be as large and complex as one of the many multi-corps, joint services activities like Operation Killer, designed to change the course of the war. A large number, however, were fairly small and limited to geographically-local expectations. Some operations were conducted to accomplish a highly specific goal. Some were simply humanitarian.

As the years fade the memories of unit names and specific villages or map coordinates pass away, what many of these veterans remember is that their unit — their squad or platoon or company — was a part of an operation whose name recalls their service. In these cases they want to know where they were, or what units participated in the action or what had been the expectations of the operation in which they had been involved. Some were in-

terested in knowing if their operation had been successful, if it changed the course of the war, or if it made any difference at all.

It quickly became apparent that it was not as easy to locate this information as might have been expected. Significant gaps still exist in the research done on the Korean War. While there are excellent narrative histories now available, they are, by design, far more generalized and quite often lack any mention of these smaller operations. Even when the larger operations are identified, Operation Tomahawk or Chromite for example, little detailed information is provided. Smaller actions, Operation Kiddie Car or Operation Slam for example, are not mentioned at all. A second problem for the researcher is that by design most of the official service histories reflect only the reporting service's own participation. What is provided is a description of the involvement of the single service rather than the combined effort that actually occurred. Air Force histories, for example, mention a good many of these operations but only discuss the Air Force assignment, leaving one to assume much about the role of the Army, Navy, or Marine units that also participated.

So when one older veteran remembered that he had been involved in something called Operation Native Son Dog and wanted more information about it, I discovered that rather

1

expanded research was necessary. This particular operation — the movement of an early warning detachment of a Marine Ground Interceptor Squadron — was harder to locate than many. While these operations were significant to those individuals, and even of importance to the general war effort, narrative history has no room to reflect on them and they have been fading from the public memory. Over time it became apparent that it would be helpful, to provide an account of as many of these operations as could be located. While there were hundreds of operations, many have little historical recognition, some are totally undocumented, and a few appear to have been planned but not executed.

The Korean War was fought from 25 June 1950 until 27 July 1953. While these are considered the combat dates, there was military activity, including operations, going on in Korea both before and after. Prior to the North Korean invasion were numerous border disputes. After the armistice dates, combat activities of a limited nature continued for some time, though these are generally ignored by historians. The combat phase is usually defined with the above dates, though the Korean War Veterans Association recognizes the combat period as extending to January 1954. Known intermittently as the Korean Conflict, the forgotten war or as a police action, or even as Harry Truman's War, the fight in Korea was long, intense, and dirty. America's involvement, much like that of the other nations who participated in this the first of the United Nations actions, came as a surprise to the nation. America's immediate response to the outbreak of war was both reactionary and severely limited. Yet, as Americans have always done, men and women throughout the country answered the call and troops, ammunition and equipment quickly began to flow toward this far distant nation.

Most of the military leaders of the time had their skills honed on the battlefields of World War II, and to a large extent still thought in

those dimensions. The nation, long sick of war, had allowed its armed forces to dwindle, its production to decline, and its availability to be challenged. In less than five years the character of war had changed, and in this new war the United States was fighting a different kind of enemy in a much different place. These new events called for many adjustments, changes, tests and trials before any sort of victory could be carved out of the events. Notwithstanding, the United States, along with 16 other nations, met the challenge.

All of the services, even the Coast Guard, were involved. This was the first war in which the Air Force functioned as an independent service, having only been separated from the Army in 1947. Caught as they were between the conventional forces of World War II and the emergence of jet power and electronic intervention, they were neither equipped nor trained for what they found. The Navy, just coming out of a long conflict with the other services and the resulting "revolt of the admirals," was ill-prepared; its measure of available craft was not nearly enough to meet the increasing demands. The Marine Corps had been downsized to the point of potential nonexistence and required a massive recall of reservists to reform the 1st Marine Division. The Army, cut to a minimum and increasingly staffed with occupational forces, was short on experience, training, and equipment. The Coast Guard, restricted because the events in Korea were not "really a war," stood long watches in isolated positions in unaccustomed duty, making it safer for other men. Lacking a great deal of forethought, first American and then United Nations involvement was certainly a gamble and the outcome was not all that clear. On several occasions serious consideration was given to the idea of evacuating Korea, leaving it to the enemy, and removing American troops to Japan to make the necessary line of defense there. Yet, slowly, as men fought and died to provide the time needed, the resources of the United States and those of the United Nations began to flow into Korea and the trend of battle changed.

Many would argue that the course of action in Korea was never really clear, and that much of what lies behind the "forgotten" character of this war is the result of having failed to identify what was happening. It was not then, nor is it now, all that well understood; there were serious questions about whether the war was necessary, or what was at stake in the conflict. The missions and the goals were not well defined for the average fighting man, and the military leadership was limited, if not often stymied, by the shifting nature of the political winds. The problems within Korea were exaggerated by the increasing sense of indifference found among those outside of Korea, for there was not really any "home front" during this war. As the war settled down to a prolonged series of small unit affairs, acknowledgment of the events soon fell to the back page in news reporting. Because America had not gone on a war footing, and such a small percentage of her population was involved in the war compared to World War II, there was not even enough interest in what was happening to incur any significant opposition.

Nevertheless, the military mission was addressed, and to a large extent it was accomplished. The war, which was conducted in a series of campaigns, consisted of the daily routine of armies facing each other across a disputed field, and was colored by a series of specialized operations carried out by fine men, and occasionally women, who went when called and did what was asked and expected. When it was over most came home to pick up their lives where they had left off. Many thousands, of course, did not return.

The Korean War, pale in comparison to the massive efforts of World War II and overshadowed by the events in Vietnam, was a very expensive war both in terms of dollars and lives. It cost the world nearly six million lives. It was, as well, a watershed in American history and is the lens through which much of the 21st century military and political expectations must be understood. The irony of the Demilitarized Zone that divides these nations is that it is the most heavily militarized frontier in the world and remains so today after more than sixty years. If the war in Korea is forgotten, as some suggest, then it has been forgotten by those uninterested masses unaware of either the significance or the cost, for it most certainly has not been forgotten among those who fought it out on that difficult peninsula. This was a war too costly to forget.

Introduction

Many historians are inclined to think of the Korean War in two distinct phases, even going so far as to identify them as different wars. This bifurcation is strengthened by the often expressed belief that while the United Nations submitted to a cease-fire in the second phase, it clearly won the first one.

The first war, generally between the invasion in June 1950 and November 1950, was a mobile, quick, decisive, and costly war that was turned by the X Corps invasion of Inchon in September 1950 and Eighth Army's return to the 38th parallel. At this point the military had fulfilled the United Nations' assignment to expel the invading North Korean forces from South Korea. The war might well have stopped there and victory declared. But it did not. The second war would then be defined as beginning with the military and political decision to cross the 38th parallel and take the United Nations Command all the way to the Yalu River. In this case the goal was the total destruction of the North Korean Army and the unification of Korea. As it turned out, this second phase was to be much less a mobile war, and in fact was rather reminiscent of World War I, a hazardous, long-and-drawn-out static fight between two armies, neither of which was willing to invest enough to win, nor willing to lose.

From then on it is harder to define what happened. Perhaps no one has said it better than Bevin Alexander in *Korea: The First War We Lost;* Alexander suggests the case could be made that the Korean War in fact "ended when the peace talks started at Kaesong. Both the Chinese and the Americans had obtained what they had originally set out to get, and they were never to obtain anything more" (436). What followed was two years of doleful, almost inconceivable, battle that could scarcely be called a war, because it was pursued essentially without purpose. The cost in terms of men and materiel was immense.

Those not familiar with military history, or with military service, are sometimes inclined to think of war as one long, continuous battle running from beginning to end in which the entire military force available is involved. This is not the case. Wars are sporadic, they are usually fought in phases, often seen as campaigns, and their battles are primarily limited in time and separated by long periods taken up with stretches of boredom and tension. The Korean War was fought in such campaigns often identified with the seasons such as the Chinese Communist Forces Spring Offensive. However, running parallel with campaigns are much shorter, more closely defined, one-shot encounters termed operations. Generally these operations are named. The terms are not restrictive and sometimes operations are defined as operational plans, as well as the other way around. Some operations were so massive, as was Operation Killer, as to be better understood as a campaign. Some of the more significant operations were in place during much of the war, but are only referenced on those occasions when they cross the chronological narratives of other events. Others were more immediate and localized, lasting only a short period of time. In order to deal with this diversity, the selection of operations has been totally dependent on the military's reference to the event; if the military called it an operation it is included here.

What might be considered the first operation of the Korean War, though not listed as such, occurred on Sunday morning after Washington, D.C., received its flash concerning the North Korean attack on the Republic of (South) Korea. The time in the nation's capital was 14 hours earlier than it was in Seoul, Korea. General J. Lawton Collins, the Army chief of staff, along with Secretary of State Dean Acheson and others announced that with the approval of President Harry Truman, a protective air zone would be identified over Seoul and Kimpo airfield. This was necessary in order to speed the evacuation of American dependents. They also recommended that ammunition and equipment stored in Japan be sent to support the Republic of Korea Army.

Military operations are the combat execution of plans with a specific military goal in mind, often referred to by code names. In the most technical sense a military operation consists of seven phases that include conception, intelligence, planning, administration, commencement, defeating, and ending. While some operations are carefully and cautiously planned, in practice most operations are less rather than more defined, and often quickly planned and promoted. Military operations can also be classified by the scale and scope of the force employed and the area in which they unfold, but these lines are very vague, and in the Korean War the term was used for everything from engagements to campaigns.

Where the military is involved there have always been operations. But it was not really until the German High Command began to name their operations during the final years of World War I that they were so well identified. At first the names were used as codes, but after that operations tended to be identified in such a way as to provide motivation for the soldiers involved or to attract public attention to the deed. The Americans got into the naming business during the early days of World War II by using color codes for war plans like Operation Indigo, the military support of Iceland, then moved on to use one of the 10,000 common nouns and adjectives listed in an adopted code word list that was provided. During World War II, British Prime Minister Winston Churchill saw such value in the names given to military operations that he issued instructions, among them that the name should not be such as to bring shame to some mother whose son had died in the effort; there was to be no operation "Pink Night Gown" or the like.

During the Korean War General Douglas MacArthur, United Nations commander, maintained the use of named operations. The names were generally to be taken from an established code list. However, General Matthew B. Ridgway, who replaced MacArthur in April 1951, pushed for more aggressive names. He wanted names that reflected the intentions of his exercises, and he allowed more freedom in the naming of a variety of more localized operations. Some of the names used eventually attracted displeasure among his critics, including members of congress. These legislators found names like "Operation Killer" offensive to the public. General Ridgway would later wonder in his autobiography why the American people were reluctant to name what they were not reluctant to do.

Operations are most often filler movements between other more established campaigns. Sometimes they are a part or a phase of a larger operation. A large number of these operations, at least the majority, took place during the "stalemate" period of the Korean War. During the early stages when the war was one of movement and characterized by attack and

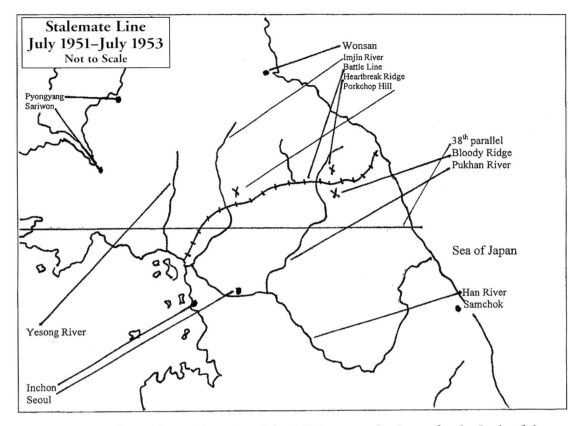

**Stalemate Line
July 1951–July 1953**
Not to Scale

Wonsan
Imjin River
Battle Line
Heartbreak Ridge
Porkchop Hill

Pyongyang
Sariwon

38th parallel
Bloody Ridge
Pukhan River

Sea of Japan

Han River
Samchok

Yesong River

Inchon
Seoul

Approximate stalemate lines, July 1951 to July 1953 (courtesy the Center for the Study of the Korean War).

counterattack, the need for more specialized operations was smaller. But as the war ground down to a series of small skirmishes, small unit fights for individual hills and outposts and the struggle for supplies, special operations became more effective.

A surprising number of these operations were unsuccessful. That is, they did not accomplish the lofty goals established by the planners. This should not come as a surprise, for a good deal of combat is unsuccessful. Besides that, the goals of operational planners were often unrealistic, quite often the enemy was far too well prepared or anticipated the event, and sometimes the operation was simply deemed too costly to continue. But it is important to remember that it is not the battle but the war that is important, and operations by their very nature tended to exist out-side the bounds of the larger, more basic military situations. Success or failure, operations often molded the face of the war, making the war in Korea uniquely what it was.

One other point perhaps should be made: the Korean War is not over nor has there been an end to military operations there. Over that past half-century there have been numerous military and semi-military operations in Korea. Most of them are unrecorded and deliberately unpublicized. While the Korean War still goes on, the July 1953 cutoff date in the present work for the inclusion of operations follow the dates given for the combat phase. It can only be hoped that a qualified scholar will sometime write a history of the Korean War from 1953 to the present. If so, it will contain a different, but strangely familiar, story.

In determining the breadth of this book,

two early decisions had to be made. One was how broad a scope was to be used in order to include military and related operations initiated by entities other than the United Nations Command. Because of the lack of information, and because the Communist forces did not seem to use the concept "operation" in the same fashion as the UN, the decision was made to limited the compilation to operations under United Nations Command.

The second decision was determining which of the many operations to include. The decision was by necessity subjective, but every effort has been made to include all operations discovered during a rather massive search of sources. I am sure that some have been missed, that others have received less attention than they deserve, and that some included are perhaps of little or no significance. Nothing about the selection process should be seen as an evaluation of the event discussed. The length of an entry is generally dependent on what information is available and is not intended to suggest any degree of importance. Each in its own way was significant to the overall outcome of the war.

Some comment needs to be made about duplications. Half a dozen or so operations appear here under more than one name and an explanation might help. In the references — histories, documents, plans, operational orders, and even after-action-reports — the various commands often referred to the same operation by different names. What is more important, however, is that their descriptions of that event are different. It is not necessarily the basic facts that are different, but from the disposition of the recorders the operations are seen quite differently, with different participants emphasized or outcomes considered. A prime example of this is the rescue of a group of Korean orphans from Seoul during late December 1950. The rescue is seen differently, and reported differently, from the eyes of participants and non-participants, Air Force or civilians, official histories or memoirs. Another

example would be the several operational names used for the transfer of X Corps to Wonsan, which had various descriptions depending on how the reporter was involved. In each case different information or perhaps an alternative point of view is provided. Thus events are reported under their own operational name. Whenever possible these operations have been cross-referenced.

The dates provided are those most associated with the event (usually a beginning date). Few military operations have as clear a closing date as they will have an opening date, so final dates are generally not given except in the narrative; when different dates are recorded for the same operation, those used are the ones provided by the U.S. Army. Dates are presented in the standard military format (day, month, year); the same is true for military time, which operates on a twenty-four hour clock. Time, in Korea and Japan, is half a day later than in the United States. All times are given as being the time registered at the location where the event took place.

A distinction has been made between an operation order and an operation. The first consists of the planning and the essence of execution, while the second defines the operation as a whole. In most cases the distinction is very clear. In two or three places I have included an Operations Order when it later went on to be defined as an executed operation. On the other hand, general operational plans, like Vice Admiral C. Turner Joy's 27 July 1950 Operations Order 11-50, are not included. This one directed naval forces to conduct harassing and demolition raids and execute deceptive operations to disrupt North Korean lines of communication and supply, and to deceive the enemy. It called on Vice Admiral Arthur D. Struble's Combined Joint Task Force to attack enemy positions, and it provided guidance and direction that were in order through the war. While operational, it never identified any specific endeavor.

A comment about how the etymology is

perceived. In the Republic of South Korea the war is usually referred to by the date it began, 6-25, and more formally as the Korean War. In the Democratic People's Republic of Korea it is called *Joguk haebang jeonjaeng* or Fatherland Liberation War. In China the conflict was originally called the War to Resist America and Aid Korea, but in the past few years it is generally referred to as the Korean War. The United States does not know really what to call it: police action, forgotten war, Mr. Truman's War, the Korean Conflict; but today most histories simply call it the Korean War. That is the phrase used in this volume.

Military ranks are given as they were at the time of the event. Occasionally when the individual involved has risen to a higher command status, their final rank is also given. Reference is made to winners of the Medal of Honor when they relate directly to an operation being discussed. While the names of commanders naturally appear in relation to their commands, other significant individuals are included in the discussion of operation when possible.

First names are provided for individuals whenever possible. No disrespect is intended by calling leading commanders by their last name only. It is done out of concern for the length of the manuscript, as repeating lengthy titles can take up a lot of room. Oriental names are given as they are spoken; that is with the surname (family name) first. Generally the more prominent persons are listed by the name most recognized, even if they have several names or ways of spelling their names. Again, when a variety of spellings are present, the Army reference is used. The common Korean suffixes that are used include:

pong	hill or mountain
chon	small river or tributary of larger river
dan/tan	point
do/to	island
gang	river
ni/ri	township or several villages together
nae	dam
ryong	mountain pass

Notes, documentation, and suggestions for further reading have been listed at the end of each entry. Full accounting and other sources are listed in the bibliography. Please be aware of the fact that the U.S. Marines, the Army, the Navy, and the United States Air Force do not always use the same names or descriptions, or provide the same dates, for what seem to be like events. Note a difference in campaign names and dates listed in Appendix 4. In those cases arbitrary preference has been given to names and dates listed by the U.S. Army.

Every effort has been made to avoid nationalistic comments. Phrases like "the enemy" — meaning those fighting in opposition to the United Nations Command — are used only to provide some identification while not being too repetitious. The official name for those living north of the 38th parallel is the Democratic People's Republic of Korea (DPRK) but the term North Korea is commonly used. The same is true for the Republic of Korea (ROK) when using the term South Korea. The term Communist in this work refers to any troops fighting against the United Nations in Korea. Occasionally I have used the term Red, meaning Communist, as it was popular terminology at the time.

At least 21 nations supported the United Nations cause and 16 of them provided military assistance. Most of these units fought alongside other UN commands and thus often lost their individual identities. These national commitments, however, played a highly significant role in the outcome of the war, and when the term "United Nations" is used it needs to be recognized for the breadth of participation. For a listing of those nations involved, see Appendix 1.

Since, in the case of these reported operations, 98.9 percent of the participants are male, the term men has been used to mean the troops involved. On that rare occasion when women were involved great care has been given to acknowledge their participation. Most of the women serving in Korea itself were nurses or associated with the medical profession, and while several lost their lives because of their service, these casualties were not associated with operations. No gender bias is intended.

In considering the casualty figures it is wise to remember that the military uses the term casualty to include all those killed (KIA), wounded (WIA), and those missing in action (MIA). As such, all figures are subject to interpretation, for different sources provided different figures. The figures used are the most conservative of those located.

Brief History
of the Korean War

The United States' involvement with the nation of Korea goes back to the 1860s with American trade efforts and "the first Korean war." Since then the two nations have had indirect ties and while relations have not always been positive — the American supported the Japanese annexation of Korea in the 1900s, for example — the late 20th century saw the fate of the two nations drawn together both politically and militarily. More immediate was America's role in the decision to divide Korea between Soviet and American forces at the end of World War II, and later its UN assigned responsibility for the development of the Republic of Korea Army. American troops had been in Korea since 1945 and had only been withdrawn for a couple of years when President Harry Truman called them back in a move presented to the American people as "drawing a line in the sand" to stop the growth of Communism.

With the Soviet Union occupying North Korea and local control in the hands of the Communist leader Kim Il Sung, and United States troops gathering to the south where leadership of the Republic of Korea was in the hands of Syngman Rhee's unification party, there was little hope for peace in Korea. The divided nation was fated to be a pawn in the international troubles that were brewing across the world. Both sides were determined to unify the nation, though under vastly differ-

ent concepts of government, and as quickly as the two protectorate powers pulled out their troops, the border clashes began. The fighting continued, during which hundreds of Koreans on both sides of the 38th parallel lost their lives.

The Korean War began on 25 June 1950 with an attack by Communist North Korean forces that crossed the 38th parallel in force and entered the Republic of Korea (ROK). Some revisionists today suggest that the outbreak of war was the result of provocative actions taken by South Korea, but that case has not yet been made. There is no doubt that Syngman Rhee's government was aggressive and difficult, but the decision for war seems to have been that of Kim Il Sung, with the reluctant support of China and the Soviet Union. On being informed of the attack, President Harry S Truman, who was at the summer White House in Independence, Missouri, rushed back to Washington where he and his staff committed the United States to military action in Korea. In anticipation of a move by either Communist or Nationalist China, the Seventh Fleet was sent to patrol the waters of the Formosa Strait. Swift action on the part of the U.S. put the problem before the United Nations and they immediately responded with a resolution condemning the action and, eventually, supporting military assistance to South Korea.

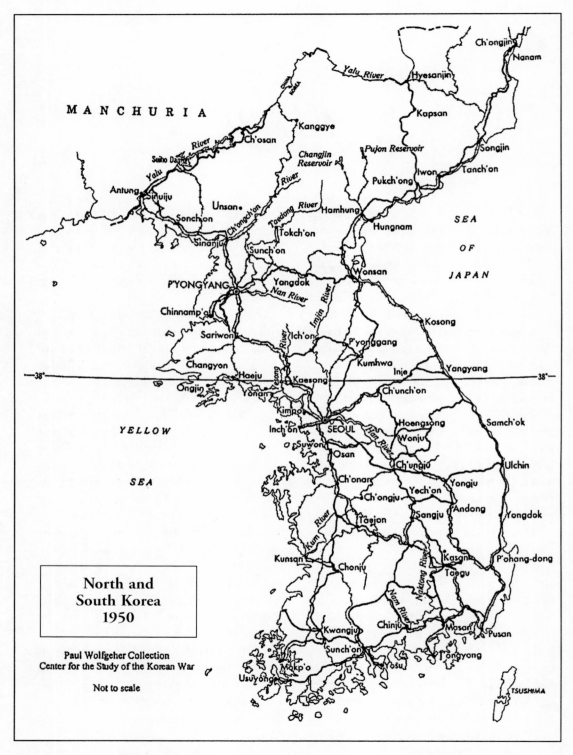

North and South Korea, 1950 (courtesy Paul Wolfgeher Collection, Center for the Study of the Korean War).

At first the United States was simply to supply enough military assistance to protect the evacuation of American and foreign dependents, and to provide much needed ammunition for troops of the Republic of Korean Army. Concern by President Truman and many of his military advisors, who believed the outbreak in Korea was but the opening guns of a Soviet inspired World War III, made the U.S. cautious. But the rapid advance of North Korean troops, and the inability of the ROK Army to hold them, led to a visit by the Pacific Commander, General Douglas MacArthur, and by President's Truman's special eyes, Major General John Church, to evaluate the situation. Both agreed that more was needed and that it was needed quickly.

Other than a few anti-aircraft gunners sent to protect the ports, the first American ground involvement was Task Force Smith, pulled together from the 24th Infantry Division. The Task Force was sent to Korea to show the flag and, hopefully, to stop the Communist advance. Unfortunately these early troops were primarily untrained and poorly equipped soldiers who were suddenly brought face to face with well-trained, combat-hardened North Korean troops, spearheaded by Russian-made T-34 tanks. The efforts at stopping, and then delaying, the Communists was not successful and it was increasingly obvious that the United States, as well as the United Nations, either had to meet the challenge or get out. At the United Nations' request President Truman named General MacArthur to establish the United Nations' Command and in turn MacArthur named Lieutenant General Walton H. Walker as ground commander for the United States Eighth Army in Korea. Walker arrived in Taejon, Korea, on 7 July 1950.

As the organization of the military defense was being established and the first of a few additional troops began to arrive, the North Koreans managed to move steadily south. The Republic of Korea Army (ROKA) fought as much of a delaying action as possible, but they were outnumbered and fighting a highly aggressive and well disciplined army. With the ROKA being unable to slow them much, the Communists quickly took the capital city of Seoul and moved on so that by 20 July 1950 they had occupied the city of Taejon.

At this time, and in the first major response, the UN conducted an unopposed amphibious landing of the 1st Cavalry Division at Pohang-dong. The troops were sent to the fight at Pusan, but were unable to land in that suddenly overwhelmed port. Arriving at Pohang-dong they were thrown into the battle to preserve Pusan and maintain some military presence in Korea. As North Koreans drove forces south, there were simply not enough men and equipment to stop them. Slowly, Eighth Army broke contact with the enemy and on the night of 31 July withdrew to the relative safety of the Naktong River. Beyond that they took up a defensive line that has become known in history as the Pusan Perimeter. For six weeks — by the rapid movement of his troops by rail inside the perimeter, the assignment of the newly arrived 1st Marine Provisional Brigade, as well as early stores of ammunition and vehicles — General Walker's Eighth Army made its last stand in a half-circle defense around the port of Pusan.

In one of the great stories of military leadership, determination, and individual courage, the defenders — at this time still the ROK and U.S. Army — managed to hold on. They had one advantage working for them. The farther the North Koreans advanced the longer and less secure were their supply lines, while at the same time the U.S. was delivering men and equipment as quickly as they could be located and transported. During the battle the defending troops not only held out but managed to make a significant stand in early August when Task Force Keen pushed the Koreans back to Chinju. The pressure both remained and grew, and in the heaviest attack of all, the North Koreans hit the UN on the night of 31 August on the extreme flanks. The situation was shaky for some time, and consideration was given to pulling out, retreating back to Japan, and making whatever stand was necessary from there. But the United Nations managed to hold. As it did, more and more troops, ammunition, and equipment were coming ashore.

By the middle of September 1950 enough troops had arrived, and adequate supplies accumulated, so that General MacArthur felt ready to attempt one of the more risky of amphibious operations in military history. In a dramatic move he pulled the 1st Provincial Marines out of the Pusan Perimeter, linked them up with the re-formed 1st Marine Division and joined them with the 7th Infantry Division to form X Corps. Under the command of Lieutenant General Edward Almond, X Corps was assigned the responsibility for Operation Chromite, the invasion of Inchon. On 15 September, after heavy bombardment by UN ships in Flying Fish Channel, the invasion troops went ashore at the harbor island of Wolmi and then moved on to the mainland at Inchon. After dealing with moderate opposition, X Corps moved inland, and by 17 September, the 1st Marine Division and elements of the 7th Infantry Division were ashore and moving toward Seoul. The capital fell on 26 September. General MacArthur was there and in an elaborate ceremony on the 29th he returned the city to President Rhee.

In the south, Eighth Army broke out of the Pusan Perimeter and began to move quickly through enemy territory, pushing most of the North Korean army ahead of them. The advancing Eighth Army made contact with elements of the 7th Infantry Division on the evening of 26 September, and by the end of the month the North Korean Army had given up control of most of the land south of the 38th parallel. At this point it was not clear how much of the North Korean army had retreated to the north and how many had simply changed clothes and melted into the population.

The war might well have stopped at this point, for it was here that the United Nations' mandate had been fulfilled. The invading North Korean forces had been driven out of South Korea. But instead, for complex political as well as immediate military reasons, the decision was made to destroy the North Korean Army and reunite Korea. The United Nations Command (UNC) began its drive north, crossing the 38th parallel in October 1950. In a planned amphibious operation to encircle the enemy through a landing on the east coast, X Corps was pulled out of the fighting around Seoul and transported east to the city of Wonsan. Difficulties with sea mines sown by the North Koreans delayed the 1st Marine Division effort, and the 7th Infantry had to land at Iwon to the north. So by the time the Marines were ready to come ashore on the east, the UN on the west coast had advanced north and taken the city of Pyongyang, the North Korean capital, which fell on 19 October. On the east the ROKA moved forward rapidly and in a series of quick successes took Wonsan and then Hamhung and Hungnam.

Once X Corps was on the ground it struck out, the Marines toward the Chosin Reservoir and the 7th Infantry Division to the northwest. By the morning of 21 November a small task force of the 17th Infantry Regiment (7th Infantry Division) reached the Yalu River at Hyesanjin. Elsewhere, Eighth Army was within striking distance of the Yalu. Again it seemed that the war was about to be over, the mission to have been accomplished.

But here the war changed. Either ignoring the warnings from the Chinese or somehow unaware of the danger they imposed, the UN Command saw fit to downplay the increasing evidence, appearing late October and early November, that Chinese troops had crossed the Yalu and were involved in the war in Korea. Just after Thanksgiving Day was celebrated, on 24 November 1950, the Chinese Communist Forces attacked Eighth Army and X Corps in full force, hitting them with hundreds of thousands of fresh and well-equipped troops. In the east X Corps was addressed by twelve Chinese divisions and forced to withdraw all its units into a bridgehead around Hamhung and Hungnam. It was a glorious "advance in the other direction," well executed and rampant with stories of great courage, but a serious retreat nevertheless. This left Eighth Army with an unprotected flank as well as an advancing enemy that meant it had to move out as well. General Walton Walker, not as confident as MacArthur, had moved a little slower and was able to break contact with the enemy and began his own orderly withdrawal, fighting as he retreated.

The Navy set up an invasion in reverse and prepared for an evacuation of X Corps by water. On the west coast Eighth Army was making every effort to destroy what it could not take, as it moved rapidly south. In the process of the withdrawal some troops were taken out by sea — the British admiralty, using smaller ships at incidental inlets, evacuated more than 7,000 soldiers from the Pyongyang area — as they pulled back more than 150 miles and took up positions across the peninsula south of the 38th parallel. On the east coast, the 3rd Division held the final perimeter and naval guns lay down a curtain of fire around Hungnam, allowing X Corps to get out. Carrier planes from Task Force 77 filled the skies with dive bombers holding back the Chinese as X Corps was able to evacuate more than 105,000 military personnel and nearly as many civilians.

General Walton Walker, who had commanded Eighth Army through much of this crisis, was killed in a jeep accident on 23 December. He was replaced by Lieutenant General Matthew B. Ridgway, a military hero from World War II and a seasoned strategist, who arrived on the day after Christmas. He came in command of an army that had just experienced a massive retreat, was in limited defensive positions, and was facing a renewed enemy attack which, as intelligence had anticipated, came on New Year's Eve. Before

Ridgway had a chance to check things out, the Communists hit the 6th ROK Division south of Yonchon. There was little at this point that could be done to stop them and the Chinese advanced quickly, finally taking the capital at Seoul on 4 January.

General Ridgway was not the sort of leader to stand back and wait, and in a remarkable case of morale boosting and command shake-ups, he managed to gear up his forces to launch back. The UNC established a new offensive and pushed back against the advancing Chinese who, by now, were also suffering the difficulties of long range supply. Hitting hard, the UN force was once again able to push their way back north until they reached the Han River, achieved finally on 12 February 1951. In response the Chinese struck hard at the central sector hoping to split the UN forces down the center. There was some progress in this regard, and many casualties, but attack after attack was beaten off as the UN forces, soundly supported by Air Force cover and Navy bombardment, held their ground and advanced when they could. Following up in Operation Killer, General Ridgway swept the Communists back so that by the end of February, Eighth Army was once again on line overlooking the Han River.

The sea war, which had primarily consisted of controlling the sea lanes and shore bombardment, was expanded when it was announced the UN would blockade Korea as well as taking up the siege of the significant port city of Wonsan. On 16 February 1951 the destroyers USS *Lind* and *Ozbourn* moved into the harbor and fired their 5 inch guns at the city. The siege, so simply begun, would continue until the end of the war.

While General Ridgway was more interested in creating casualties among the Communist forces than he was taking land, he was nevertheless able to return to the 38th parallel. There he forced a strong defensive position by the creation of a series of phase lines from which he could launch devastating offensive maneuvers. The line, just north of the 38th parallel, ran 115 miles across Korea. From there he moved forward in an effort to neutralize the infamous Iron Triangle an enemy supply, communication, and transportation center, and by 20 April 1951 UN forces had reached a phase line just south of the triangle.

Because of basic disagreements that went too deep to ignore, President Truman relieved General Douglas MacArthur in April 1951 and named General Ridgway to the United Nations Command. Lieutenant General James Van Fleet, who took over command of the Eighth Army, continued to move slowly but essentially forward. Nevertheless, the Communists were not done yet. They struck in late April with a force so powerful and determined that it penetrated the UN lines in the west-central section, forcing the UN to withdraw as much as 40 miles. But in each case the UN withdrawal was preplanned and they moved back into prepared defense lines from which it was possible to stop the enemy. When the Communist attack ended on 29 April, the UN line still formed an arc north of Seoul. The Chinese Fifth Phase offensive had been stopped.

At this time Communist reversals on the field led some to believe that they might be willing to consider a negotiated settlement. Then, when the Soviet delegate to the UN, Jacob A. Malik, hinted that his nation would favor such a move, the Truman Administration took it to heart and suggested an appeal be broadcast. The response was positive and on 10 July 1951 the first session of a negotiation team met. Admiral C. Turner Joy, commander of Naval Forces Far East, headed the UN delegation. But the hopes that had been generated so quickly were swiftly dashed, for the Communist concept of negotiation was not what the UN had in mind. In well over 100 plenary sessions that began first at Kaesong, and then later continued on at Panmunjom, there was little evidence that the Communists were seeking a serious agreement.

Nevertheless the war entered a different stage as more and more of the military decisions were dictated by political considerations. And the war, no longer the mobile drive for possessions, became less aggressive and turned into a war of defensive lines, a stalemate of sorts, as political leaders began to think of "fighting for an armistice." In this case the opposing sides took root, dug in to protect what they had so far gained and took a stand, determined not to lose on the field of battle what they might win at the negotiation table. Facing one another across barren valleys and rocky hills, they took out their anger and frustration with small objectives, limited campaigns, and an increasing number of restricted patrols. These became small but deadly fights over bits and pieces of land where occupancy was not as important as the threat of doing so.

Because of the changing nature of the war, and the end to large campaigns, as well as the defensive attitude and execution, many historians pass over this phase of the conflict, not realizing that it was in many ways the bloodiest, that it cost the most lives, and left us with the legacy of such infamous names as Old Baldy, Heartbreak Ridge, and Pork Chop. Some of these locations, like Pork Chop, would change hands nearly a dozen times, the ownership alternatively determined by war and by politics. Patrols and ambushes continued, but from the beginning of negotiations in July of 1951 until April of 1953, no major ground offensives were launched by either side. These limited actions did not seem small to those involved, however, and were extremely costly in terms of men and equipment. Fought over well-defended terrain against an enemy that had plenty of time to dig in and become prepared, the hill wars, as this phase was often called, sent squads and platoons, sometimes companies, against stable and entrenched targets.

When General Van Fleet relinquished command to Lieutenant General Maxwell Taylor on 11 February 1953, the war continued but it

Communist representatives on their way to negotiations at Kaesong, June 1951 (Joseph Adams Collection: Center for the Study of the Korean War).

seemed to have no purpose. The military demanded action when the negotiators wanted talk, and the opposite, and there was little dialogue between the two. True to the GI's cryptic comment, it appeared to have become a war that we could not win, could not quit, and could not leave.

The end of combat began when it became increasingly obvious to all sides that the war had become far too costly in terms of both money and lives, and that there was not now all that much either to win or to lose. A crack began to appear in the hard line attitudes of those seeking a cease-fire. First there was a positive response to the international Red Cross suggestion of an exchange of sick and wounded prisoners of war. This was worked out in Operation Little Switch amid charges of mistreatment and skullduggery, but accomplished nevertheless. Coincidental with, or as

a result of, the death of Soviet Premier Joseph Stalin on 28 March 1953, the negotiations took on a more serous note and it was not long before a final armistice agreement was reached. The cease-fire was signed with the fighting to be stopped officially at 2000 hours on 27 July 1953. Both sides in the agreement continued to fire artillery until the very last moments of the conflict. The agreement was signed by the Chinese Communists, Democratic People's Republic of Korea, and the United Nations Command, but not by the Republic of Korea. The combat stopped, but the hostilities and some of the shooting have been going on ever since.

The United Nations

The Korean War was in most respects a United Nations war. Once the United States decided on a military response to the Democratic People's Republic of Korea, it appealed to the UN for support. The United Nations Security Council Resolution of 25 June 1950, and the second resolution of 27 June, authorized the UN intervention in the developing war in Korea. It called for "an immediate cessation of hostilities" and urged the member nations to "render every assistance." The passage of these resolutions was a diplomatic success for the Truman Administration but was aided by the strong support for action led by UN Secretary-General Trygve Lie. Most historians believe, as well, that the absence of the Soviet delegate Jacob A. Malik, who might well have vetoed the action, was a significant factor. The nation of Yugoslavia offered the only serious objections.

In time sixteen nations sent participating troops and many were involved in the various campaigns and operations of the war. They were: Australia, Belgium, Canada, Colombia, Ethiopia, France, Greece, Luxembourg, Netherlands, New Zealand, Philippines, Thailand, Turkey, South Africa, United Kingdom and the United States. Five nations provided medical units: Denmark, Italy, India, Norway, and Sweden. Overall military command for these troops was given to the United States, under General Douglas MacArthur, simply because the United States was providing most of the men and equipment. The breakdown of participation was: the U.S., 50.3 percent; other UN nations, 9.6 percent; and the ROK, 40.1 percent when accounting for ground troops. In terms of naval support, the U.S. provided 85.9 percent, other UN nations 6.7 percent and the ROKN 7.4 percent. In the air 93.4 percent of the total force was from the U.S. and 1.0 percent was from other UN members. The ROK air contribution was 5.6 percent.*

*Paul J. Morton, "United Nations Command." In James I. Matray, Historical Dictionary of the Korean War. Westport, CT: Greenwood Press, 1991, pp. 507–508.

Brief Chronology
of Korean War Operations

Pre-War

1943 December	Cairo Declaration promises future independence for Korea
1945 August	Soviet-American agreement divides Korea at 38th parallel
1945 September 8	Operation Black List Forty
1947	Operation Rollup
1948 August	Republic of Korea established
1948 September	Democratic People's Republic of Korea established
1948 December	Soviet troops withdraw
1949 June	United States troops withdraw

1950

June	Operation Chow Chow
25 June	North Korea invades the Republic of Korea
26 June	Seventh Fleet deploys to Korean waters
27 June	Authorized combat air and naval operations
28 June	Seoul taken by NK forces
29 June	Naval blockade of Korea authorized
July	Operation Bout One
	Operation Flush Out
	Operation Salamander
1 July	Task Force Smith deployed
4 July	24th Infantry Division arrives in Korea
8 July	General Douglas MacArthur named UN Commander in Chief
10 July	25th Infantry Division arrives in Korea
14 July	ROK forces placed under UN command
18 July	1st Cavalry Division arrives in Korea
27 July	Operation Hawk
29 July	Operation Nannie Able
31 July	5th Regimental Combat Team arrives in Korea
August	Operation Rebuild
1 August	Operation Nannie Baker
2 August	1st Provisional Marine Brigade arrives in Korea
3 August	2nd Infantry Division arrives in Korea
	Operation Nannie Charles
8–18 August	Battle of Naktong

1950 (cont.)

10–20 August	Battle of Pohang
15–20 August	Battle of Bowling Alley
17 August	Operation Lee
26 August	Tenth Corps arrives in Korea
29 August	27th British Infantry Brigade arrives in Korea
31 August–19 Sept.	Second Battle of the Naktong
September	Operation Trudy Jackson
15 September	Tenth Corps lands at Inchon — Operation Chromite
	Operation Booklift
16–22 September	Eighth Army breaks out of Pusan Perimeter
17 September	7th Infantry Division lands at Inchon
26 September	Operation Aviary
27 September	Seoul liberated by UN Forces
30 September	ROK forces cross the 38th parallel
October	Operation Comback
4 October	China decides to enter Korean War
7 October	UN authorizes UN troops north of 38th parallel
15 October	Wake Island conference
19 October	Pyongyang, North Korean capital, secured by ROK
20 October	187th Airborne jumps at Sukch'on and Such'on
25 October	Phase One of Chinese offensive begins
	Operation Tailboard
26 October	ROK elements reach Yalu River
26–29 October	Tenth Corps lands at Wonsan and Iwon
10 November	3rd Infantry Division arrives in Korea
13 November	Operation Plan 116-50
24 November	Operation Defrost
27 November	UN forces begin withdrawal from Chosin Reservoir area
December	Operation Long Johns
	Operation Sleigh Ride
	Operation Snap
5 December	Pyongyang recaptured by North Korea
	Operation Pink
7 December	Operation Turnaround
16 December	State of national emergency declared by Truman
20 December	Operation Christmas Kidlift
	Operation Kiddie Car
	Operation Kiddie Car Lift
	Operation Santa Claus
	Operation Little Orphan Annie
28 December	Tenth Corps assigned to Eighth Army
30 December	Operation Relax

1951

January	Operation Downpour
	Operation Stole
	Operation Leopard
4 January	Seoul evacuated

1951 (cont.)

5 January	Inchon evacuated
15 January	Operation Wolfhound
23 January	Operation Thunderbolt
25 January	UN counteroffensive
29 January	Operation Ascendant
February	Operation Tack
5 February	Operation Roundup met with counterattack
	Operation Exploitation
	Operation Punch
19 February	Operation P
21 February	Operation Killer
21–28 February	UN clears south of Han River
24 February	Operation Rotate
4 March	Operation Wellsend
	Operation Shining Moon
7 March	Operation Ripper
14 March	Seoul liberated again
15 March	Operation Virginia I
22 March	Operation Courageous
23 March	187th Airborne drops at Munsan-ni — Operation Tomahawk
	Operation Courageous
27 March	UN Forces reach the 38th parallel
29 March	Operation Hawk
April	Operation Sea Dragon
3 April	Operation Rugged
6 April	Operation Dauntless
7 April	Operation Iron Triangle
11 April	Operation Audacious
11 April	Truman relieves MacArthur of command
May	Operation Squeegee
10 May	Operation Ashcan
12 May	Operation Detonate
16 May	Chinese begin Fifth Phase of offensive
24 May	Operation Mousetrap
25 May	Operation Initiate
26 May	Operation Chopper
29 May	Operation Follow-Up
June	Operation Amphibious Kojo
	Operation Wolfpack
1 June	Operation Piledriver moves UN to Wyoming Line
2 June	Operation Strangle
13 June	Operation Goose
14 June	Communists accept UN cease-fire negotiation proposal
18 June	Operation Spitfire
23 June	Cease-fire talks proposed by Soviet delegates
26 June	Operation Cat and Dog
	Operation Maindy
29 June	Operation Firefly

1951 (cont.)

30 June	Operation Order 8-50
July	Operation Mustang I
1 July	Operation Doughnut
10 July	Cease-fire talks begin at Kaesong
12 July	Operation Cave Dweller
18 July	Operation Kickoff
28 July	First Commonwealth Division activated
August	Operation Dirk
	Operation Punchbowl
2 August	Operation Cow Puncher
4 August	Operation Slam
19 August	Operation Citadel
23 August	Operation Claymore
September	Operation Mustang II
7 September	Operation Boomerang
	Operation Minden
8 September	Operation Ohio Sloan
13 Sept.–15 Oct.	Battle of Heartbreak Ridge
13 September	Operation Windmill I
17 September	Operation Clean Up I
19 September	Operation Cudgel
	Operation Windmill II
21 September	Operation Cleaver
	Operation Summit
22 September	Operation Snatch
27 September	Operation Blackbird
	Operation Pelican
28 September	Operation Commando
29 September	Operation Clean Up II
October	Operation Hudson Harbor
	Operation Rabbit Hunt
1 October	Korean based units of army integrated
	Operation Snowball
3 October	Operation Retribution
5 October	Operation Touchdown
11 October	Operation Bumblebee
13 October	Operation Nomad-Polar
15 October	Operating Polecharge
	Operation Wedge
22 October	Operation Bushbeater
26 October	Operation House Burning I
27 October	Operation Sundial
31 October	Operation House Burning II
9 November	Operation Touchy
11 November	Operation Switch
12 November	Operation Ratkiller
13 November	Operation Counter Punch
December	Operation Freeze Out

1951 (cont.)

15 December	Operation Shunkhunt
17 December	Operation Cheerful
19 December	Operation Farewell
21 December	Operation Helicopter
28 December	45th Infantry Division relieves 1st Cavalry

1952

January	Operation Highboy
	Operation Derail
	Operation Broken Reed
1 January	Operation Moonlight Sonata
2 January	Operation Mustang III
10 January	Operation Changie Changie
11 January	Operation Package
13 January	Operation Junket
18 January	Operation Chicken Stealer
3 February	40th Infantry Division relieves 24th Division
10 February	Operation Clam Up
	Operation Snare
16 February	Operation Liverpool
18 February	Operation Polecat
March	Operation Saturate
1 March	Operation Get Well
6 March	Operation Roof Lifter
	Operation Muletrain
	Operation Native Son Dog
12 March	Operation Alcatraz
16 March	Operation Mustang IV
April	Operation Clobber
	Operation Westminster
	Operation Fishnet
	Operation Tropic
1 April	Operation Chopstick 6
3 April	Operation Scatter
5 April	Operation Pronto
15 April	Operation Chopstick 16
17 April	Operation MiG
18 April	Operation Leapfrog
19 April	Operation Spreadout
23 April	Operation Circus
May	Operation Removal
	Operation Timber
7 May	Operation Breakup
7–11 May	Battle of Old Baldy
13 May	Operation Insomnia
14 May	Operation Mustang V
15 May	Operation Mustang VI
22 May	Operation Skyhook

1952 (cont.)

June	Operation Butterfly
12 June	Operation Amazon
25 June	Operation Everready planned
July	Operation Pressure Pump
1 July	Operation Homecoming releases 27,000 civilians
2 July	Operation Blaze
4 July	Operation Firecracker
8 July	Operation Buckshot
12 August	Operation Panther
13 August	Operation Buffalo
19 August	Operation Ripple I
25 August	Operation Manchu
2 September	Operation Get Ready
22 September	Operation Haylift I
28 September	Operation Plan Blast
October	Operation Overwhelming
	Operation Wrangler
	Operation Cat Whiskers
	Operation Red Frog
8 October	Operation Red Cow
12 October	Operation Feint
13 October	Operation Showdown
	Operation Nebraska
15 October	Operation Decoy
24 October	Operation Mustang VII
	Operation Mustang VIII
25 November	Operation Beat Up
December	Operation Janus
	Operation War Dance
	Operation Thanksgiving
11 December	Operation Fauna
28 December	Operation Jesse James

1953

8 January	Operation Bimbo
9 January	Operation Paralysis
23 January	Operation Doorstop
25 January	Operation Smack tests air support
	Operation Green Dragon
February	Operation Ripple V
	Operation Silent Redline V
3 February	Operation Clambake
7 February	Operation Boxer
23 February	Operation Haylift II
25 February	Operation Charlie
March	Operation Terry Blue
5 March	Joseph Stalin dies
20 March	Operation Moolah approved

1953 (cont.)

21 March	Operation Spring Thaw
23 March	Battle of Pork Chop
30 March	Operation Hurricane
31 March	Operation Rabbit I
April	Operation Moolah
5 April	Operation Rainbow
7 April	Operation Rabbit II
11 April	Operation Little Switch approved
12 April	Operation Fast Shuffle
18 April	Operation Once Again
20 April	Exchange of sick and wounded POWs
23 April	Operation Left Hook
May	Operation Shakedown
25 May	Operation Beehive
June	Operation Pandora
	Operation No Doze
	Operation Skyway
4 June	Communists accept UN cease-fire proposal
6 June	Operation Counter begins
12 June	Operation PAPPY
27 July	Cease-fire agreement signed, effective 2200 local
	Operation Camel
August	Operation Spyglass
5 August	Operation Big Switch
September	Operation Back Door
8 September	Operation Once Again

1954

February	Operation Quicksilver
20 February	Operation Haul Ass
22 July	Operation Glory

OPERATIONS

A significant number of the operations conducted during the Korean War were joint operations in which two or more of the services cooperated and participated. In these operations the vast difference that had risen between the services, and the near open warfare between them that marked the post World War II period, were quickly pushed into the background. Cooperation was excellent and when they worked together their efforts were very effective. The diversity of their philosophies made it difficult at time, especially in regard to command and control of air-ground support. The Air Force put far more emphasis on destroying the enemy's war-making facilities than did the Navy, which tended to focus on the interdiction of supply lines to and from the front. The Air Force disagreed with the Navy and Marines on ground support, and had developed its military strategy on long-range bombing, whereas the Navy, based on its own experiences in World War II, considered close air support as essential. These differences, while substantial, however, did not seriously disrupt the role each would play in support of the land war. The difficulties inherent in any complex joint activities can't be ignored and the success of any mission under joint command is a tribute to the efforts of those involved working toward a common goal.

In the organization of this material, however, the joint participation aspect has been downplayed in order to identify operations by the predominance of the service involved. In most cases the Air Force or the Navy was a partner in ground operations, and the Navy and the Air Force worked together on their own operations. For the sake of presentation, however, operations have been listed under the primary participant.

I. Primarily
Ground Operations

At first General Douglas MacArthur believed that the conflict in Korea would be primarily an air war, convinced that through dominant air power the invasion could be halted almost before it began. But, of course, this was not to be the case and soon even MacArthur knew it.

The war in Korea was a ground war and despite the highly significant contribution of the Air Force and the Navy, this war, like all wars, was fought primarily on the ground by men of the Army and Marines. It was on the ground that the majority of the casualties appeared and the progress of the war was determined. It was on the ground where eventual success or failure was identified. It was on the ground where the movement and the stagnation were felt and where the outcome of the war was often held in the balance. And even as the war stalemated, both on the front lines and at the negotiation table, it remained a ground war. A large segment of the operations identified in this volume are those conducted primarily by ground troops.

When the North Korean troops crossed the 38th parallel and invaded the Republic of Korea, the United States was ill-prepared for an offensive war, especially one so far away. Four divisions of U.S. troops were on occupation duty in Japan, a couple more in Europe, and six in the United States. But all of these divisions were under-strength and seriously short of equipment. In late June 1950 the Army was authorized a force of 610, 000 men and women, but had a strength of only 593,000. More than 111,400 of these troops were in the Far East. The infantry regiments were set up with only four rifle companies rather than the authorized nine, thus providing only 36 rather than the table of organization and equipment (TO&E) authorized 81 rifle platoons in a division. In addition the United States was ill suited to fight a war of the kind that the Korean turned out to be, for it would prove to be a different kind.

On the day of the invasion the estimated strength of the army of the People's Democratic Republic of Korea were 135,000 men in eight infantry divisions, plus two Boarder Constabulary brigades with about 10,000 in total. It had as well 6,000 artillery and armored troops, and 124 Russian made T34 tanks, and artillery built around mortars and up to 122mm howitzers. Nearly a third of the troops were veterans, having fought both the Japanese and in the Chinese Civil War. It was, contrary to some beliefs, not a rag-tag peasant army but a well trained coherent military force. To meet the invasion, South Korea possessed an army of about 65,000 men, a small coast guard, about 45,000 men in constabularies, and an air force of about 2,000. They were advised and trained by the Korean Military Advisory Group (KMAG), and therein

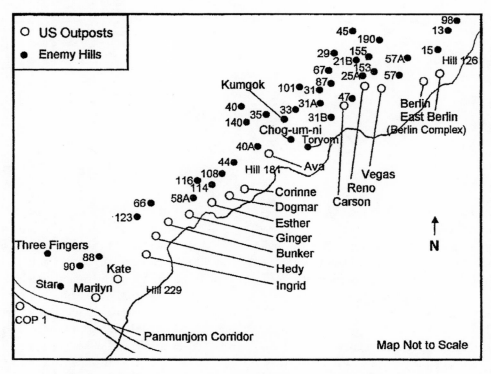

Concentration of outposts and bunkers along UN Lines (Megan Bethel).

lay part of the problem, for the KMAG was designed to train a defensive army, while Syngman Rhee, the president of South Korea, was determined to develop an offensive armed force. Therefore, according to American policy, the South Koreans possessed little heavy artillery (the largest a 105mm howitzer), and even fewer tanks.

On Tuesday, 20 June 1950, Dean Rusk, the assistant secretary of state for Far Eastern affairs, testified before the House Foreign Affairs Committee and was asked about the North Korean intentions in terms of the unification of the nation. He replied: "We see no present intention that the people across the border have any intention of fighting a major war for that purpose [and if they did we] could meet credibly the kind of force which the North Koreans have established" (Goulden 14, 41). As Joseph Goulden points out, Rusk was wrong, for the Democratic People's Republic of Korea had already issued the order to attack. And for some time after they did, the

question of our ability to meet the challenge was in serious doubt.

During the course of the war the ground fighting was done by soldiers and Marines of the Regular Army, the Army Reserves, the Marine and Marine Reserves, as well as National Guard units. The Marines, both a semi-independent body and a naval unit, fought on the ground and generally in conjunction with Army personnel, and side by side with the forces of the Republic of Korea and of sixteen other nations that responded to the United Nations' call for participation.

Certainly the largest number of these operations was designed and executed by the staff and men of Eighth Army and under subsequent commands below them, and they included men from all the United Nations Command as well as a significant number of partisans who were involved in numerous clandestine activities.

Joseph C. Goulden, *Korea: The Untold Story of the War*. New York: Times Books, 1982, p. 14, 41.

A temporary bridge built over the Han River in preparation for a summer campaign (Joseph Adams Collection: Center for the Study of the Korean War).

Russell Gugeler, *Combat Action in Korea: Infantry, Artillery, Armor*. Washington, D.C.: Combat Forces Press, 1954.

S.L.A. Marshall, *The Military History of the Korean War*. New York: Franklin Watts, 1963.

James L. Stokesbury, *A Short History of the Korean War*. New York: William Morrow, 1988, pp. 33–39.

Operation Amazon   12 June 1952

In the summer of 1952, Eighth Army was involved in the second phase of **Operation Counter**, a plan of Major General David L. Ruffner, commander of the 45th Infantry Division (a National Guard outfit), who was facing an untenable situation. The Communists were holding the high ground in front of his position on the flank of I Corps. Their observation posts were overlooking much of his sector and their artillery impact had increased considerably. To combat this he decided to advance his own forward outpost line in a series of offensive sweeps called Operation Counter.

The hills he was facing were in a line from the southeast to the northeast and included several spots which had taken on infamous names: White Horse, Arrowhead, Pork Chop and Old Baldy, and the Chinese were responding with a series of limited counterattacks.

In anticipation of a greater movement by the Communist forces, Operation Amazon was activated. This operation, published by I Corps on 12 June 1952, ordered that preparations be made for bridging the higher waters expected with the summer flood season. Of major concern was the logistical problem facing the units on the main line of resistance in case the bridges necessary for their supply were made impassable by the annual flood. Eighth Army was aware that helicopter supply was becoming more effective in delivering goods, but even they would not be able to provide all that was necessary. The plan required that tank-transport capabilities be established at least for the medium tanks. In order to meet this requirement it would be necessary to both strengthen the existing bridge spans and be ready to erect emergency river spans in case it became necessary. The efforts included the employment of 60 inch searchlights to light up the area for night work, the development and operation of an M-4 ferry, and the continued removal of debris from the river. And, finally, the positioning of 13,000 life-saving floatation devices for use by troops if they were caught away from the established evacuation routes.

Pat Meid and James M. Yingling, *U.S. Marine Operations in Korea, Volume V. Operations in West Korea.* Washington, D.C.: Historical Division, Headquarters U.S. Marine Corps, 1972, p. 101.

Operation Audacious   11–12 April 1951

In mid–April 1951, **Operation Rugged** had been completed and Eighth Army was hovering around Line Kansas. **Operation Dauntless,** to be conducted by General "Shrimp" Milburn's I Corps, was set to start on 11 April 1951, and it was expected the advance would set off the long anticipated Communist counterattack. It had been reported that 274,000 Chinese and about 158,000 North Korean troops were gathering and preparing to launch an offensive in force. In anticipation of the potential attack, Eighth Army was ordered to conduct no operations north of Line Wyoming. In fact plans were being drawn up for a withdrawal. This plan, Operation Audacious, described the process by which Eighth Army anticipated an orderly withdrawal during which they could impose heavy losses on the enemy. The withdrawal was to consist of a series of phase lines running south of Line Kansas. The

lines established were Delta, Golden and Nevada. Golden was to serve as a heavily fortified defensive line around the capital of Seoul. The withdrawal was to be conducted in an orderly fashion, maintaining unit contact and integrity, during which troops would move into well prepared defensive positions. The anticipated attack arrived about as expected, and the withdrawal commenced. Line Delta was the first line and ran from coast to coast almost due east and west from Chunchon. On the night of 25 April, General Milburn ordered a pullback to Line Delta that ran between four and twelve miles below Line Kansas. Line Golden formed a loop around the city of Seoul and paralleled No Name Line beginning at the Han River, crossed route 1, and continued east to cross the Pukhan River. Milburn planned to make his withdrawal from Lines Delta to Golden in increments, with Line Golden holding. Line Nevada was the second withdrawal line set up behind Line Delta.

Clay Blair, *The Forgotten War: America in Korea 1950–1953.* New York: Times Books, 1987, pp. 794–832.

Operation Avalanche   March 1952

While most of the harassing fire directed at enemy locations was delivered in the daytime, not all of it was. In Operation Avalanche, the gunners of the 16th Field Regiment, Royal New Zealand Artillery, were called on to provide harassing fire that consisted of a concerted three-day program of delivering fire between 1900 hours and 0600 hours each day. The gunners were required to fire off 1,200 rounds in all, with an additional 300 rounds in a series at first and last light. While the fire harassed the enemy, it was not terribly effective, as the New Zealanders were firing twenty-five pounders and they were virtually useless against any facility with five meters or more of overhead cover

Ian McGibbon, *New Zealand and the Korean War: Combat Operations.* Melbourne: Oxford University Press, 1996, p. 263.

Operation Barbula   March 1953

When the call went out for members of the United Nations to supply military assistance to the war in Korea, the only South American country to respond positively was Colombia. On 21 May 1950 a Colombian battalion sailed for Korea and on 13 October was assigned to the 21st Infantry Regiment. While the Colombians were involved on several occasions, the major action of the battalion took place during Operation Barbula, a company sized exercise designed to destroy two Communist positions. The Colombians ran into heavy Chinese opposition that resulted in numerous casualties. After putting up a good fight they were forced to withdraw in the face of arriving Chinese reinforcements. The Colombian medics were overwhelmed and to make matters worse the Korean Service Corps personnel serving as stretcher-bearers fled in the face of the odds. The third Colombian platoon returned to the fight to get their casualties and with considerable risk managed to drive their way back to their own lines, bringing their dead and wounded out with them. The action cost the lives of nineteen, forty-four were wounded and eight were listed as missing in action.

Russell W. Ramsey, "The Colombian Battalion in Korea and Suez." *Journal of Inter-American Studies* (October 1967).

Operation Big Stick   February 1952

During the long cold winter of 1952 the foot soldier was occupied with seemingly endless patrols, but the contact with the enemy was limited. Seeking more action, General James Van Fleet kept his staff busy forwarding a series of plans for limited operations to General Matthew Ridgway. In each case General Ridgway's office discarded them as being too costly or by suggesting that they might affect the delicate negotiations going on at the peace table. Plans for Operation Big Stick arrived early in February. The goal behind this was to destroy the Chinese Communist supply base

on Sibyon-ri and to advance Eighth Army's flank as far as the Yesong River and retake Kaesong. If this ambitious plan worked as outlined, it would provoke the dispersal of four Chinese armies and capture the city of Kaesong. The staff estimated that preparation could be made in time to launch the operation by 15 April, beginning with an amphibious feint on the east coast of Korea provided by the 1st Marine Division. The estimated casualties for the endeavor were 11,000. However, it was met with little encouragement by Ridgway's headquarters, which eventually replaced it with another much more restricted plan called **Operation Homecoming**. The more limited plan dropped the anticipated amphibious feint on Korean's east coast and the attack on Sibyong-ni. It did, however, maintain the drive against Kaesong.

Tracy D. Connors, "Truckbusters from Dogpatch." *The Combat Diary of the 18th Fighter Bomber Wing in the Korean War.* http://www.truckbustersfrom-dogpatch.com/index.php?.id=9.

Operation Bimbo   18 January 1953

During the end of the year 1952, the Marines, like the rest of Eighth Army, maintained a regular, somewhat reduced wintertime schedule. At times it seemed to be too quiet for the Marines and so several efforts were made to bring the Chinese out of their fortifications. Operation Bimbo was a Marine exercise that attempted to combine an infantry-artillery-tank-air action to create the impression that the Chinese Communist Forces were under heavy attack. It was another of the several efforts to bait a trap for the Chinese. It began with a heavy concentration of artillery fire by the 11th Marines. On 18 January two participating infantry regiments opened fire. Armored vehicles added to the general effect by shelling Chinese emplacements. Marine attack planes swooped in to unload napalm. The Chinese responded by directing mortar fire into suspected Marine areas, and there was some Chinese troop movement but not as much as anticipated. The operation, which lasted approximately an hour and a half, failed to bring the Chinese out in the open.

Pat Meid and James M. Yingling, *U.S. Marine Operations in Korea, Volume V: Operations in West Korea*. Washington, D.C.: Historical Division, Headquarters, U.S. Marine Corps, 1972, p. 232.

Operation Black List Forty
8 September 1945

The partition of the Korean peninsula was made at the Cairo Conference in December 1943 and was the result of President Franklin D. Roosevelt's belief that the Koreans were unable to govern themselves. Korea, he promised, would be freed "in due course." The situation was verified at the Potsdam Conference in July 1945. In General Order No. 1 (2 September 1945), which was issued by the Allied Commander in the Pacific General of the Army Douglas MacArthur, the rules for the Japanese surrender were set forth. It acknowledged the earlier and nearly unilateral decision that it would be easiest for the Russians to swarm over Manchuria and then to occupy the northern portion of Korea. The American troops would take the surrender of the Japanese in the area south of the 38th parallel.

General MacArthur anticipated that there might be trouble with the Soviet Union, and on 29 August he warned Lieutenant General John R. Hodge, who had been selected to command the occupation troops, that the Russians might already have taken Seoul when he arrived. It was apparent that MacArthur still believed that Korea would be occupied under a quadripartite agreement of some kind with the United States participating with China, Russia, and Great Britain. Despite this, Hodge was given little or no guidance about U.S. policy in Korea.

Called to the job was Hodge's XXIV Corps that was located on Okinawa. He was ordered to rush his 45,000 troops to southern Korea as quickly as possible in a movement that was identified as Operation Black List Forty. At this point the necessary shipping was not available and it was the 9th of September before any significant number of troops arrived. However, on 4 September a small advanced party arrived at Kimpo Airfield near Seoul. There it was discovered that while isolated units of Russian troops were on the south side of the parallel, they were not organized and showed no intention of trying to stay. On the 8 September, and more than a month after the arrival of Russian troops, a fourteen man advance unit of the 7th Infantry Division sailed into the small harbor at Inchon. There Hodge was informed that the Russians, as promised, had halted at the 38th parallel.

The United States was not really all that interested in Korea, leaving most of the postwar decisions to MacArthur, who was already overloaded with occupied Japan. His orders instructed General Hodge to maintain a "harsh" occupation. On 7 September, MacArthur had issued a proclamation establishing military control over the area. General Hodge was not a good choice for this assignment. While an excellent military commander, he was generally short on tact and had even fewer diplomatic skills. To begin with he had instructed his men that they were to treat the Koreans as enemies.

There is little doubt that he disliked Koreans. From then on a series of large mistakes were made. Because of a shortage of troops and his scant knowledge of the Korean culture, Hodge allowed the Japanese police to remain armed and used them to control Korean crowds. The occupation was complete, however, and soon elements of the 6th, 7th and 40th Infantry divisions arrived and spread out across the southern portion of the Korean peninsula. Perhaps the most significant of the actions taken by Hodge during this highly sensitive period was to align the occupation government with the wealthy anti–Communist political faction and allow men who had previously collaborated with the Japanese to be promoted into positions of authority.

Clay Blair, *The Forgotten War: America in Korea 1950–1953*. New York: Times Books, 1987, pp. 36–38.

James F. Schnabel, *United States Army in the Korean War: Policy and Direction: The First Year.* Washington, D.C.: Office of the Chief of Military History, United States Army, 1973, pp. 14–17.

James Stokesbury, *A Short History of the Korean War.* New York: William Morrow, 1988, pp. 25–26.

Operation Blaze   2 July 1952

The First Royal Australian Regiment arrived in Korea on 4 March 1952, and after some months of training it took up station on 17 June 1950 south of Line Kansas. Operation Blaze was one of their first actions. It was a raid on Hill 227 occupied by the Chinese Communists. The hill was a significant piece of terrain, for it dominated the crossing site of the Sangpo ferry. The purpose of the raid, carried out by the regiment's A Company under Major D. S. Thomson, was to capture a prisoner and to destroy what fortifications they could. This daylight raid started at 0900 hours and lasted only 90 minutes. The fighting was tough right from the beginning, and after the initial assault the raiding party realized they were facing considerable Chinese opposition. The Australians were running low on ammunition, so the unit was finally ordered to withdraw. Major D. S. Thomson was awarded the Military Cross, and Corporal H. E. Patch was awarded the American Silver Star. Operation Blaze was not considered successful and cost the Regiment 36 casualties, nearly 33 percent of those involved.

Royal Australian Regiment, *War Diary*. http://www.kmike.com/oz/charlie/ green4.htm.

Operation Bluehearts   18 July 1950

By mid–July 1950 it was obvious that an amphibious landing was necessary; not only was there a drastic need for additional troops, but it was also necessary to get them into Korea without going through the port at Pusan. By this time Pusan had already handled more than fifty ships and there were many more on the way. The port facility was dangerously overloaded. Such a landing, which was to be on the southeastern coast, had to have access to the interior near Pusan where the enemy was gathering. Admiral J. H. Doyle was given the responsibility for a plan for the landing of two regimental combat teams of the 1st Cavalry and on 10 July his suggestion that they land at Pohang was accepted. Pohang was a town of some 50,000 residents located 60 plus miles from Pusan. Prior to the decision, on the 10th and 11th an LST full of amphibious and weather experts landed to do the necessary reconnaissance. Though limited, some jetties were available for landing craft, and the rail and communication lines to Pusan were intact. The landing, which would take place a scant eight days later, was named Operation Bluehearts.

Just a few days after the final decision, and to the tunes of the Army band, the Army's 1st Cavalry Division embarked at Yokosuka. While the 1st Cavalry Division had no experience in an amphibious landing, the Amphibious Group that was handling it was well-trained and capable. Fifteen LSTs were borrowed from Shipping Control Administration, Japan (Scajap) and two cargo attack ships, the *Oglethorpe* and *Titania,* were provided, as well as miscellaneous support vessels. Many of these vessels were chartered Japanese merchant ships, manned by Japanese crews who, at least technically, were still at war with the United States. Close air support was provided from Seventh Fleet, deep air support from Far East Air Force, and patrol aircraft from Task Group 96.2. The landing force was under the command of Major General Hobart Gay and consisted of the 5th and 8th Regimental Combat Teams of the 1st Cavalry Division, an artillery group made up of three battalions, and some minor support groups. They were preceded by a minesweeping group of seven sweepers and a gunfire support group made up of the American ships USS *Juneau*, *Kyes*, *Higbee*, and *Collett* and the Australian *Bataan*.

Early in the morning of the 18th the convoy moved into Yongil Man. When it was acknowledged that Pohang was still in the hands of the ROK 3rd Division, Admiral Doyle made the signal to land. Landing began at 0715 hours and the unloading was quickly completed. The initial landing went off unopposed. In the process more than 10,000 troops, 2,000 vehicles, and nearly 3,000 tons of cargo were brought ashore. Once ashore, General Walton Walker's crews were waiting to take them to the front. By noon on the 19th General Gay took command ashore. "Only the press was disappointed that this was not a guns-blazing near thing like the great amphibious assaults of just a few years before" (Miralda). Within a week the regiment was in combat on the Taegu-Taejon Road, having relieved the battered 25th Infantry Division.

The third echelon of the amphibious force arrived late, on 26 and 29 August, having been delayed by the appearance of typhoon Grace that came up the coast with its gusts of 50 knots. As the first, and the quickest, of the amphibious efforts, Operation Bluehearts must be considered a major success. It was the first sizable planned and executed naval effort of the war, and while it did not seem to attract a lot of attention from the press, military planners were well aware of the value of the operation and what was to be learned from it.

Clay Blair, *The Forgotten War: America in Korea 1950–1953*. New York: Times Books, 1987, pp. 87–89.

James A. Field, Jr., *History of United States Naval Operations: Korea*. Washington, D.C.: Government Printing Office, 1962, pp. 106–110.

Edward J. Miralda (ed), *The U.S. Navy in the Korean War*. Annapolis, MD: Naval Institute Press, 2007, p. 27.

Operation Bluehearts   22 July 1950

This was the name given to General Douglas MacArthur's plan for an amphibious landing behind enemy lines. The general reported that he had first conceived of the idea on his initial visit to Korea as he watched the massive lines of retreating soldiers and refugees. Operation Bluehearts was to be a landing on the west coast in an effort to cut across Korea, thus suffocating the enemy by denying its anticipated sources of supplies and reinforcements. The initial plan called for the invasion to take place on 22 July 1950, and General MacArthur's staff was sent into an all-out effort to compete the numerous details. However, despite the initial planning, Eighth Army simply did not have enough troops. The rapid success of North Korean troops and their quick and decisive victory at the Han River simply did not allow MacArthur to obligate troops elsewhere. What forces he had available were redirected to General Walton Walker's defense of the Pusan Perimeter, including the 1st Cavalry Division that landed at Pohang-dong to counteract the North Korean forces in the southwest sector of the defense at Pusan. MacArthur postponed the plan only long enough to increase his troop strength and build up supplies, and then initiated the plan in an altered form on 15 September 1950 as **Operation Chromite**, the invasion of Inchon, North Korea.

Clay Blair, *The Forgotten War: America in Korea 1950–1953*. New York: Times Books, 1987, pp. 84–87.

Walt Sheldon, *Hell or High Water: MacArthur's Landing at Inchon*. New York: Macmillan, 1968.

Operation Boomerang
7 September 1951

From 7 to 17 September the 161st Battery of the New Zealand Artillery had been pulled off line to calibrate twelve new guns. In addition, they spend a lot of time in what they defined as "housekeeping duties." They also provided support for the 28th Commonwealth Brigade that had conducted a series of raids just before going into reserves. On 7 September 1951, however, the New Zealanders of the Third Royal Australian Regiment were pulled back into service and, supported by a troop of tanks, crossed the Imjin River at a point known as "Pintail." Once across they advanced without much opposition for about five miles to the northwest. Once there, and for the next three days, the New Zealanders in Operation Boomerang continued to send out patrols to the north. During this time they were strongly supported by well-defined artillery fire by 163rd Battery. But the Communists had considerable artillery capacity of their own, and the patrol finally had to withdraw, doing so under the fire from its own guns set up in a predetermined fire plan. They came out being sure that there was no follow-up by the Chinese infantry. During the brief operation two men were killed and four wounded.

Ian McGibbon, *New Zealand and the Korean War.* Melbourne: Oxford University Press, 1996, p. 203.

Operation Buckshot 8 July 1952

Getting prisoners of war for interrogation was more of a problem during 1952 than it had been earlier in the war. The fact was so obvious that Major General Clark F. Ruffner sent a letter to his troops promising an R & R leave in Japan to any solder that captured a prisoner. In responding to the need, yet another attempt to take prisoners was set up in Operation Buckshot, approved in July by General Mark Clark. The assignment went to elements of the 11th ROK Division of the ROK I Corps. A reinforced battalion was sent west of the Nam River on 8 July seeking prisoners. They ran into trouble almost immediately and suffered 33 killed, 157 wounded, and 36 missing from the battalion. The enemy losses were estimated at 90 killed and 82

wounded, but equally important, not a single prisoner was taken. These unrewarded losses were not acceptable to General Clark and he turned down General James Van Fleet's request for a similar kind of operation, this time in the area controlled by the 1st Commonwealth Division.

Paul Wolfgeher, "The Battle Hills, Outposts, Operations and Battle Lines of the Korean War." Unpublished manuscript in the Wolfgeher Collection at the Center for the Study of the Korean War.

Operation Buckshot 22 January 1953

During the month of January 1953, 40th Division remained in X U.S. Corps reserve. On 22 January Operation Buckshot began as a relief exercise when the 180th Infantry Regiment relieved the 224th Infantry Regiment of the 40th U.S. Division in the center section of X Corps command at Nambakchon. The infantry regiment was placed in the left sector, leaving the 5th U.S. Regimental Combat Team occupying the right. The 245th Tank Battalion was attached to the 40th U.S. Division, which along with the Division Artillery (placed under corps command) were put in support of the 12th ROK Division. The following day they completed Operation Buckshot by sending the 179th Infantry Regiment in relief of the 223rd Regiment. The 40th Division was at this time completely deployed between Paeam and Ihyon-ni.

http://www.history.army.mil/reference/code.htm.

Operation Buffalo 13 August 1952

In the early morning of 13 August the hard-driving Marines were able to push the Chinese from Hill 122 (Bunker Hill) and take the post. At the same time, Operation Buffalo, directed toward Hill 75, 1200 meters to the west of the 3rd Royal Australian Regiment sector, was a small unit action designed to capture prisoners. The hill was the high point on a ridge about 500 yards from the Chinese main defensive line. It was believed that it was held by two Chinese platoons supported by two machine guns. Company B, under the command of Captain R. P. Richardson, left their sector on 2100 hours on the 13 and attacked at 2345. Supporting Centurion tanks, artillery, and mortar fire opened up. When the fire lifted the men from A Company moved up the flanks without much opposition. Those who moved into the center of the line, however, ran into considerable Chinese fire that resulted in the wounding of several of the advancing Australians. Shortly after midnight the Chinese withdrew into tunnels and directed 81 mm mortar fire in to the defenses.

The prime mission of the raid was to capture prisoners, but the defense was much stronger than anticipated, and the chance to get prisoners was gone. When the company losses became serious a withdrawal was ordered. Captain Richardson was awarded the Military Cross and Lieutenant Zwolanski (known as Lt. George by the Diggers) received the U.S. Bronze Star. All but one of the dead and all the 24 wounded were brought out. One more died of wounds after the battle.

Ian McGibbon, *New Zealand and the Korean War: Combat Operations.* Melbourne: Oxford University Press, 1996, p. 258.

Robert O'Neil, "Operation Buffalo: An Aussie Op in Korea." *Bulletin*, Vol. 3, 1999.

Operation Bushbeater

22 October 1951

While the navy was called on to increase its "bridge busting and roof lifting" campaigns to slow down enemy supplies and the Panmunjom Security Agreement was being signed by Vice Admiral C. Turner Joy in preparation for a new phase of cease-fire discussions, teams from the 1st Battalion, 1st Marine Regiment, were involved in Operation Bushbeater. The operation was designed to sweep up units of enemy troops that had been operating behind

the United Nations lines. During October several Marine ground efforts had been directed toward limiting the guerrilla activity near Line Minnesota. On the 22nd the 1st Marine Battalion, using helicopters from HMR-161 headquarters, pursued Operation Bushbeater on the east flank with orders to move toward the town of Soyang as teams from the battalion's Reconnaissance Company came in from the other direction. Able and Baker Companies of the 1st Marines were to be landed at ten points along the line at the division's east flank and were to sweep westward toward the Soyang River.

In the meantime 60 troops from the Recon Company were being landed on the west to deploy and patrol from the opposite directions. They were to drop by climbing ropes into Red and White zones. Bad weather caused two helicopters to lose power and crash, and another machine was damaged. All were recovered and flew again; no one was badly injured during the flight. Despite these setbacks, Operation Bushbeater proved that helicopter-borne teams were capable of carrying out many of the reconnaissance and security patrols that had previously be conducted by foot. During the operation forty flights were made to the east, where 210 troops had been landed in just under 2 hours and 21 minutes. Those going to the west flank made the trip in just an hour, having encountered little difficulty. From the exercise it was also determined that debarking from knotted ropes was dangerous both to the men and the helicopter and should be used only when no other means of landing was possible. While the areas were never completely cleared of the enemy, the operation was nevertheless considered successful.

Lynn Montross, *Cavalry of the Sky: The Story of U.S. Marine Combat Helicopters.* New York: Harper and Brothers, 1954, p. 173.

Lynn Montross, *U.S. Marine Operations in Korea 1950–1953: The East-Central Front.* Washington, D.C.: Historical Branch, Headquarters, U.S. Marine Corps, 1962, p. 217.

Operation Cat and Dog 26–28
June 1951

After Generals Matthew Ridgway and James Van Fleet had toured the battlefield, they decided there was no value in trying to advance beyond Line Wyoming. The cost in casualties anticipated in taking additional land was not worth it. Nevertheless, they needed prisoners for interrogation and thus launched Operation Cat and Dog with the primary goal of capturing as many enemy prisoners as possible. The operation lasted three days, and while some Communist facilities in the IX Corps sector were destroyed in the process, the primarily goal, the taking of prisoners, was not accomplished.

Paul M. Edwards, *Korean War Almanac*. New York: Facts on File, 2006, p. 217.

Operation Cat Whiskers
October 1952

During the summer of 1952 the 1st Amphibian Tractor Battalion had taken part in the defense of the Kansas Line. In late August it had sent 58 of its members to help the 1st Marines, who had lost so many men in the fight for Bunker Hill that they required reinforcements. The battalion had set up a system whereby they could patrol the Han River by tractor. Several of the troops were involved in laying a signal cable across the river, and some were assigned to man outposts along the river. Throughout the end of 1952 they maintained their Kansas Line defense mission. In October, however, Company B was sent out on an amphibious mission to capture enemy prisoners. This was titled Operation Cat Whiskers. The plan was for the unit to cross the Han River in a rubber boat, and for the troops to set up an ambush somewhere on the far shore in hope they could pick up a prisoner. Bad weather on the river, however, prevented them from landing the boat and Operation Cat Whiskers withdrew unsuccessfully.

Pat Meid and James M. Yingling, *U.S. Marine Operations in Korea, Volume V: Operations in West Korea*. Washington, D.C.: Historical Division, Headquarters, U.S. Marine Corps, 1972, p. 250.

Operation Charlie 25 February
1953

Carried out by the 5th Marines, Operation Charlie was a two-reinforced platoon- size unit that executed an attack during the daylight hours of 25 February 1953. The object was a single hill (Hill 15, generally called Detroit), two miles east of the objectives sought in **Operation Clambake**. It was considered a routine kill, capture and destroy mission and was given to Company F. Launched early in the morning to screen the movement, bad weather prevented almost all phases of the d-day air strikes, but the artillery fire was continued. In nearly three hours of firing by the 11th Marine Regiment and the 1st Royal Canadian Horse Artillery, 11,881 rounds were expended. Upon reaching Hill Detroit the Marines found that most of the enemy fortifications were undamaged despite the earlier bombardment, but the artillery had successfully isolated the battlefield.

Lee Ballenger, *U.S. Marines in Korea, Volume 2: 1953*. Washington, D.C.: Brassey's, 2001, pp. 83–86.

Operation Cheerful 17 December
1951

The Communists had taken Chongyong-do as well as some of the smaller islands in a surprise raid at 0800 hours on 16 December 1951, but they had only held it a few hours. Then the Canadians were assigned the job of clearing them. Operation Cheerful, in keeping with the Christmas season, was proposed to launch a two prong attack in order to retake the islands simultaneously. It was to be accomplished by a combined force of Leopard and Salamander (partisan) units. This was not a wise decision, as the groups had never worked together before and it was generally believed that both units showed a significant lack of discipline. The landings were under the direction of Commander J. Plomer on board the HMCS *Cayuga* and on-the-site command by Lieutenant Pack, the commander of the ROKN minesweeper *JMI 302*. At first the islands were shelled and then four junks filled with guerrillas were taken in tow. One of the junks began to leak, however, and the fighting force was cut by a forth. At first they seemed to have landed without opposition, but this was not to be the case, and heavy Chinese fire sank another of the junks. From the bridge of the *Cayuga,* Commander Plomer could see that the plan was not working. While they had established a small beachhead it was obvious that they were outnumbered and he ordered the evacuation of all of the attackers. On the return to the shelter of the convoy, one of the junks with all aboard deserted. Operation Cheerful had failed.

Edward C. Meyers, *Thunder in the Morning Calm*. St. Catharines, Ontario: Vanwell Publishing, 1991, pp. 163–165.

Operation Chopper   26 May 1951

The order for Operation Chopper was initiated by X Corps and was set up to send the 1st Marine Division to seize the area of Yanggu. The U.S. 2nd Infantry Division was to move forward, then secure and occupy the Hyon-ni to Inje road. A third prong, this time Task Force Baker, was to advance toward the northeast, moving to the coast in such a way as to cut off, and hopefully destroy, significant elements of the enemy troops trying to escape to the north. The execution of Operation Chopper was not quick enough to allow it to be as successful as intended. Apparently some of the commanding officers involved were hesitant because of the boldness of the plan advanced, and did not act quickly enough.

Roy E. Appleman, *Ridgway Duels for Korea*. College Station: Texas A&M University Press, 1990, p. 543.

Operation Chopstick 6   1 April 1952

Since the negotiations at Panmunjom were showing signs of some progress by the end of February 1952, General Matthew Ridgway was not in favor of any operations that would result in a high rate of casualties. At this point the Chinese Communists were directing much of their effort in limited attacks against front line areas held by the Korean Marine Corps, where they would briefly penetrate the main line of resistance and then pull back. Wanting to control the situation, Ridgway informed General James Van Fleet that he wanted any offensive action to be limited to reconnaissance and counter-offensive measures. On the other hand, General Van Fleet envisioned an expanded offensive plan that would focus on the use of his Republic of Korea divisions acting in a series of limited objectives. In proposing Operation Chopstick 6, Van Fleet envisioned the envelopment of the high ground that was south of Pyongyang by a reinforced ROK division, designed to destroy fortifications and inflict casualties. The plan was to support the ROK by air and artillery and to take advantage of surprise and mobility. However, General Ridgway did not like the terrain they would need to cross, feeling that it was too difficult, and did not approve the plan.

Tracy D. Commons, *The Combat Diary of the 18th Fighter Bomber Wing in the Korean War*. http://www.truckbustersfromdogpatch.com/index.php?.id=9.

Operation Chopstick 16   15 April 1952

This operation was a part of General James Van Fleet's offensive plan using the ROK divisions at his disposal in a series of limited objectives. Operation Chopstick 16 laid out a two-division attack to drive the enemy from the area east and south of the Nam River in eastern Korea. While not much more impressed with Operation Chopsticks 16 than he had been with **Operation Chopsticks 6**, General Ridgway nevertheless approved it with the agreement that no U.S. troops would be used, and that he would be told as soon as the operation was launched. As it turned out General Van Fleet suspended it indefinitely, himself, on 29 April in light of some slight but encouraging changes in the negotiation process.

Tracy D. Commons, *The Combat Diary of the 18th Fighter Bomber Wing in the Korean War.* http:// www.truckbustersfromdogpatch.com/index.php?.id =9.

Paul Wolfgeher, "The Battle Hills, Outposts, Operations and Battle Lines of the Korean War." Unpublished manuscript in the Wolfgeher Collection at the Center for the Study of the Korean War.

Operation Chromite

15 September 1950

The military situation in early September 1950 was tantamount to a disaster; the United Nations forces were holding on to a perimeter at Pusan by the skin of their teeth. Aware that much of a potential victory lay in restricting the Communist supply lines, MacArthur had considered, as early as late June 1950, an end-around amphibious assault designed to cut off the lines of supply and reinforcements which were already considerably strained as the North Koreans moved steadily south. To General MacArthur, at least, the obvious point of such an attack would be the port city of Inchon, tied to the capital at Seoul by 20 miles or so of rail and highway. Having decided, he set in motion preparations for a landing "near Seoul" that was called **Operation Bluehearts** (22 July 1950). At the time the idea was unworkable, for he was barely holding on at Pusan and did not have enough American troops to mount any such attack.

As well, problems resident in any attack on Inchon were numerous. In the first place the sea route to the port was treacherous and went through Flying Fish Channel, one of the highest tide reaches in the world with tides that rose and fell more than thirty feet and a water surge of five to six knots. The port itself was divided and guarded by Wolmi-do, a small island connected to the mainland by a causeway that would have to be taken before moving any farther. To add to the difficulties, the maps in use were primarily Japanese and the area was not well marked, meaning that much of the planning was based on less than accurate information.

In the background of much of this were the remaining hostilities created in the late 1940s as the various services fought for predominance and in the some cases for survival. The Marines were not only in disfavor with General Omar Bradley but with President Truman as well, and his remark "They have a propaganda machine that is almost equal to Stalin" left many a hard feelings. And the reality of the situation was that the 1st Marines existed only on paper; the core of its manpower was situated in reserve units.

But, while MacArthur did not have the facilities to wage such an invasion in June, primarily because the 1st Marine division was not

LST 833 (*La Moure County*) unloading in Operation Chromite (**Center for the Study of the Korean War**).

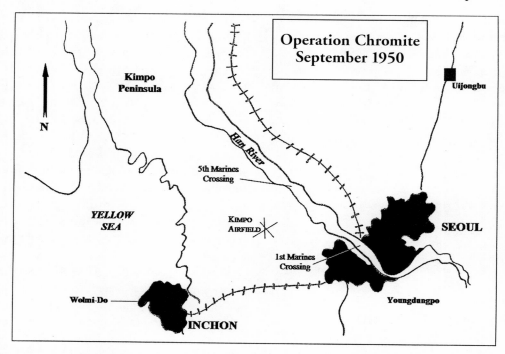

Operation Chromite, September 1950 (courtesy Paul Wolfgeher Collection, Center for the Study of the Korean War).

yet fully manned and what reinforcements were coming in were quickly drained off for the expanding crisis at Pusan, it was never far from his mind. In early September when he felt he could mount the attack, he ran into considerable opposition from other officers as well as the Joint Chiefs of Staff. Generals Omar Bradley and J. Lawton Collins, themselves no strangers to massive infantry assaults, were opposed, as was the Navy, which felt the technical requirements were too high. The best the general was able to get from a high-pressure meeting to discuss the idea was from Rear Admiral James H. Doyle: "It is not impossible."

The primary alternative being considered was Kunsan and a strike there would have been far less risky. On the other hand, it was MacArthur's contention that it would not serve the purpose, for it would not cut the enemy's logistics lines. Instead he offered to risk his professional reputation by acknowledging that if things did not go as planned he would be willing to withdraw as soon as it became evident.

To pull off his plan MacArthur created X Corps, composed of the 1st Marine Division and the 7th Infantry Division under the command of his chief-of-staff, Major General Edward M. Almond. This was to be a separate organization and would report to Tokyo, not to Eighth Army. This divided command would remain one of the hotly contested questions in the analysis of General MacArthur's military role in Korea. It also created disagreements with General Oliver P. Smith, leading the Marines, who had to go head-to-head with General Walker about pulling the 1st Marine Brigade out of Pusan. A compromise of sorts was reached with Walker getting a regiment of the 7th Infantry Division as a replacement.

Joint Task Force 7 with Admiral Struble in command would provide air cover, shore bombardment, blockade, minesweeping and logistics support for Admiral Doyle's attack force. All in all the fleet consisted of 230 vessels. It was finally determined that Operation Chromite would begin with bombardment and the Marines heading for shore at Wolmi-do at high tide on the morning of 15 September, and the main elements at Inchon on the tide.

After an intense bombardment, the 3rd and 5th Marine Regiments went ashore, meeting little resistance. They were able to take control of Wolmi-do within several hours, at the cost of 20 wounded Marines. Later in the afternoon the Marines went ahead to the mainland, climbing a sea wall with hastily constructed ladders, and landing their LSTs on the beach where they would be grounded overnight. At first there was considerable confusion and opposition, but within an hour the Marines had taken Cemetery Hill that overlooked Red Beach, and by the next morning the two landing beaches were linked. Inchon was eventually taken with fewer than 200 casualties. The 7th Infantry Division came ashore at Green Beach and linked up with the Marines heading for Kimpo Airfield and Seoul. In the meantime, General Walton Walker had broken out of the Pusan Perimeter and was moving north in an effort to link up with X Corps as the culmination of MacArthur's anvil plan.

There can be little doubt that the concept, the planning, and the execution of the landing at Inchon was a remarkable achievement, and that MacArthur deserves whatever credit is coming. And, at least on the surface, it marked the turning point in this early phase of the war. But historian James Stokesbury makes the important point that while the results of the Inchon landing had been magnificent, it only "meant the North Koreans were finished as an army, but not as soldiers." See **Operation Common Knowledge.**

James A. Field, Jr., *History of United States Naval Operations: Korea*. Washington, D.C.: Government Printing Office, 1962, see Inchon.
Joseph C. Goulden, *Korea: The Untold Story of the War*. New York: Times Books, 1982, Chapter Seven.
James L. Stokesbury, *A Short History of the Korean War*. New York: William Morrow, 1988, p. 76.

Operation Citadel   19 August 1951

Eighth Army was focused on a mountain range, about 17 miles north of the 38th Parallel and thirty miles east of Kumhwa, that was know as Bloody Ridge. While involved there against the North Korean 45th, 13th, and 2nd Divisions, Operation Citadel was set in motion. It was a plan to move the main line of resistance closer to the outpost line of resistance. The operation was completed successfully.

"Overview of Korean War Battle/Offensive." Korean War. http://www.Korea.War.com.
Paul M. Edwards, *Korean War Almanac*. New York: Facts on File, 2006, p. 229.

Operation Clam Up   10 February 1952

Certainly this was one of the more bizarre of the operations conducted by Eighth Army. In January 1952 General James Van Fleet had implemented a month long artillery-air campaign designed to impress the Communists with the power the United Nations could deliver. In response the Communists dug deeper, reinforced their fortifications, and stayed off the battlefield. In an effort to get them to come out and fight, Van Fleet ordered Eighth Army to implement Operation Clam Up. It was a difficult plan to execute, for it called for silence on the battlefield in hope that the enemy would believe the UN had gone away. The 4 August order stated "a policy of aggressive patrolling has led the enemy to rely upon our patrols for the maintenance of contact" which the general concluded was allowing them to avoid the hazard of capture. Therefore, he ordered an "attempt to decoy the enemy into dispatching patrols against our lines and ambush and capture such patrols" (Montross). If they believed the ruse then they might come out of their various defenses and allow the UN to seize a significant number of North Korean and Chinese prisoners. The set up included three regiments on the main line of resistance: the Korean Marine Corps, the 1st Marine Regiment, and the 7th Marine Regiment.

First, the 1st Marine Division's 11th Marines fired harassing and interdiction missions as if they were covering up a withdrawal. All air strikes within 20,000 yards of the line were abandoned, all artillery fire stopped, no patrols went out, and even ground fire was greatly reduced. Reserve battalions were sent on long daylight marches to the rear and returned by motor lift each night to give the impression of a withdrawal. The plan was that sensing the quiet, the Communists would emerge, but they did not. The Communists sent out night patrols attempting to draw Marine fire near Hill 812 but when it was not returned they attacked. Finally, in self-defense, the Marines fought them off. While Operation Clam Up continued for several days the Communists either did not recognize the quiet, or at least did not believe it. The few patrols that the Communists sent out were not significant enough to meet Van Fleet's expectations. When Operation Clam Up came to an end on 15 February, it had fallen considerably short of expectations. The enemy loses among their patrols were high, but they had fewer in the rear areas, and besides, the enemy had enjoyed a five day period in which to bring up ammunition and supplies without interference. It was finally conceded that despite the effort, the Communists had most likely lost fewer prisoners during this operation than they had in the five previous days.

Lynn Montross, *U.S. Marine Operations in Korea 1950–1953: The East-Central Front.* Washington, D.C.: Historical Branch, Headquarters, U.S. Marine Corps, 1962, pp. 2–43.

Operation Claymore   22–24 August 1951

This was conducted by the 25th Brigade of the Commonwealth Division just a week after the completion of **Operation Dirk**. In Operation Claymore the advance was conducted with 2nd Royal 22e Regiment and the 2nd Princess Patricia Canadian Light Infantry against Hill 208, a landmass near Mabang-ri on the highway southeast of Ascom City and Hill 187, a much disputed enemy vantage point. The advance was made at night with little opposition. Much of it covered terrain that had not been reconnoitered and the units were prepared to withdraw if there was heavy opposition. The enemy's main position was some three miles north of the Imjin and the location jeopardized the UN supply lines. This patrol, and many others like it, was always hampered by the unpredictability of the Imjin River, which at this time of year was the first major hurdle to be faced. Consideration was given to moving the Commonwealth Division to the north side of the river in order to avoid this ongoing problem. This crossing was attempted in **Operation Minden.**

Les Peate, *The War That Wasn't: Canadians in Korea.* Ottawa, Canada: Esprit de Corps Books, 2005, pp. 39–40.

Operation Clean Up I
17 September 1951

As a part of the overall operations in the Iron Triangle, and in keeping with Lieutenant General Matthew Ridgway's limited objectives policy, Operation Clean Up I (as well as **Operation Clean Up II**) was to take and hold the hill complex west of Chorwon. What was most important was to secure the rail line between Kumhwa and Chorwon because the continuing rains had made the roads nearly impassable. This meant UN control of the area called Bloody Angle. The goal of Operation Clean Up I was to take the ridge that ran west of Hill 487 in order to disrupt Communist supply lines. The battle that was fought on the western approaches to Hill 477 and Twin Peaks, just northeast of Hill 487, eventually

Defensive bunker on Line Jamestown, 1952 (Center for the Study of the Korean War).

fell to the 3rd Infantry Division. However, despite the coordinated attacks on 18 September, they were unable to take Hill 487. This operation only achieved a limited success, but the follow up in Clean Up II advanced all of I Corps' components to near Line Jamestown and assured the safety of the Kumhwa to Chorwon rail line.

"Overview of Korean War Battle/Offensive." http://Korean War.com.

Operation Clean Up II

29 September 1951

Keeping with Lieutenant General Ridgway's limited operations policy and as a part of the overall operations in the Iron Triangle, Operation Clean Up II was launched to complete the job started by **Operation Clean Up I**; to take and hold the hill complex west of Chorwon. Operation Clean Up II was an assault on the entire five-hill complex. The attack was preceded by nine days of bombardment that took more than 45,000 rounds of artillery, primarily from tanks so placed as to fire directly into Communist bunkers. On the 29 September, A and B Companies of the 1st Battalion and Company E of the 2nd Battalion, 15th Regiment, took on Hill 487. The battle lasted seven days. All three companies encountered strong Chinese Communist resistance but were able to take Hill 487. The Communists poured in artillery, and undertook several counterattacks. At the same time, the 3rd Battalion of the 65th Regiment was on Twin Peaks and two other related hills. Finally, joined by G Company of the 15th Regiment, they were able to take the associated hill. In early October 1951, Operation Clean Up II merged with **Operation Commando**.

"Overview of Korean War Battle/Offensive." http://Korean War.com.

Operation Cleaver   21 September 1951

The only record listed suggests this operation was a joint tank and infantry raid that moved into the Iron Triangle.

Paul Wolfgeher, "The Battle Hills, Outposts, Operations and Battle Lines of the Korean War." Unpublished manuscript in the Wolfgeher Collection at the Center for Studies of the Korean War.

Operation Clobber   April 1952

As the second Korean Winter phase came to an end, the 1st Marine Division decided that the Chinese Communists were holding back and showing little interest in conducting any kind of significant ground action. This definite lack of commitment continued into April 1952. The Marines instituted a plan they hoped would either shake them loose, or if not that, then inflict serous casualties. Toward the end of the month the Marines, in conjunction with elements of other I Corps divisions, deluged the Chinese with artillery and tank fire. The exercise was called Operation Clobber. The 11th Marines, supported by Company D of the 1st Tank Battalion and nine of the battalion's 105mm howitzers, blasted Chinese command posts, bivouac areas, gun positions, and observation posts. Most of the firing was done at night and was designed to inflict maximum casualties and damage on any Chinese who might be preparing to launch a surprise attack. However, it did not result in any major changes in the placement of the Chinese Communist Forces.

Pat Meid and James M. Yingling, *U.S. Marine Operations in Korea, Volume V: Operations in West Korea.* Washington, D.C.: Historical Division, Headquarters, U.S. Marine Corps, 1972, p. 73.

Operation Commando
3 October 1951

Carried out by I Corps, on Eighth Army's left flank, Operation Commando was commanded by Lieutenant General "Iron Mike" O'Daniel. The primary mission of the operation was to maintain pressure on the Communists. This operation involved several U.S. divisions: the 3rd and 25th Infantry Divisions, the 1st Cavalry Division, the newly organized 1st Commonwealth Division and the 1st Republic of Korea Division. The more immediate and practical goal for the operation was an assault designed to extend the Commonwealth Division position along the Jamestown Line. Another aim was to provide protection for the Chorwon-Seoul-Kumhwa railroad, which was the primary military supply route to the front. Moving forward between 3 and 8 October, the divisions advanced the line about 8,000 yards, including the area of Maryang-san. The goal was to establish a new defensive line and to destroy elements of the Communist 42nd, 47th, 64th, and 65th Army.

It required nearly sixteen days for the 1st Cavalry Division to make it the six miles to Line Jamestown. During the assault, I Corps experienced nearly 4,000 casualties, more than half in the 1st Cavalry. Once they reached Line Jamestown General O'Daniel called for a halt. As it turned out, there would be no more major offensives of this nature.

Operation Commando involved an Australian battalion in one of its major roles. The Third Royal Australian Regiment, assigned to the Commonwealth Division, was on the forefront of the attack. This action has been called "one of the most impressive victories by any Australian battalion. The outnumbered regiment dislodged an enemy that was in a superior position during the five days of heavy fighting. Australian casualties were 20 dead and 89 wounded.

Also taking a critical role was the 1st Cavalry Division, which was resisted at every yard as they drove toward the 139th and 141st Division of the Chinese 47th Army. By 8 October, however, they were able to gain the high ground on the northeast half of the Jamestown Line. The fighting did not end until the 19th with I Corps forward of the line. Operation Commando was followed up by an advance against the hills south of the line in **Operation Polecharge**.

Clay Blair, *The Forgotten War: America in Korea 1950–1953.* New York: Times Books, 1987, pp. 948–949.
James Stokesbury, *A Short History of the Korean War.* New York: William Morrow, 1988, p. 163.

Operation Common Knowledge 15 September 1950

Despite all the effort expended by MacArthur's headquarters to keep the invasion a secret, war correspondents in Japan were openly discussing the anticipated invasion of North Korea, calling it Operation Common Knowledge. Even before X Corps began preparing to board the invasion fleet, the *New York Times* was running articles discussing the probability of a landing behind the lines. The best that MacArthur and his staff could do was to try and keep the location a secret. Headquarters launched a series of complicated deception schemes designed to confuse the North Koreans about possible targets. This included feints, unassociated bombardments, and naval gunfire at places like Kunsan, Ongjin, Chinnampo, all designed to keep the Communists guessing.

Clay Blair, *The Forgotten War: America in Korea 1950–1953.* New York: Times Books, 1987, pp. 238.

Operation Counter 6 June 1953

In the summer of 1952, Major General David L. Ruffner, commander of the 45th Infantry Division, a National Guard outfit, was facing an unpleasant situation. The enemy was holding the high ground in front of his position on the flank of I Corps. Their observation posts were overlooking much of his sec-

tor and their artillery impact had increased considerably. He decided to advance his own forward outpost line in a plan called Operation Counter. The hills he was facing were in a line from the southeast to the northeast and included spots that had taken on infamous names: White Horse, Arrowhead, Pork Chop and Old Baldy. The six outposts to the north were assigned to the 278th Infantry Regiment while the 180th Infantry Regiment was sent to the south. The men from the 45th Division moved out on 6 June 1952. The attacks were successful, as Company A of the 180th was finally able to take Old Baldy and I Company, after an hour of heavy fighting, took Pork Chop. The twelve identified outposts had been overrun. Once the land was occupied the soldiers began the job of setting up their own outposts, building new bunkers and laying communications wire.

The Chinese responded almost immediately with company sized counterattacks, trying to push the United Nations Command away from the newly acquired ground. The highest of the peaks, Old Baldy, found the fighting particularly hard and it took an advance by the 179th Infantry, a replacement for the 180th, to secure a Chinese post that had been established less than 1,000 yards from the UN controlled ridge. Three companies supported by two tanks were able to climb a portion of the hill, where they slugged it out with the Chinese. In the action one of tanks lost a tread and the other tipped over. The probes went on daily after that and toward the end of the month the Chinese grew increasingly determined. On the 28th and 29th they launched four separate battalion-size attacks on all points held by the 179th. The Chinese actually broke through at one point, but calling in artillery almost on top of them, the UN was able to drive the enemy away and held the ridge. The Communists tried again during the first few days of July but when that failed, they apparently gave up on retaking the ridge at once and focused elsewhere.

While the immediate operation was successful and did deny the Communists an outpost for more direct artillery fire, it did not last long. In the give-and-take of the ridge-line fighting, the Chinese were able to retake Old Baldy in July. It changed hands again in August and September.

James Stokesbury, *A Short History of the Korean War.* New York: William Morrow, 1988, pp. 205–206.

Operation Courageous
23–28 March 1951

Initially the events of Operation Courageous, to expand on the success of **Operation Killer,** perhaps hinged as much on its political importance as it did on the military events. The concern in Washington was how to approach the Communists with the UN desire for a cease-fire. The Truman administration believed the Chinese might have come to the conclusion that the war could not be won and would be willing to negotiate. President Harry S Truman was planning to make a public statement suggesting a willingness to end the war. The timing of the statement was set up to coincide with the fact that General Ridgway's forces were approaching the 38th parallel. On the other hand, General Ridgway's military intentions were not so much to occupy additional territory as they were to advance and trap a significant number of Chinese Communist and North Korean troops between the Han and Imjin Rivers, and destroy them.

Operation Courageous was a part of Ridgway's "meat grinder policy" designed to keep his units intact and his casualties at the bare minimum as he inflicted the greatest amount of damage on the enemy. He was well aware of the restraints imposed on him by his own

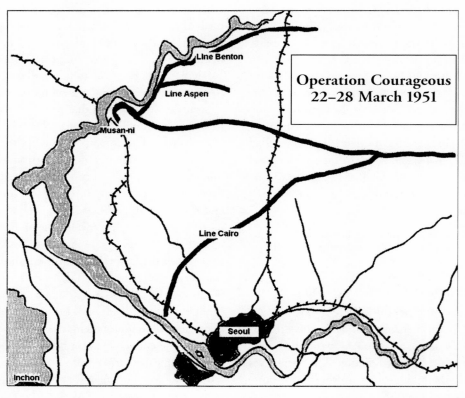

Operation Courageous, March 1951 (courtesy the Center for the Study of the Korean War).

logistic problems, and had no intention of outrunning them. General Milburn of I Corps, which was composed of the U.S. 25th and 3rd Infantry Divisions and ROK 1st Infantry, would be operating in conjunction with the 187th Airborne Regimental Combat Team and their attached 2nd and 4th Rangers companies, who were planning to drop near Munsan-ni on the morning of 23 March (**Operation Tomahawk**). The plan was for a link up between the attacking forces that would converge toward the final objective of Operation Courageous, a point some ten miles north of Line Benton, virtually to the 38th parallel.

The attack was launched on time, with the C-46 and C-119 of the 315th Air Division lifting the airborne from Taegu just before 0700. The timetable was upset by mechanical problems with one of the planes and a miscalculated drop zone, but despite this and some unanticipated Chinese resistance, the linkup of UN forces occurred generally as planned. The operation initiated a large number of Communist casualties, and the success of the movement was considered assured as most of the area, with one small exception, was cleared of all Communists forces. On reaching the operation's objectives the stage was set for the launching of **Operation Ripper**.

Clay Blair, *The Forgotten War: America in Korea 1950–1953.* New York: Times Books, 1987, pp. 729–752.

Ian McGibbon, *New Zealand and the Korean War: Combat Operations.* Melbourne: Oxford University Press 1996, p. 100.

Operation Cow Puncher

2–3 August 1951

General Van Fleet decided to deepen his defensive field and ordered Line Wyoming to become a permanent defensive line. In the process, Operation Cow Puncher was invoked to move IX Corps forward from phase Line Utah to Line Wyoming.

Paul M. Edwards, *Korean War Almanac.* New York: Facts on File, 2006, p. 226.

Paul Wolfgeher, "The Battle Hills, Outposts, Operations and Battle Lines of the Korean War." Unpublished manuscript in the Wolfgeher Collection at the Center for the Study of the Korean War.

Operation Cudgel   19 September 1951

Shortly after the successful conclusion of **Operation Touchdown** in mid–September 1951, Operation Cudgel was drawn up by General James Van Fleet and his staff seeking an advance in the sections held by the U.S. I and IX Corps. It anticipated a drive north of about 15 miles from the Wyoming Line to protect the highly important Chorwon-Kumhwa railway line and to force the enemy out of the forward fortifications. The Eighth Army command intended to use the railway as a part of a follow up attack, to be named **Operation Wrangler**, and sought immediate permission from General Matthew Ridgway. Even while considering the plan, he was aware of the potential danger of such an advance if the Communists initiated a counterthrust while the operation was in effect. Therefore, almost immediately after making his request, Van Fleet discarded both Operation Cudgel and Operation Wrangler, having reconsidered the probable casualty costs of the plans.

Terry D. Connors, *The Combat Diary of the 18th Fighter Bomber Wing in the Korean War.* http://www.truckbustersfromdogpatch.com/index.php?.id=9.

Operation Dauntless   6 April 1951

This operation was carried out in two phases. The first was to move out from Line Kansas and forward to Line Utah; the second was to advance from there to Line Wyoming toward Line Quantico. The underlying assumptions of this move were as much defensive as offensive since Ridgway believed that the Communists were preparing for a massive attack, probably in mid to late April. Rumors had it, as well, that the Chinese Communist Forces (CCF) were finally committed to bringing their air power to bear; some estimates suggested that they had as many as 800 planes waiting to attack. There was also the long-range possibility always hanging in the background that this might be a time when the Soviet Union would decide to enter the war. And aside from these fears, there was the immediate reality that the weather was going to get worse.

The mission goal was threefold: destroy as much of the enemy's equipment as possible, keep those enemy units in front of the U.S. I and IX Corps off balance, and advance the two corps towards to what would later be identified as Line Utah. At that point the advanced troops would be within six miles of Chorwon and at the edge of the Iron Triangle. Since General Ridgway had replaced General MacArthur by the time the plan went into operation, General James Van Fleet was in command.

The second phase of Operation Dauntless had two main objectives: to advance General Milburn's I Corps from Line Utah on the left of Eighth Army to Line Wyoming at the Iron Triangle and at the same time advance IX Corps under General William F. Hoge at the center from Line Kansas to Line Quantico, the line that lay just above the Hwachon Reservoir. It was expected that this second phase would invoke a Communist counterattack. It was also Van Fleet's expectation that there would be no northerly advance further than Line Quantico. He was limited by General Ridgway's concern and the orders issued: "Your mission is to repel aggression against so much of the territory (and the people therein) of the Republic of Korea as you now occupy and ... to maintain and establish order" (Blair). But any action beyond Line Wyoming was to be cleared with Ridgway.

I Corps attacked with six infantry regiments toward Line Wyoming. They moved forward slowly against very light enemy resistance,

with most regiments crossing more than a mile and half. In the center IX moved forward with the ROK 6th and 1st Marine Divisions, again without much enemy opposition, and entered the town of Hwachon. General Ridgway was pretty well convinced by this time that the combination of poor weather, terrible terrain, and potential enemy counterattacks made any further advance unrealistic, so no further movement was planned. At 1000 hours on 22 April the Chinese Communist Forces attacked Eighth Army across a front that was forty miles wide, using elements from 27 divisions.

Clay Blair, *The Forgotten War: America in Korea 1950–1953.* New York: Times Books, 1987, pp. 780–814.

James F. Schnabel, *United States Army in the Korean War, Policy and Direction: The First Year.* Washington, D.C.: Office of the Chief of Military History, United States Army, 1972, p. 363.

Operation Detonate   12 May 1951

Even as the first spring offensive was being carried out, Communist leader Chairman Mao Tse-tung was planning the second step of his Fifth Campaign. UN reconnaissance planes had located nearly four thousand enemy vehicles gathering, the largest number of them heading south. By 10 May 1951, General James C. Tarkenton, G2 for General James Van Fleet, felt he needed to warn the general that he was expecting an imminent Chinese attack on Seoul. The next day Van Fleet cancelled his own offensive that had been planned as Operation Detonate and informed General Ridgway that the Chinese were planning an attack of large portions. The Ridgway offensive that followed on 12 June was called **Operation Piledriver**.

Clay Blair, *The Forgotten War: America in Korea 1950–1953.* New York: Times Books, 1987, p. 867–900.

Operation Dirk   August 1951

Though it was officially in reserves during August of 1951, the Canadian 25th Brigade took part in the Commonwealth Division's program of long range patrols. And on 13 August 1951 it crossed the Imjin River as a battalion-sized patrol identified as Operation Dirk. The four infantry companies of the 2nd Royal Canadian Regiment were supported by engineers from the 57th Field Squadron, a troop of Strathcona tanks, and elements of the division artillery. The goal of the operation was to drive the Communists across the river, capture a prisoner or two, and establish a location on the main line of resistance. By 1900 hours on the 13th they had crossed the river and established a base about a mile north. Leapfrogging companies through the hot and humid day, the Canadians completed the anticipated four mile advance unopposed. The Chinese did not react until that night when they sent several small probes against the entrenched Canadian units. On the morning of the 14th, moving the last mile toward their final destination at Hill 187, it became obvious that the Chinese had the hill well defended. No further attempt was made to take it. The brigade made an unhurried withdrawal through sporadic enemy fire. During the advance the Canadian artillery and tank fire support was continuous and effective enough to be mentioned in dispatches. Operation Dirk had cost four wounded. The entire operation was observed and guided by Lieutenant Colonel Keane, acting brigade commander, flying overhead in a reconnaissance plane.

Ted Barris, *Deadlock in Korea: Canadians at War, 1950–1953*. Toronto: Macmillan Canada, 1999, pp. 134, 136.
Les Peate, *The War That Wasn't: Canadians in Korea*. Ottawa, Canada: Esprit de Corps Books, 2005, pp. 39–40.

Operation Dog   23 February 1953

This operation was designed to be a frontal assault at night against the Boot. The focus of the attack was about 2,000 yards in front of the main line of resistance near Hills 92 (Marilyn) and 64A (Ingrid). The object was to sur-

round the area on three sides and sent Easy Company, 2nd Battalion, 7th Regiment, supported by tanks, to soften up the Boot and then Baker Company, 1st Battalion, 7th Regiment, would reinforce the assault. Once attacked the entire area came under Chinese fire and enemy troops were seen arriving from Three Fingers. During the firefight the Chinese established control between Hill 90 and Outpost Marilyn. Just as quickly, as the initiative turned, Operation Dog became the battle for Hill 90. The Chinese were held back but were not finished and managed to set up an ambush on the evacuation route laid out by the Marines to remove their wounded. While it did not stop the orderly withdrawal it did result in additional casualties.

The fight for Hill 90 went on with the Chinese attacking again at the cost of numerous wounded. The Chinese finally ceased their activity at about 0140 and the Marines destroyed the emplacements on Hill 90 and began moving away. As it turned out the fight for Hill 90 was a good fight but, as Lee Ballenger describes it, against "the wrong objective perhaps, but in battle one has to expect the unexpected." Casualties were 5 killed and 22 wounded and 96 of the Chinese killed and 123 wounded.

Lee Ballenger, *U.S. Marines in Korea, Vol. 2: 1953*. Washington, D.C.: Brassey's, 2001, pp. 80–83.

Operation Doughnut   1 July 1951

Conducted in the U.S. 3rd Division area, Operation Doughnut began on the evening of 30 June as units moved to the debarkation point, scheduled to jump off the following day. The objective was to seize Hill 717 and the nearby high ground found at Hills 682, 608, and 581 in the area northwest of Kumhwa. Accumulated for the attack were the 1st and 2nd Battalion of the 7th Infantry and the 3rd Battalion of the 65th Infantry, K Company of the 15th Infantry and the 64th Tank Battalion with several attached units. On 1 July, the

7th Infantry supported by 23 flights of 90 fighters and got under way toward Hill 717, but failed to dislodge the Communists, nor were they able to do so on the second day of fighting. On the third, however, the 7th, with the help of the 10th Philippine Battalion Combat Team, was able to take hills 717 and 682, but was repulsed during the night. During the day the 65th Infantry had managed to take Hill 608.

For a repulse of counterattacks on the 4th Sergeant LeRoy A. Mendonca of B Company, 7th Infantry, was awarded the Medal of Honor posthumously. By daylight on the 4th all units had gained their objectives. There were no further enemy efforts to take the hills and the 3rd Division used them as a basis of operation. The cost of this four day battle was 196 casualties. The Communist loss numbered near 2,000 casualties.

Roy E. Appleman, *Ridgway Duels for Korea*. College Station: Texas A&M University Press, 1990, pp. 572–573.

Operation Downpour   January 1951

General Matthew Ridgway's plan **Operation Thunderbolt** called for I and IX Corps to take the offensive and attack north, line abreast, for about twenty miles. To facilitate this operation the Navy conceived of two amphibious landing deceptions, one on the west coast at Inchon and one on the east coast at either Kansong or Kosong. These would be supported by the cruiser USS *St. Paul* and the battleship USS *Missouri*. In addition, Ridgway considered an airborne maneuver that he called Operation Downpour. This was designed to drop airborne troops north of Suwon at Ayang in an effort to capture superior ranking military leaders and their staffs as they tried to escape the advance of Thunderbolt. Brigadier General Frank S. Bowen was asked to provide a battalion from the 187th Airborne Regimental Combat Team, but they were still

attached to X Corps and involved, and so he placed the 4th Ranger Company on standby. This aspect of the operation never went into effect.

Clay Blair, *The Forgotten War: America in Korea 1950–1953*. Berryville, VA: Time Books, 1987, p. 654.

Operation Exploitation
5–11 February 1951

In February of 1951 Lieutenant General Matthew Ridgway, Eighth Army commander, determined it was necessary to advance the center of his lines in order to prepare for an assault on the capital city of Seoul. The key to the assignment was Lieutenant General Edward Almond's X Corps, which was to make contact and determine the disposition and intentions of the Chinese Communist Forces. General Almond was alerted to take advantage of any opportunity that became available to disrupt any Chinese offensive that might be in the beginning stages. The advance was to be made in conjunction with I and IX Corps in **Operation Thunderbolt**. The final expectation was for Eighth Army to be in sole control of the Han River on its left flank. The success would be followed by **Operation Roundup**.

Clay Blair, *The Forgotten War: America in Korea 1950–1953*. Berryville, VA: Time Books, 1987, pp. 658–685.

Operation Fauna   11–12 December 1952

During the night of 11–12 December 1952, the gunners of the Royal New Zealand Artillery were providing fire support for a company of the 1st Royal Australian Regiment that was involved in a raid identified as Operation Fauna in the area of the Jamestown Line. Company B, 1 RAR, was assigned to take an enemy position that was situated on a spur just across the valley from Hill 355 (Little Gibraltar). The primary mission was to capture a prisoner for interrogation. While there, they were to destroy what fortification they could. Intelligence had suggested that the area was held by no more than fifteen enemy soldiers and one or two mortar crews. Extensive artillery support was provided and additional artillery support could be called into play via the code name "Capstan." At midnight on 10 December, 4th Platoon, 6th Platoon, and a section of the Assault Pioneer Platoon and Headquarters Company attacked the rise. They took the hill and held it long enough to destroy some of the fortification but they were unable to get a prisoner. It was becoming increasingly evident that taking Chinese prisoners was extremely costly. When the Chinese finally reacted, the troops called for "Capstan" and the shelling began. The raiding force began to pull back and along the slopes of Hill 355. The operation was the deepest penetration the Commonwealth Division had made in more than a year. In the action the New Zealand regiment fired more than 2,400 shells. The attacking force suffered 22 wounded and 3 missing in action. Major A. O. Mann received the Distinguished Service Order for his leadership and courage.

Ian McGibbon, *New Zealand and the Korean War.* Melbourne: Oxford University Press, 1996, pp. 258–259.

Operation Follow-up 29 May 1951

Planned as a follow up to **Operation Initiate**, this event began in late May and consisted of the tanks of C Company, Royal 22e Regiment, in association with Philippine troops. In the operation the units managed to overtake and run down some Chinese troops who were still involved in a retreat. The Royal tanks occupied a burned out village at the foot of Kakhul-Bong (sometimes identified as Hill 467), a small mountain that overlooked the village of Chail-li. There they were responsi-

ble for the disruption of Chinese communication. The continued operation, however, was slowed, as the Chinese were determined to hold on. As the battle progressed the other companies found themselves in untenable positions and by 1300 hours on the 30th, Major Richard Medlands realized that Chinese infiltrators had surrounded his force. At 1430 hours it was decided that the offensive had achieved enough and it was ordered to disengage and fall back; it proved to be a most difficult operation. The withdrawal was not complete until 2100 hours on 31 May, but most of the equipment was taken out with the troops. The cost of Operation Follow-up was six Canadians dead and 54 wounded.

Les Peate, *The War That Wasn't: Canadians in Korea.* Ottawa, Canada: Esprit de Corps Books, 2005, p. 35.

Operation Freeze Out December 1951–January 1952

Primarily due to the inescapable weather conditions, few large unit engagements were conducted during the winter months, but the front line units were kept occupied with running a variety of operations designed to harass the enemy. One of these was Operation Freeze Out, executed by members of the 9th Regiment of the 2nd Infantry Division. Special trained small patrols of roving units, carrying demolitions, would cross over into no-man's land, locate fortifications the enemy had been using as patrol bases, and destroy them. The units went out almost every night during the months of December and January. During a single night Company A destroyed 19 enemy bunkers with demolitions. During the whole of Operation Freeze Out, 368 enemy fortifications were destroyed.

Paul Wolfgeher, "The Battle Hills, Outposts, Operations and Battle Lines of the Korean War." Unpublished manuscript in the Wolfgeher Collection at the Center for the Study of the Korean War.

Operation Goose   13 June 1951

In mid–June 1951 as hope for success at the peace talks was growing, General Matthew Ridgway was concerned with the location of the demilitarized zone that would be established if and when a settlement was reached. He wanted to move north eight miles or so from what was identified as Line Wyoming. It was assumed that when the fighting stopped, the current main line of resistance would become the "battle line" and from it each side would withdraw ten miles. The general believed that for military reasons it was important to occupy the territory, for it was much more defensible and thus advantageous to the United Nations cause. With this in mind General Van Fleet launched one of the more ambitious of a series of hit-and-run attacks on the Chinese Communist Forces. Operation Goose, as it was called, began on 13 June 1951 with the object of taking Pyonggang, a town located at the apex of the Iron Triangle. The raid was launched with support from armored elements from the 3rd Infantry Division located at Chorwon, and the 25th Infantry Division then at Kumhwa. But while it moved the line north and was greeted with some acclaim, it had less than expected effects since the Communists had apparently already decided to make a tactical withdrawal from that area.

Clay Blair, *The Forgotten War: American in Korea 1950–1953*. Berryville, VA; Times Books, 1987, p. 921.

Operation Greek II

11 November 1952

This operation was conducted by the 2nd Battalion, 5th Regiment, of the 1st Marines against Hill 104 that lay north of Outpost Ava. Led by a reinforced platoon from Easy Company, the unit moved against a hill where the Chinese had dug in and prepared for battle. When the assault squad engaged the enemy, they took many casualties and were unable to move forward. They were aided by two more squads but they also sustained casualties. It was determined that the hill was not worth additional costs and the platoon was ordered to withdraw and return to Outpost Ava. The Marines had lost six dead and seventeen wounded.

Lee Ballenger, *U.S. Marines in Korea, Vol. 1: 1952*. Washington, D.C.: Brassey's, 2000, p. 220.

Operation Highboy   January 1952

In response to General James Van Fleet's reported disappointment in the efficiency of his artillery units, and taking advantage of the lessened activity then on the battlefield, U.S. I Corps undertook Operation Highboy. The problem was that existing artillery and mortar fire was not hitting the enemy fortifications at an angle that would inflict the heaviest damage. In an effort to increase the efficiency of the fire an experiment was set up where heavy artillery and armored vehicles would be lo-

Operation Highboy is set up for direct fire into enemy bunkers, January 1952 (Center for the Study of the Korean War).

cated on hilltops where they could send direct fire into enemy positions. The targets were bunkers and fortifications that, up to this time, had been surviving hits by more traditional artillery and mortar fire. Van Fleet acknowledged some success in this effort and the missions continued on and off for some time, but the basic problem was not solved.

Paul M. Edwards, *Korean War Almanac*. New York: Facts on File, 2006, p. 273.

Operation House Burning I

26 October 1951

There was always the problem of infiltrators and sympathizers who were located behind the United Nations line, and a variety of operations set up during the war were intended to limit the guerrilla activity. In October 1951 Operation House Burning I was launched. It was designed as an anti-guerrilla raid against Communists that were located behind the main line of resistance. Transported by Marine Helicopter Squadron 161, combat teams set out to deprive the guerrillas of shelter for the coming winter by burning any Korean home that might be used. Two helicopters were deployed, each carrying a four-man demolition team with incendiary equipment, satchel charges, flame throwers and incendiary grenades. One helicopter would hover above the houses in order to provide cover as the second machine dropped down so that one of the team could spray unignited fame-thrower mixture on the roof of the house, and then an incendiary grenade was dropped to set it off. It was soon determined that it was more effective if the helicopters set down and let the two teams do their work on foot.

Lynn Montross, *Cavalry of the Sky: The Story of the U.S. Marine Combat Helicopters*. New York: Harper and Brothers, 1954, pp. 173–176.

Operation House Burning II

31 October 1951

Operation House Burning II was the second of two responses to try and solve some of the problems created by infiltrators and sympathizers located behind the lines. Continuing from **Operation House Burning I,** and transported by Marine Helicopter Squadron 161, anti-guerrilla teams set out to deprive these Communists of shelter during the winter, and proceeded to set Korean huts on fire. In House Burning II they used four helicopters in their attack on the last day of October 1941. In each ship was a four-man team equipped with satchel charges, flame throwers, and incendiary grenades. As one of the helicopters acted as cover, the second flew low over the houses so that one of the team could spray unignited fame-thrower mixture on the roof. Then an incendiary grenade was dropped to set it off. In this operation two BAR men were included in anticipation of some ground fire, and several North Korean guerrillas were flushed out and killed. The success of these efforts is hard to evaluate.

Note: During the course of Operation House Burning I and II, 113 dwellings were destroyed by teams in 20 flights amounting of 21.8 hours of flight.

Lynn Montross, *Cavalry of the Sky: The Story of the U.S. Marine Combat Helicopters*. New York: Harper and Brothers, Publishers, 1954, pp. 173–176.

Operation Initiate   25 May 1951

On 20 May, I Corps began to advance along the west coast. Within five days the corps reached a line about four miles north of Musan-ni. Leading them was Task Force Dolvin (Lt. Colonel Welborn G. Dolvin), a U.S. regimental combat team whose mission was to drive to the parallel with all speed. The next phase of the advance was Operation Initiate, undertaken by the 25th Canadian Infantry Brigade Group, formed in May 1951. It consisted of elements of the Royal Canadian Regiment, the Royal 22e Regiment, Lord Strathcona's Horse, Royal Canadian Horse Artillery, Princess Patricia Canadian Light Infantry, and the Royal Canadian Engineers. On 25 May they were called on to move up into the Pochon Valley. They managed to advance for thirty miles and crossed over the 38th parallel while meeting only minor resistance. On the 27th, they reached the line some 2,500 yards south of Yangpyong River at the junction with Pochon. By the 28th they took over from Dolvin Force on the high ground south of the 38th parallel and the Canadian Brigade followed them the next day. Once accomplished, the successful drive was further expanded into **Operation Follow-up.**

Les Peate, *The War that Wasn't: Canadians in Korea.* Ottawa, Canada: Esprit de Corps, 2005, p. 35.

Operation Iron Triangle   7 April 1951

The triangle in question was formed by a line connecting the North Korean villages of Chorwon, Kumhwa, and Pyonggang. The area was the key to communications on the Korean peninsula and the shortest routes to and from the major cities in the north and south. This included the roads to and from Seoul, Pyongyang, Wonsan, and Chunchon. During the invasion North Korean troops relied on the area, as did the Chinese Communists when they entered the fight. Whoever was able to hold the triangle held a huge advantage in the war.

The overall plan to retake and hold the area was known as Operation Iron Triangle, and it was put into action during the first three months of 1951. It consisted of a series of one-time and short-time semi-coordinated operations which, all together, would carry out the larger Eighth Army plan. The first of these was **Operation Rugged,** beginning on 3 April 1951.

Paik Sun Yup, *From Pusan to Panmunjom.* Dulles, VA: Brassey's, pp. 137–138.

Operation Item   17 March 1953

In an effort to return to Ungok, Operation Item was authorized for implementation by the 1st Battalion, 5th Marine Regiment. The raid was supported by heavy aerial bombardment and was backed up with three platoons of gun tanks. It was hoped that the Communists would be confused by a feint directed toward Kumgok being created by an artillery bombardment. In preparation for the raid, reconnaissance was provided and rehearsals conducted. Two days before the raid planes from Marine Air were on station. On 19 March the raid moved forward from the main line of resistance. The unit met considerable resistance despite the flamethrowers moving up ahead. Then Chinese mortars opened up. On reaching the trenches the Marines discovered the enemy had retreated to the feeder trenches. Once the 2nd and 3rd platoons had made contact there, about 0645, they received orders to disengage. The Chinese continue to fire on the evacuation route but by dawn all units had disengaged and returned to the MLR. Six Marines were killed and 62 wounded (a 60 percent casualty rate), but the raid had reduced the enemy held area of Ungok to rubble.

Lee Ballenger, *U.S. Marines in Korea, Vol. 2: 1953.* Washington, D.C.: Brassey's, 2002, pp. 112–115.

Operation Janus   December 1952

The plan was accepted on 7 December 1952 and was designed to take four nights to obtain the disposition and strength of the Chinese Communist troops that were located on the much disputed Hill 227. The patrol was a part of the preparation being made for the 1 Princess Patricia's Canadian Light Infantry attack on the hill. Operation Janus called for each of the four Canadian battalions to send a reconnaissance and ambush force into enemy territory. The raid was conducted by 1 PPCLI against the high ground west of Hill 227, a position held by the enemy and one that had posed a special problem for companies holding positions on the surrounding hills. For two nights prior to the attack, reconnaissance patrols determined the enemy strength and tried to capture some prisoners. The front line had been divided into specific patrol areas that had been named for Greek and Roman gods: Mars, Janus, Atlas, and Bacchus, with each of those divided into three segments. Operation Janus was then identified as I, II, and III. After a slow and careful advance, a four man patrol from the Princess Patricia unit reached the high ground, where they encountered four Communist soldiers snug down in a bunker. The

Operation Killer: A spotter plane is ready to deliver artillery support (Center for the Study of the Korean War).

advancing unit was able to kill the enemy soldiers but was unable to capture a prisoner. For the next two days the raids continued in the search for a prisoner, but as the resistance grew ever stronger the cost of continuing was too high. Several were killed and more than thirty wounded, including the commander, Major D. H. George. No prisoner was taken.

Brent Byron Watson, *Far Eastern Tour: The Canadian Infantry in Korea 1950–1953.* Montreal: McGill-Queen's University Press, 2002, pp. 44–93.

Operation Killer   21 February 1951

This was one of the few operations for which General Matthew Ridgway provided advance information to the press. He did so with their agreement not to publish until it was launched. However, in a press conference on 20 February, General Douglas MacArthur announced that he was going to launch this offensive. It was not MacArthur's plan nor should he have announced it, but fortunately, when Operation Killer was unleashed on 21 February, the enemy was not waiting as feared. In fact, in this case, they seem to have faded away. Operation Killer was a part of Ridgway's

major thrust following the disastrous retreat from the Yalu. It called for the slow, steady advance of about 100,000 troops, members of four army divisions and the 1st Marine Division, at a rate of about ten miles a day. The idea was to destroy the Communists east of the Han River and south of a line that ran through Yangpyong, Hyonchon-ni, and Haanmi-ri.

When Ridgway took command of Eighth Army morale was low and the military resolve had been lost. It was essential for Eighth Army to secure a victory. The operation sent the 1st Marine Division to attack to the northeast, supported by the Commonwealth Division, the 1st Cavalry Division and the 24th Infantry Division. The ROK 3rd and 5th Divisions as well as the U.S. 2nd and 7th Infantry Divisions were also involved. The 25th was to hold the Han River at Line Boston. Ridgway had given strict orders that this was not to be a runaway movement toward the north, but rather strict coordination was to be maintained between IX and X Corps as the attack progressed.

While the Communist forces fell back, heavy rains, deep mud, and the evasive tactics of the enemy meant that the operation was not as successful as Ridgway had hoped. It did, however, reaffirm the United Nations line and established General Ridgway as an aggressive military leader. Within eight days Operation Killer had fulfilled its objective to destroy the enemy east of the Han River line and south of the general line Yangpyong-Hyonchon-ni-Haanmi-ri. And, despite the fact that it was a massive frontal assault, casualties were much lighter than had been feared: 181 killed and 84 wounded. There were, as well, several Marine losses, and two Navy corpsmen gave their lives.

The advance was to have other significant consequences as well, for as the UN line became stable from the lower Han northeasterly to Chumunjin on the east coast, it was possible to return many of the fighter squadrons to Korean soil and thus improve the air-ground support available.

Members of Congress and civilian authorities felt that the use of names like Killer and Ripper were too negative. They wanted something a little more positive. The name given the next phase was **Operation Courageous**. Later, in his autobiography, Ridgway expressed confusion about why people did not want to admit that they were doing what they had been sent to Korea to do.

Clay Blair, *The Forgotten War: America in Korea 1950–1953.* New York: Times Books, 1987, pp. 716–729.
James F. Schnabel, *United States Army in the Korean War: Policy and Direction: The First Year.* Washington, D.C.: Office of the Chief of Military History, United States Army, 1973, p. 340.

Operation Lee   17 August 1950

M. J. Luosey, commander, Task Group 96.7, who operated the inshore fleet, was not privy to the Inchon planning but advised his ComNavFE that he intended to seize the Tokchok Islands in the Inchon approach as a base for intelligence gathering and future operations. Thus on 17 August he launched Operation Lee, named for the commanding officer of *PC 702*. With the Republic of Korea Navy ship *Kum Kumg San*, accompanied by the Canadian destroyer HMC *Athabaskan*, Luosey put a 110 man force ashore at Tokchok. The following day the island was secure. Then, on the 19th his forces landed on Yonghung do, a small island located at the mouth of the Inchon approach channel, and from there expanded his control of several related islands. On 20 August a landing party from the HMC *Athabaskan* destroyed radio gear at the lighthouse on Palmi-do. A great deal of information had been collected by an ROKN intelligence team under Lieutenant Commander Ham Myong Su that was made available to Lieutenant Clark when his team arrived at Yonghung-do.

As Operation Lee continued *PC 703* sank a mine-laying sailboat off Haeju, North Korea, and three other small craft near the Inchon approaches. The secondary goal of Operation Lee, the hope that Communist fear of more attacks on the island structures would reduce the troop strength at Inchon, may have been less successful. However, James Field, in *History of United States Naval Operations: Korea*, states: "Weak to begin with, the forces defending the objective areas had been further weakened by their southward displacement in response to Operation Lee."

Even after the landing at Inchon, Operation Lee continued and the men pushed to clear the enemy from the islands that ran from Kunsan in the south to the Sir James Hall Archipelago on the 38th parallel. They were so effective that when **Operation Comeback** was launched on 2 October to recover some of these islands, the job had already been accomplished.

James A. Field, *History of the United States Naval Operations: Korea.* Washington, D.C.: Government Printing Office, 1962, p. 216.

Operation Left Hook   23 April 1953

This was the second of two operations that

took place during April 1953 designed primarily to harass the enemy by destroying fortifications and inflicting casualties. Following up on **Operation Once Again**, on 18 April 1953, the 2nd Infantry Division, led by Republic of Korea soldiers, attacked the Chinese held Hill 153 and took it. The hill was one of a series along the Obong-ni Ridge and it had been the location of previous battles. With the goal of destroying Chinese emplacements on the hill, the plucky South Koreans of Operation Left Hook held the hill for over an hour, during which time they destroyed almost every fortification that had been constructed. After completing their task, the troops withdrew, having accomplished its mission without serious casualties.

Second Infantry, *Korean War Roundup*. http://www. 2id/org/volume3/htm.

Operation Little Joe 31 July 1952

During the 2nd Infantry Division's fight at Old Baldy (Hill 226 [275]), the 1st Battalion of the 23rd Regiment, under the command of Lt. Colonel William Zimmerman, planned a counterattack which he hoped would put an end to the see-saw battle for the outpost. Operation Little Joe was preceded by a week of preparation as the rains continued making movement difficult. In support of his first battalion were the 37th Field Artillery, B Company of the 2nd Engineers, and elements of tank and heavy mortar companies. The preparation even included a reconnaissance fly-over as well as extra communication facilities and forward aid stations. It was decided to unleash a non-illuminated night attack without preparatory artillery fire.

The operation began as A and C Companies set out in a two-pronged push at 2200 hours on 31 July. Contact was made almost immediately, but both companies were able to advance up the slope despite the rain of small arms fire directed toward them. By dawn on 1 August, the companies had reached the crest and

joined forces. They quickly swept the area for pockets of resistance and set up for the counterattack. The expected attack was deadly but resisted and the outpost was declared secure.

After B Company had relieved A on the hill, two more Chinese attacks followed but were repulsed. On 6 August, 2nd Battalion assumed control of Old Baldy and on 23 August concentrated on rebuilding the fortifications. While casualties were heavy, Operation Little Joe was declared a success. On 6 August Colonel Joseph Stilwell, Jr., son of General Vinegar Joe Stilwell, took command of the regiment.

Second Infantry, *Korean War Roundup*. http://www. 2id/org/volume3/htm.

Operation Liverpool 16 February 1952

Operation Liverpool was a limited objective raid launched by two troops of New Zealand's Inniskilling Dragoon Guards' C Squadron. As the raid was conducted the whole of 16th Field Regiment (artillery) stood by to provide support. As the tanks of Operation Liverpool moved forward the Chinese artillery let go, allowing the UN to identify the artillery concentrations. Shortly after the identification was made the tanks pulled out. In this case, as in many others, artillery intervention could mean the difference between success and disaster and often enabled men to pull out of otherwise impossible situations.

Ian McGibbon, *New Zealand and the Korean War, Volume II: Combat Operations*. Melbourne: Oxford University Press, 1996, p. 257.

Operation Maindy 23 June 1951

The assignment was given to Company B, 1st Battalion, Royal Canadian Regiment. It was called Operation Maindy. The whole of Hill 227 was covered with the remnants of several days of fighting. In the midst of the wreckage the Chinese had constructed deep bunkers, trenches and individual foxholes connected by subterranean passages. Defensive fallback positions had been constructed on the reverse slope with a concentration of mortars and machine guns. A party of one officer and twelve other ranks cleared a minefield and made ready for the attack that was set for 0415 hours on 23 June 1951. Company B, which had been holding a forward position on Hill 355, was brought into a reserve area for preparation and was ready to move out late on the 22nd. The attack moved forward with only minor opposition, as the Chinese seemed to have been caught off guard. But soon, having recovered, the enemy let loose with mortars and machine guns. As casualties increased permission to withdraw was requested and ordered. As Chinese fire increased an orderly withdrawal was executed with the wounded coming out first. The cost of the assault was 3 killed and 23 wounded, including two platoon commanders.

Major T. J. Jackson, "The Welsh Regiment in Korea." *Men of Harlech*, No. 9352.

Operation Manchu   25 August 1950

Two reconnaissance patrols from the 9th Infantry Regiment, 2nd Infantry Division, had managed to cross over to the west side of the Naktong to a point from which they were able to watch enemy activity taking place, two miles to the west of the river. They observed the coming and going of large numbers of troops and vehicles and determined that the site was the command post of the North Korean 9th Infantry Division. Acting on this assumption, on 25 August, Colonel John G. Hill outlined Operation Manchu. The 9th Infantry Regiment had earned the nickname "Manchus" during the Boxer Rebellion. A company-sized combat unit was to cross the Naktong River, sneak up on the suspected compound, and take out whatever communication and intelligence information was there,

as well as taking some prisoners and destroying the headquarters.

The plan was to cross near the location of the Paekchin ferry. The attacking unit was composed of E Company of the 9th Infantry reserves and a section of light machine guns. Two heavy weapons companies, Dog and How from the 9th Infantry, were to furnish one section of heavy machine guns, one section of 81mm mortars, and one of their own 75mm recoilless rifles for support. They were backed up by elements of the 15th Field Artillery Battalion, 38th Field Artillery Battalion, and A and B Company of the 72nd Tank Battalion. They were to be transported across the river in assault boats on the night of 31 August. After dark that evening, Lieutenant Charles I. Caldwell, D Company, and First Lieutenant Edward Schmitt of H Company (later awarded the Distinguish Service Cross for his actions) moved their men to the base of Hill 209.

Unfortunately, the enemy was alert and on the move, and they caught the Heavy Mortar Platoon totally unaware while it was still setting up its weapons. The North Koreans also killed or captured many of the troops at the base of Hill 209. Colonel Hill was there but he managed to escape to the rear just a little after midnight, leading several others with him. Word of the enemy crossing and the assault on the waiting forces led 2nd Division Headquarters to cancel Operation Manchu five minutes before its midnight start. It was over before it began.

Roy E. Appleman, *South to the Naktong, North to the Yalu.* Washington, D.C.: Office of the Chief of Military History, Department of the Army, 1961, pp. 446–447.

Clay Blair, *The Forgotten War: America in Korea 1950–1953.* New York: Times Books, 1987, pp. 247, 253.

T. R. Fehrenbach, *This Kind of War.* Washington, D.C.: Brassey's, 1963, p. 142.

Operation Minden   7 September 1951

This operation was set up by orders from I

Corps on 7 September "to carry out an immediate advance and establish [a] new defense line approximately 5,000 yards north of River Imjin. New line to be an extension of I Corps' forward line Wyoming" (Johnston). The following day, the 28th British Commonwealth Brigade took a bridgehead and began the construction of two bridges for tanks to support the unit. For the next few days, in a series of planned phases, the line advanced toward its objective with the 29th Brigade guarding the left flank and the 25th Brigade defending the right. On 12 September the Communists mounted their only serious defense when they tried to prevent the attack on three hills to the front, but the advance continued under help from Canadian tanks. The overhead fire was so close to the men of the R22eR that the following day members of the unit shaved a strip through the middle of the hair on their heads and called themselves the "Iroquois Company." The power of the Canadian attack led the Chinese to abandon their position. The assigned area and the mission of Operation Minden were completed on 13 September.

William Johnston, *A War of Patrols: Canadian Army Operations in Korea.* Vancouver: UBC Press, 2003, page 153.
Ian McGibbon, *New Zealand and the Korean War: Combat Operations.* Melbourne: Oxford University Press, 1996, pp. 203–205.

Operation Mixmaster 17 March 1952

In early spring 1952 the 1st Marine Division moved from the eastern to the western sector, where it was to defend parts of the Jamestown Line. It was a complicated movement rearranging UN divisions across the length of the front, requiring the shuffling of about 200,000 men and their equipment for a distance that ran from 25 to 180 miles. The Marines were to relieve the 1st ROK Division and take over the left flank of Eighth Army. In Operation Mixmaster they were responsible for the difficult area in front of them, dotted with ridges and hills in which the Chinese 63rd and 65th armies were located. Their line straddled the main approaches to Seoul and they remained under considerable pressure. The Marines were to prepare this location with fall-back positions on lines Wyoming and Kansas. They had a secondary mission as well, to be prepared to rescue the United Nations truce negotiators just in case the enemy attempted to trap them at Panmunjom.

The units that were to move consisted of the 1st, 5th, and 7th Marine Regiments, the 1st Korean Marine Corps Regiment, the 11th Marine Artillery and several other service and support units. The transportation required nearly 6,000 truck loads that carried the troops along the dangerous and nearly impassible trails to the west. They utilized 83 railroad cars, 63 flat-bed trailers, and 14 Landing Ship Docks (LSDs), Landing Ship Tanks (LSTs), and DUKWs (Ducks), all which sailed from Soloho-re and landed at Inchon. The move was amazingly successful and the units arrived on line on 25 March. The exercise also illustrated the fact that the division was over-equipped, having picked up considerable equipment along the way.

Lynn Montross, Hubard D. Kuokka, and Norman W. Hicks, *U.S. Marine Operations in Korea. Volume IV.* Washington, D.C.: Historical Branch G-3, Headquarters U.S. Marine Corps, 1962, p. 251.

Operation Moonbeam

Operation Moonbeam is reported as being an exercise in which a huge spotlight was set up behind the main line of resistance with the result that the light would bounce off the clouds and light up the area in front of the line. The snow on the ground intensified the impact.

Paul Wolfgeher, "The Battle Hills, Outposts, Operations and Battle Lines of the Korean War." Unpublished manuscript in the Wolfgeher Collection at the Center for the Study of the Korean War.

Operation Nomad-Polar

13 October 1951

Talks at the negotiation table had broken down less than a month after they started, and General Matthew Ridgway believed some military action was in order to get them started again. At the same time, General James Van Fleet, commanding Eighth Army, felt a series of limited offensive actions were necessary to keep his men on the alert and to harden the many replacements coming onto the line. As General Van Fleet was to say, "A sit down army is subject to collapse at the first sign of an enemy effort.... As Commander of the Eighth Army, I couldn't allow my forces to become soft and dormant" (Hermes). In order to meet these concerns, a series of operations were launched. The last of these, in the central sector about 30 miles north of the 38th parallel and south of Kumsong, North Korea, was called Operation Nomad. The advancing force consisted of three allied divisions (U.S. 24th and ROK 2nd and 6th) and moved along a 14 mile wide front. Many consider the operation to be the most brutal and costly ever faced by the 24th Infantry Division. Many of the veterans involved remember this only as the "Big Fall Push."

It started with an aggressive movement against the Chinese Communists that were dug in the mountains that lay before them. The hope was to clear the Chinese from their fortified line and to take the city of Kumsong. Standing in their way was Hill 770, known as the Pearl, where the Chinese had prepared winter quarters for their troops. The terrain was extremely steep and the Chinese and North Koreans were stubborn fighters. At the end of the first day the 24th had suffered heavy losses. Nevertheless, they reached Line Nomad by 17 October, but rather than being allowed to regroup, they were sent on to a new objective called Line Polar, which they were finally able to secure on the 22nd. As they advanced the Communist forces slowly withdrew. Several Communist counter-attacks were made but the resistance finally collapsed. The cost of the effort was high at an estimated 1,784 casualties during the ten days. Some historians have speculated that Operation Nomad-Polar was skewed and buried by the press and that this caused persons looking at the highly significant operation to show more indifference than it deserved.

In terms of its success it must be stated that the 24th did indeed reach its objectives against harsh resistance, and on 22 October, the same day the division reached Line Polar, the Communists agreed to return to the cease-fire talks.

Walter G. Hermes, *Truce Tent and Fighting Front: United States Army in the Korean War.* Washington, D.C.: U.S. Army Center of Military History.

Operation Ohio Sloan

8–12 September 1951

Though the name is listed in several narrative histories as occurring during September of 1951, there is little known about what troops were involved in Operation Ohio-Sloan. The operation was conducted coincidentally with **Operation Clean Up**, and during the time UN forces were engaged in the Battle of Heartbreak Ridge. The recorded mission was to secure new positions on Phase Line Wyoming.

Norman O. Nelson, "Battles, Operations, and Outposts Found in the Korean War." Unpublished manuscript in the Nelson Collection, Center for the Study of the Korean War.

Operation Once Again 18 April 1953

This was the first of two operations carried out by the 2nd Infantry Division and its associated 1st ROK Division designed to capture and destroy Chinese fortifications on Hill 153. The hill was part of a series known as the Obong-ni Ridge in an area called Little Italy. Operation Once Again was a daring daylight raid by the 1st ROK Division, supported by

2nd Infantry Division artillery. In a short, quick attack they smashed through the defenses of Little Italy, moved ahead, held the hill for a little over an hour, and in this time destroyed the Chinese fortifications and defenses. The mission was accomplished without serious casualties.

Second Infantry, *Korean War Roundup*. http://www. 2id/volume2/htm.

Operation Order 9-50
29 September 1950

In Operation Order 9-50, General Douglas MacArthur assigned priority for the loading of the 1st Marine Division, the amphibious element of X Corps, from the port at Inchon in order to make a landing at Wonsan, North Korea. The Marines were to establish a base of operations while the 7th Infantry Division, to join them later after embarking at Pusan, was to move west to join with Eighth Army. It was envisioned as a two-pronged attack to move north of the 38th Parallel. It was necessary for the two divisions involved to break off with the enemy from the fighting around Seoul and make their way to the coast. By 16 October the Marines had gathered at the assembly at Inchon and 23,591 of them were loaded up at the cost of withholding all other activity not directly related. The 31 foot tides and mud flats made the operation difficult, and all loading was done via assault ship to the transports (APAs).

In addition to the men and their equipment were 32,000 assault rations and 100,000 C rations sent from Japan, and the heavy vehicles belonging to the 7th Infantry Division. The Marines began loading on 9 October. On 11 October the shore command post closed and X Corps headquarters was opened aboard the USS *Mount McKinley*. The amphibious unit set sail on 19 October and was scheduled to land at Wonsan in **Operation Tailboard**.

Malcolm W. Cagle and Frank A. Manson, *The Sea War in Korea*. Annapolis, MD: Naval Institute Press, 1957.

Operation Overwhelming
October 1952

General James Van Fleet, Eighth Army commander, believed that the best results might be achieved by meeting the enemy along the Kansas-Wyoming Line. He was also concerned about the vulnerability of an army that was not moving forward, as talk of peace and the constant turnover caused by the Army's rotation system made soldiers reluctant to be the last one killed in Korea. Instead, at the request of General Matthew Ridgway, some aggressive offensive operations were planned, including **Operation Wrangler** and Operation Overwhelming. Overwhelming was a revised version of a previous plan that called for Eighth Army to make an all-out attack at the waist of Korea on a line from Pyongyang to Wonsan. It was based on several provisions, however, including a decline or withdrawal in the anticipated enemy strength or the allocation of additional forces to Eighth Army. As it was, neither of these seemed to be happening. There were other concerns over the plan, however; one was that a large-scale operation might jeopardize the hope for negotiations to be carried out. Operation Overwhelming was never carried out, leaving Van Fleet to rely instead on a series of limited objective operations to be executed on the initiative of the corps commanders.

Clay Blair, *The Forgotten War: American in Korea 1950–1953*. Berryville, VA: Times Books, 1987, p. 947.

Operation P   19 February 1951

The 2nd Marine Battalion, 5th Regiment, joined with X Corps in an aggressive action that began on 19 February 1951. It was called Operation P. The mission was to take the two massive hills east of the Chinju Pass that lay just in front of them. From this high position the Communists were able to control the movement along Mansan Road that ran between the two hills. The first of these, Hill

687, was 2254 feet in height and rose on the northeast of Chinju Pass. The second, Hill 738, was 2421 feet high and was also known as Sobuk-san. In the lead, Captain Picket's Company Fox was assigned Hill 687 which, after a brief rest, they attacked and managed to take the following day. The second objective was taken shortly after. Both of these hills had been the scenes of major fighting in August of 1950.

Paul Wolfgeher, "The Battle Hills, Outposts, Operations and Battle Lines of the Korean War." Unpublished manuscript in the Wolfgeher Collection at the Center for the Study of the Korean War.

Operation Pandora   June 1953

In April 1953 the cease-fire discussions were heating up again. If they were included under the draft arrangement, many of the islands that had been so determinedly defended would be relinquished to the Communists. This involved all the islands north of a line that ran southwest from the Han Estuary. Colonel Harry N. Shea conferred with both American and British commanders about the need to launch Operation Pandora. In the meantime, Marine garrison personnel stationed on the two islands, as well as the patrol ships operating in the area, were busy neutralizing Communist mainland fire. The plan was to provide evacuation and refuge for anyone who wanted to leave the islands, assuming this was to be accomplished immediately following any armistice.

The operation called for the evacuation of Sok-to and Cho-do islands north of the 38th parallel. The problem was complicated by the fact that according to the repatriation clauses, no civilian who had not been a South Korean resident before the outbreak of the war could cross over to South Korea after the armistice was signed. In June, as it was believed that some sort of armistice was in sight, the first phase got underway and Task Force 95 evacuated approximately 19,425 partisans, their families, and refugees from these two islands. The New Zealand ships HMNZS *Kaniere* and *Hawea* were both involved early on and then again when some of the islands had to be reoccupied to keep them from falling into North Korean hands too early. Elements of the 6th Partisan Regiment were sent back to Tok-to and Hach'wira-do during the night of 24–25 June in expectation of Communist activities. The operation was carried out smoothly considering all the complications imposed by the changing attitudes during the final stages of the war

Ian McGibbon, *New Zealand and the Korean War: Combat Operations.* Melbourne: Oxford University Press, 1996, p. 341.
Pat Meid and James M. Yingling, *U.S. Marine Operations in Korea, Volume V: Operations in West Korea.* Washington, D.C.: Historical Division, Headquarters, U.S. Marine Corps, 1972, p. 235.

Operation Panther   12–13 August 1952

This operation was set up to try to capture some enemy soldiers for interrogation. The operation, if it was to succeed, would be particularly demanding on its artillery support. When New Zealand troops headed out in Operation Panther, artillery fire plans and counter-mortar programs had been prepared in advance, and the division artillery had the additional support of the American 936th Field Artillery Battalion. The artillery plan was designed to neutralize the Chinese Communist Forces in the vicinity so the raid could get in, and then out, quickly. By this time in the war these small hit-and-run raids into no man's land were become increasingly dangerous. The Communists had become more aggressive and were sending raiding parties into this sector. In this particular raid, successfully completed, the New Zealanders fired more than 4,800 rounds.

Ian McGibbon, *New Zealand and the Korean War: Combat Operations.* Melbourne: Oxford University Press, 1996, p. 258.

Operation Pepperpot
23 October 1951

Two weeks before it officially entered the line, the men of one company of 1st Princess Patricia Canadian Light Infantry were called into action as participants in Operation Pepperpot. In this case the operational plan came from the ground up and called for them to inflict damage and casualties on the enemy while at the same time trying to gain as much intelligence as they could. The Canadian brigade provided one company from each battalion. After the 1st PPCLI and the 2 R22eR had occupied the hills on the left of the divisional front with relative ease, they went on to complete a series of reconnaissance patrols through the Nabu-ri valley.

But Lieutenant Colonel Dextraze wanted more action and informed the brigade major that he would like to take a company to attack Hill 166 on Sunday, 21 October. Not only did the commander approve the plan but expanded the action to include all three battalions. The objectives of Operation Pepperpot were to locate enemy dispositions, capture prisoners, and maintain the offensive keeping the Chinese from having time to dig in. If they captured the hill, they were to booby-trap it and then withdraw. The advancing group involved elements of 2R22eR, the PPCDI, and the tanks of Lord Strathcona's Horse. The raid was to be conducted in daylight beginning at 0630 on 23 October. After a long assault Hill 156 was secured. The fight for Hill 166 was more difficult, and despite shelling and continued assault, the UN force could get no closer than about 140 yards. They failed to take the hill and at 1115 were ordered to withdraw. This was done carefully, coming out with five killed and 21 wounded. The estimated enemy casualties were 37.

Les Peate, *The War That Wasn't: Canadians in Korea*. Ottawa, Canada: Esprit de Corps, 2005, p. 50.
"Canada Remembers," Veteran Affairs of Canada, October-November 1951. www.vac-acc.gc.ca.

Operation Piledriver   3 June 1951

The assignment was for I Corps to undergo an offensive that would relocate at Lines Utah and Wyoming, with the intention of moving forward about twelve miles to occupy an area known as the Iron Triangle. To accomplish this General "Shrimp" Milburn's offensive units would be formed by Major General Charles Palmer's 1st Cavalry, Major General Robert Soule's 3rd Division, and Brigadier General Sladen Bradley's 25th Division. Their mission included "inflicting maximum casualties on a defeated and retiring enemy," (Blair, p. 901). Operation Piledriver was conceived in late May 1951 as the Communist forces were pulling back in order to replenish their supplies, and General Matthew Ridgway believed that Eighth Army was ready to move forward without a great deal of resistance.

Billed as a "last ditch" (Wright) effort to solidify its position along the Kansas-Wyoming Line, he ordered an attack on the Iron Triangle, that difficult area bordered by Pyonggang to the north, Chorwon to the west, and Kumhwa to the east. Operation Piledriver was set up so that I Corps would hit the area bounded by Chorwon and Kimhwa; IX Corps would take the area from Hwachon north to Samyang-ni; and X Corps was to attack north from the east. The ROK Army I Corps was to seize the area of Kojin-ni. The attacks began on 3 June 1951 but contrary to Ridgway's intelligence, the UN forces ran into hard resistance focused on the I Corps area. By 10 June after 24 hour air support, the 3rd Infantry Division, the ROKA 9th Division and the 10th Philippine Battalion took the high ground south of Chorwon on the west of the triangle. The following day the Communists abandoned Chorwon and Kimhwa, and on 13 June two tank infantry forces entered the ruins of Pyonggang, the apex of the triangle.

Several things were holding back the advance of Operation Piledriver, factors which would be illustrative of future actions. The officers and men who had fought the war so far

Operation Piledriver, approaching the deserted city of Chorwon, Korea (Center for the Study of the Korean War).

were being rotated out according to the new policy, leaving men either vastly new or cautiously waiting for release. To many, the effort to advance so far beyond the 38th parallel seemed foolish when the rumored armistice might set the demarcation line at the 38th. These, as well as the weather and the increasing fatigue of the divisions, made this particularly heavy going. Undoubtedly of the divisions assigned Milburn's I Corps, the 3rd Division had the hardest time, being first across the Hantan River into what the corps historian would call a "hornet's nest." Finally on 14 June all the divisions reached Line Wyoming and the 1st Cavalry and 3rd Division occupied the deserted city of Chorwon.

At this point, because the heights dominated the triangle, neither the Communists nor the UN could hold much of the lower ground. Nevertheless, the Chinese struck back and on 17 June retook Pyonggang. Operation Piledriver was the last major offensive of the war prior to the settling of the lines north of the 38th parallel. A second significant outcome of the operation was that the Iron Triangle became sort of a no-man's land, available to neither side. Clay Blair suggests that the resistance offered during Operation Piledriver cooled General Van Fleet's desire to execute any additional Eighth Army offensives deep into North Korean territory. As it turned out, this was pretty much the case.

Clay Blair, *The Forgotten War: America in Korea 1950–1953*. New York: Times Books, 1987, pp. 789–922.

David J. Wright, "Operation Piledriver," in James I Matray, *Historical Dictionary of the Korean War*. Westport, CT: Greenwood Press, 1991, pp. 354–355.

Operation Plan Eightbind

21 September 1952

This operation was planned as a relief for the 8th ROK Division that was to be undertaken by elements of the 45th Division. The relief took place during the nights of 21–25 September, and when completed the 45th occupied a sector on Line Minnesota between the 1st ROK and the 25th U.S. Infantry Division that ran from Ihyon-ni to Sachon-ni.

Paul Wolfgeher, "The Battle Hills, Outposts, Operations and Battle Lines of the Korean War." Unpublished manuscript in the Wolfgeher Collection at the Center for the Study of the Korean War.

Operation Polecat   18 February

1952

The operation called Polecat was a follow up of the not-too-successful **Operation Skunkhunt** in December 1951. The problem was increasing guerrilla raids in the area held by the Commonwealth Division. The earlier effort had done a great deal to move civilians out of the area but it did not stop either the raids or the effects of booby-traps that were left behind. As the attacks continued through January 1952, it was determined to do an additional sweep, this time called Operation Polecat, beginning on 18 February 1952. The force consisted of an officer, ten men from 10th Company, and some of the gunners from the 64th Field Artillery. The area was swept with little or nothing to show for it. It did result, however, in an increase in local protection provided by the 904th Field Security Squadron and the establishment of check points for the Korean Service Corps workers who had previously moved freely about camp. These measures were more successful than the sweeps and the number of guerrilla incidents decreased.

Ian McGibbon, *New Zealand and the Korean War: Combat Operations.* Melbourne: Oxford University Press, 1996, p. 243.

Operation Polecharge

15 October 1951

The mission assigned to Operation Polecharge, that of reaching the Jamestown Line as the enemy retreated north of the Yokkok-chon, was accomplished on 19 October 1951. Operation Polecharge was designed to capture the hills as a part of the larger **Operation Commando**. It called on the 5th Cavalry Regiment, the 1st Cavalry Division, working with its assigned Belgian Battalion from the 3rd Infantry Division, to take Hill 346. After accomplishing this they were to take Hill 230 to provide protection for the Jamestown Line. Previously they had taken Hills 418, 313, 334, 287, and 347 in order to secure the high ground to the northeast of the Jamestown Line. The fight for Hill 272, which was on the eastern approach to the enemy defense line on Hill 346, was highly contested by the enemy, who had apparently decided to make a determined stand. These four to five days of combat were some of the most deadly of the Korean War; and the Chinese Communists losses were estimated 16,000 during the fight. The First Cavalry reported casualties of 2,900. The Chinese were forced to their next line of defense, the Yokkok-chon.

Tracey D. Connors, "Truckbusters from Dogpatch." *The Combat Diary of the 18thFighter Bomber Wing in the Korean War.* http://www.truckbustersfrom dogpatchcom/index.php?.id=9.

Operation Punch   5 February 1951

This operation was a phase of **Operation Roundup**, an extension of I and IX Corps' drive on Seoul. It consisted of a task force made up of the 24th Infantry Division with heavy armor and artillery support. The focus of the operation was to destroy the enemy in the vicinity of Hill 440 just south of Seoul. Operation Roundup was launched as the United Nations Command advanced northward from Hoengsong toward Hongchon-ni. The battle continued on through 7 February.

It was for action during this fighting that Captain Lewis L. Millett was awarded the Medal of Honor for his services near Soam-ni. On 8 February the UN forces finally dislodged the Communists from the area around Hill 440, forcing the Chinese back across the Han River and opening the way for I Corps to assault Seoul.

David Rees, *Korea: The Limited War*. New York: St. Martin's Press, 1964, p. 185.

David J. Wright, "Operation Punch," in James I. Matray *Historical Dictionary of the Korean War*. Westport, CT: Greenwood Press, 1991, p. 355.

Operation Punchbowl
1951/52/53

During the Korean War there was a great deal of activity in an area known as the Punchbowl. Also, the Punchbowl is the final home in

Korean Service Corp's carries ammunition up Hill 702 in Operation Punchbowl (Center for the Study of the Korean War).

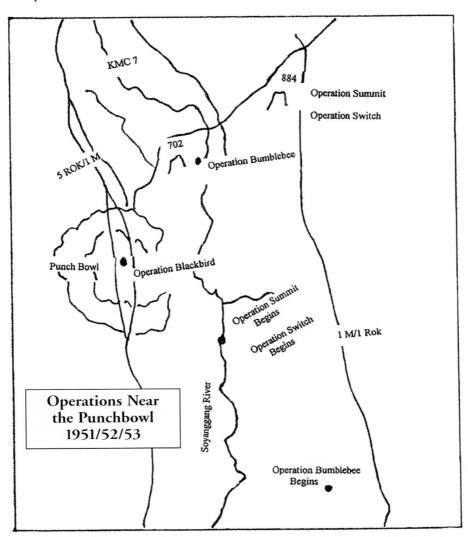

Operations near the Punchbowl (courtesy the Center for the Study of the Korean War).

Hawaii of many American soldiers from this, and other, wars. In the literature there are many mentions of Punchbowl operations. There were several battles for the Punchbowl in North Korea, and a good many of the operations included in this volume took place in and around the Punchbowl. But, there is no record of an Operation Punchbowl per se. The only mention found is a reference by Bill Goodman, 1st Marine Division combat photographer, who had so labeled a photograph that shows a Marine rocket company firing "during Operation Punchbowl" near Hwa-

chon Reservoir, North Korea, in August of 1951.

Photographic Collection, p. 301.14, Center for the Study of the Korean War.

Operation Ratkiller   December 1950–January 1951

The early months of the Korean War were a time of quick and massive movement. Yet the ability to traverse large territories, even occupied areas, was often hampered by the existence of large and well-equipped Communist guerrilla units. These units operated as organized and disciplined groups and were able to inflict considerable damage. In order to relieve some of this pressure on Eighth Army, the government of South Korea declared martial law in the southwestern part of the Chirisan Mountain regions. With General James Van Fleet's approval Task Force Paik, named after its commander, Major General Paik Sun Yup (chief of staff, ROK Army) and consisting of the Republic of Korea 8th Infantry and Capital Divisions, moved into the area with the intention of cutting off most communications and movement in and out of the restricted zone. Operation Ratkiller was launched to finish the job.

The operation was an anti-guerrilla pincer movement that moved along a perimeter 163 miles in length. It was conducted in three phases: 1 to 4 December, 19 December to 4 January, and from 6 to 31 January 1951. In each of these phases the ROK 8th Division came in from the northwest, the Capital Division from the south, and the National Police covered the gap, squeezing the Communists between them. The action moved slowly and clean-up continued until 15 March 1953. In this last sweep the operation returned to the village of Chirisan to flush out the North Korean guerrillas who returned to the area after the earlier raids. Operation Ratkiller was considered a great success. General Matthew Ridgway estimated that more than 10,000 guerrillas were captured. While some claimed this is too low, suggesting that as many as 19,000 rebels had been killed, the success of the operation nevertheless provided some relief from guerrilla activities in the area. However, it was also true that guerrilla activity continued in the south with much of it directed against the political antics of President Syngman Rhee.

Jon Halliday and Bruce Cumings, *Korea: The Unknown War*. New York, 1989.
Matthew Ridgway, *The Korean War*. Garden City, NY: Doubleday, 1967.

Operation Ripper 7 March 1951

The heavy rain and snow had slowed **Operation Killer**. At this point the Chinese were considerably weakened by the UN command's aggressive action but were getting some relief as supply and communication lines shortened. The next phase in General Matthew Ridgway's plan was called Operation Ripper and it was launched on 7 May 1951. General Ridgway was not pleased with the number of enemy dead resulting from Operation Killer, and Ripper was designed to inflict as many Communist casualties as possible, keeping the pressure on the Communists and making it more difficult for them to launch any sort of new offensive. It was designed so that IX and X Corps would bring the line in central Korea almost to the 38th parallel, rather than making a frontal assault across the wide and partially frozen Han River. For several days the 2nd Infantry Division fought hard to develop a bridgehead across the Han River, but once that was done the ROK 1st Division moved past Seoul and the city was liberated for the second time when elements of the 1st Marine Division entered the nearly deserted capital. Outflanked, the enemy had moved out with little opposition. Operations had been slowed somewhat by the shortage of ammunition suffered by the 11th Marines, which was finally corrected by a series of air drops. The Communists, relying on well designed and often used tactics, put up a limited defense and then pulled back, but the withdrawal was constant.

The operation moved on to secure its objective at phase Line Buffalo on 20 March. This time General Douglas MacArthur did not return to the city for a ceremonial liberation. During the operation UN destroyers continue to provide fire support at Inchon, and the Air Force flew an average of 182 close-air support missions a day.

By this time the existence of the 38th parallel carried very little military or political significance, and after discussions with General MacArthur, General Ridgway decided to push on to the parallel and expand the mission of Operation Ripper. The U.S. 1st Cavalry, supported by a Canadian battalion along with the 1st Marine Division, found the movement hard, but continued to press forward. Eighth Army dropped the 187th Regimental Combat Team at Munsan-ni more than twenty miles north of Seoul, but as before it failed to trap significant numbers of enemy troops or governmental leaders. While the operation must be considered a success, Ridgway decided that it was now best to establish a series of defensive liens running across the peninsula roughly from Munsan-ni to Yangyant on the east. From these points he would hold the Communists and launch whatever offensive operations were possible, while maintaining a defensive fall-back position.

Clay Blair, *The Forgotten War: America in Korea 1950–1953*. New York: Times Books, 1987, pp. 729–758.

Lynn Montross, Hubard D. Kuokka, and Norman W. Hicks, *U.S. Marine Operations in Korea 1950–1953*. Volume IV. Washington, D.C.: Historical Branch, G-3, Headquarters, U.S. Marine Corps, 1962, pp. 88–93.

Operation Roundup
5–11 February 1951

Tenth Corps had not, as yet, developed full confrontation with the Chinese Communist Forces. General Matthew Ridgway ordered General Edward Almond to launch a simultaneous offensive, called Operation Roundup, designed to make contact with the enemy, determine its disposition, and if possible to discover its intentions. The X Corps plan was issued on 1 February for units to move out on 5 February 1951. Ridgway's overall intention was to bring Eighth Army forward to the Han River and there establish a line running east along the river to Yangpyong. During the first few days of February enemy opposition had been generally weak except for the area to the west near Chipyong-ni. Besides, those Communist units that were still on the south banks

of the Han River were increasingly isolated as the ice thinned and crossings became harder to find.

On 5 February when X Corps took off, the ROK 8th and 5th divisions were north of Hoengsong. To the east ROK III Corps and the ROK 7th and 9th divisions gradually fell behind in the advance, causing some alteration in the troops committed. On the same day the 2nd Division's Ranger Company made a night attack at 0100 hours and, surprising the enemy, managed to kill most of them and take the village of Changal. To the east the ROK Capital Division captured Kangnung. On 8 February command became aware that Chinese Communist Forces were involved in the Hongchon area. The attack continued and most units had approached to within five to eight miles north of Hoengsong. Air surveillance indicated that thousands of enemy troops were on the move toward Hongchon, one pilot reporting he had never seen so many of them in the open at one time.

Later reports indicate that General Pen Teh-huai, commander of the Chinese "volunteers" in the area, felt that the attack had to be challenged and launched a counterattack with the Chinese 40th and 66th Armies and the North Korean V Corps. Despite support by the Air Force and desperate fighting by the men of Eighth Army, Operation Roundup was pushed back. During the battle the ROK 8th Infantry Division was nearly annihilated. The Chinese were able to recapture Hoengsong. General Ridgway regrouped and from new defensive positions set in order plans for the battle of Chipyong-ni.

Roy E. Appleman, *Ridgway Duels for Korea*. College Station: Texas A&M University Press, 1990, pp. 218–306.

Clay Blair, *The Forgotten War: America in Korea 1950–1953*. New York: Times Books, 1987, pp. 679–685.

Lynn Montross, Hubard D. Kuokka, and Norman W. Hicks, *U.S. Marine Operations in Korea*. Volume IV. Washington, D.C.: Historical Branch G-3, Headquarters U.S. Marine Corps, 1962, p. 51.

Pat Meid and James M. Yingling, *U.S. Marine Oper-*

ations in Korea, Volume V: Operations in West Korea. Washington, D.C.: Historical Division, Headquarters, U.S. Marine Corps, 1972, p. 232.

Operation Rugged   3–6 April 1951

Those collecting intelligence were convinced that the Communists were planning on holding the line astride the 38th parallel in order to have the time to prepare for a major offensive. These sources included the identification of troop movements and such things as the diligent repair of bridges and supply lines. The assumption was that the Chinese Communist Forces would be launching a massive spring offensive and that they had a minimum of nine armies available. There was even some belief that Soviet intervention was a possibility. In order to slow up these preparations and maintain pressure on the Communist armies, Eighth Army determined to launch an aggressive operation. On 29 March, General Matthew Ridgway published the plans for Operation Rugged, which was to retain the Imjin River as the western base and advance the rest of the front across the parallel to shorten the line. The envisioned line would run diagonally along the Imjin River from Munsan to the Hantan River and east to the south shore of the Hwachon Reservoir. This would provide them with ten miles of water frontage at the Hwachon Reservoir. The new front would later become Line Kansas-Wyoming. General Ridgway was convinced that it was safer to continue their advance than it was to await the enemy's response.

Those units involved were the 187th Airborne Regimental Combat Team, the 1st Cavalry Division, and the 3rd, 24th and 25th Infantry Division, which were to advance from Munsan. The 1st Marine Division was to move up from reserve and into relief of the 1st Cavalry Division, supported by the Korean Marine Corps. The operation was supported by three tank battalions (6th, 64th and 89th) and artillery from both 155mm Long Toms and 155mm regulars.

In a three day assault, the units managed to cross the 38th parallel and dig in to create a defensive line at what was later called Line Kansas. By 9 April the U.S. I and IX Corps on the west and the ROK I Corps on the east had reached their positions. Tenth Corps and ROK III Corps were slowed by the rugged terrain of the Taeback Mountains, but by 9 April arrived at their assigned locations. In an attempt to slow down the UN forces, the North Koreans opened sluice gates at the Hwachon Reservoir in an attempt to flood the lower Pukhan River. The effect on the operation was negligible. Operation Rugged was a follow-up to **Operation Ripper** and overlapped with **Operation Dauntless**, designed to secure Phase Line Utah.

During the advance a significant number of Chinese Communist and North Korean prisoners were taken. From them the UN Command learned of the existence of nine CCF armies (about 270,000 men) with another ten in immediate reserve. On previous occasions the intelligence people had tended not to believe the information they received from prisoners, but by now had learned to be more attentive, as even the lowest Chinese ranks appeared to be well informed of the overall situation.

Clay Blair, *The Forgotten War: America in Korea 1950–1953.* New York: Times Books, 1987, pp. 771–793.

Lynn Montross, Hubard D. Kuokka, and Norman W. Hicks, *U.S. Marine Operations in Korea.* Volume IV. Washington, D.C.: Historical Branch G-3, Headquarters U.S. Marine Corps, 1962, p. 94.

James F. Schnabel, *The United States Army in the Korean War, Policy and Direction: The First Year.* Washington, D.C.: Office of the Chief of Military History, 1972, p. 363.

David J. Wright, "Operation Rugged," in James I. Matray, *Historical Dictionary of the Korean War.* Westport, CT: Greenwood Press, 1991, p. 357.

Operation Scatter   3 April 1952

Prior to the repatriation of prisoners of war, both sides became involved in a screening process. The Communists had proposed on 2

April 1952 at the truce talks in Panmunjom, that prisoners be screened to determine just how many soldiers might be involved in a prisoner exchange, and if they wished to be returned to their point of origin. For the United States this was Operation Scatter. Permission was received on 3 April to begin and on Ridgway's orders General James Van Fleet set the operation in motion.

The idea was to determine the actual number of prisoners available for repatriation. Each prisoner was to be individually asked and warned that once a decision had been made he could not change his mind. As the soldier came for the interview each prisoners took all their personnel possession with them so there would be no need to return to the camp. The screening began on 8 April. The following questions were established by the UN screeners: 1) Will you voluntarily be repatriated to either China or North Korea? 2) Would you forcefully resist repatriation? 3) Have you considered the impact of your decision on you family? 4) Are you aware you may remain here at Koki-do after the rest have returned home? 5) Do you understand the UN cannot promise to send you any particular place? 6) Are you still determined to resist repatriation and 7) What would you do if repatriated in spite of your decision? By 15 April General Ridgway was able to provide the Joint Chiefs of Staff with a figure that suggested of the 170,000 military and civilian prisoners the UN had on hand, only about 70,000 were interested in returning to Communism.

Despite the Communist approval of the plan there were seven prisoner compounds that held more than 37,000 hardliners who would not allow the UN teams to interview them. The UN reviewers simply recorded them all as repatriates. The People's Republic of China was upset with the numbers reported, and eventually blocked any effort at neutral screening. The effort to screen prisoners provided in Operation Scatter contributed to the unrest within the POW camps and was

part of the eventual revolt at Koje-do. In this process the United Nations had taken their stand on the return of prisoners and they patiently held this position as the war went on.

Walter G. Hermes, *Truce Ten and Fighting Front: United States Army in the Korean War.* Washington, D. C.: Office of the Chief of Military History, 1966, p. 170.

Operation Showdown
13 October 1952

Having secured General Mark Clark's approval, General James Van Fleet planned a limited Eighth Army offensive called Operation Showdown. This operation, also known as the Shangganling Campaign, was one of the boldest American offensives of the war. It was conducted by elements of the 31st, 32nd and 17th Infantry Regiments of the 7th Division. The goal of the operation was to capture Triangle Hill (Hill 598), a mountain peak three miles north of Kumhwa, as well as two adjacent elevations, Pike's Peak and Jane Russell. The original plan had called for two battalions to be engaged for five days, but eventually the job required the commitment of the whole division.

To support this renewed ground action, General Otto P. Weyland made three B-29s available to provide radio-directed close support missions each night from 10 to 16 October. In addition the 5th Air Force, combined with its attached units, flew a total of 2,217 sorties of close-air support. At the close of the operation the commander of IX Corps sent his "grateful thanks" for the 5th Air Force's magnificent help.

For the assault, the 31st Infantry was engaged and suffered the most costly single day of casualties in the entire war, with 96 killed and 337 wounded. The cost would have been even higher was it not for the fact that, for the first time in history, all the members of the assault team were wearing armored vests. Two Medals of Honor were awarded for heroic actions in Operation Showdown: 1st Lieutenant Edward R. Schowalter, Jr., and PFC Ralph E. Pomeroy.

When twelve days later the task had still not been completed and more than 1,500 Americans were casualties, other objectives of the mission were turned over to the ROK Army. While they held for a time, the area they were hoping to occupy was eventually lost. In light of the extreme casualties, General Clark informed Van Fleet, "We should not, unless absolutely necessary, initiate another action which may be a repetition of the bloody battle for Triangle Hill and Sniper Ridge" (Furnell).

Robert Furnell, FEC *Command Reports,* November 1952, pp. 6–7.
David Rees, *Korea: The Limited War.* New York: St. Martin's Press, 1964, p. 386.

Operation Slam   4 August 1951

The Commonwealth Division (COMWEL) was officially formed on 28 July 1951. Its assignment was to hold a piece of the front line about nine miles in length along the south bank of the Imjin River. The U.S. 1st Cavalry Division was on its right and the 1st ROK Division occupied the left flank. Across the river and opposing the Commonwealth was the 64th Chinese Communist Army (really about three divisions). In Operation Slam, which began on the night of 4 August 1951, four battalions — two British, one Australian, and the attached Belgian battalion — crossed over the Imjin and proceeded about three miles to the north. The operation was a reconnaissance in force seeking to locate the Chinese prime defensive positions. During its movement it met little resistance. However, during the operation the Imjin River had unexpectedly and quickly flooded and the troops were cut off by the rising water. Temporary supplies were dropped by a light liaison plane and the operation was called off. The troops, accompanied by their Korean porters, finally made it back across the

swollen river on the evening of 5 August. This operation was soon followed by **Operations Dirk** and **Claymore.**

Leslie Peate, *The War That Wasn't: Canadians in Korea.* Ottawa, Canada: Esprit de Corps Books, 2005.

Operation Snare   10 February 1952

The New Zealanders had been kept busy bunker-busting, a process made more difficult by the speed with which the North Koreans were able to repair what had been destroyed. In February 1952, however, the gunners of the 16th Field Regiment, Royal New Zealand Artillery, were put on hold by order of General James Van Fleet, who had called for a four-day unilateral United Nations cease-fire along the entire line. The idea was to lure the Communists out of their entrenchments in order to achieve a better strike, but the enemy did not seem to be fooled, most likely having been warned of the plan through captured prisoners. The Communists used the occasion to improve the defenses along their forward slope without interference from harassing fire. When Operation Snare was called off, the Commonwealth artillery went back to work trying to destroy the newly created bunkers. This Commonwealth operation was exercised in conjunction with **Operation Clam Up.**

Ian McGibbon, *New Zealand and the Korean War.* Ackland: Oxford University Press, 1996, p. 263.

Operation Snatch   22 September 1951

This operation was assigned to the 2nd Royal Canadian Regiment of the Princess Patricia's Canadian Light Infantry with the support of the 2nd Royal Canadian Horse Artillery. It was considered a routine exercise, but turned out to be highly successful. The aim was to capture one or two live Chinese prisoners. Three platoons of Captain E. K. Wildfang's B Company, approximately thirty men, were given the immediate assignment. Headquarters Company plus a platoon from A Company were assigned to hold the current position on Hill 152, code named Dog. Those who were to participate took two days of study to arrange the plan. Despite some early communications problems the operations was a success. E. K. Wildfang assembled his men before dusk on the 22nd and they moved up a covered approached and into a forming-up area near Hill 152. There they waited until dark to move out. They were in and out within three and a half hours. Leaving at 0400 hours, they arrived back at Dog by 0735. During the brief encounter they ran into considerable mortar and small arms fire. Two Chinese prisoners had been brought back to the regimental lines, and at least eighteen of the enemy had been killed. Three of the Canadians had been wounded. Despite the courage of the men involved and the success of the operation, Canadian historian Les Peate sadly acknowledged that none of the men involved were decorated.

Les Peate, *The War That Wasn't: Canadians in Korea*. Ottawa, Canada: Esprit de Corps Books, 2005, p. 41.

Operation Sundial 11 November 1951

The Communists had returned to the conference table in October following the Eighth Army offensive and General James Van Fleet felt it was important to the negotiations to keep up the pressure. Neither he nor the delegates knew if the Communists' return to the table was evidence of their interest in finally coming to an agreement, or if it was simply a way to gain time for replacement and reorganization. But, either way, operations in the field seemed essential.

Accordingly, Van Fleet set up a plan for an advance into the Iron Triangle that lay on the west and just beyond Kumsong to the east. It was determined that it was wiser to keep up the

pressure on the line rather than to let the Communists regain their balance. With the U.S. I Corps and IX Corps he planned to move to the high ground that lay north of the Chorwon-Kumhwa railway and establish a new defensive position south of Pyonggang and north of Kumsong. It was to be called Line Duluth. After establishing this position, IX Corps was to move northeast along the road to Tongchon. This operation was called Sundial. The assumption was that if it went into effect, it would eliminate the need for an amphibious operation that had been suggested as a part of **Operation Wrangler**. The operations had basically the same goals; to set up new defensive lines.

The operation was cancelled and General James Van Fleet was ordered to hold up on his attack toward Line Duluth. Partial agreements at the conference tables were suggesting that the line of demilitarization might be south of the line the UN now occupied. When negotiations continued without decision, Van Fleet again asked for permission on 5 November 1952, but by 11 November, General Matthew Ridgway had determined that the advance was not necessary and Sundial was cancelled.

Despite the poor responses at the negotiation table, the enthusiasm for aggressive action was waning and Van Fleet was ordered to assume an "active defense." Ground action would continue but without any significant attempts to gain territory.

Hermes, Walter G. *Truce Tent and Fighting Front: United States Army in the Korean War*. Washington, D.C.: U.S. Army Center of Military History, 1966, Chapter 9.

Operation Tailboard 25 October 1950

Following the successful landing at Inchon on 15 September 1950, General Douglas MacArthur decided to divide his forces and move north along both coasts. He assigned General Walton Walker's Eighth Army to

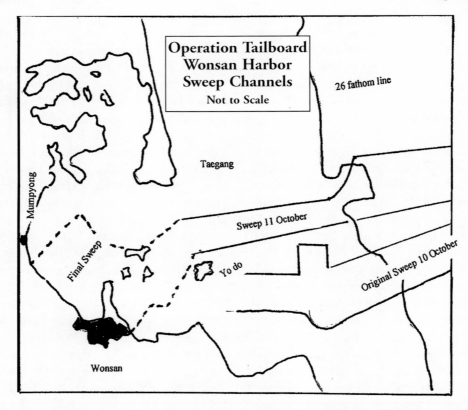

Operation Tailboard, October 1950 (courtesy the Center for the Study of the Korean War).

move northwest from the 38th parallel. General Edward Almond with X Corps was to sail to Wonsan on the further coast, and then cross the waist of Korea to join Walker in the final capture of the North Korean capital city of Pyongyang.

With the North Koreans in headlong retreat, the war, it was assumed, would soon be over. What was necessary was the final push to the Yalu River. The plan called for the 1st Marine Division to go to Wonsan by sea with the 7th Infantry Division following behind to land at Iwon. The first problem was the discovery of mines in Wonsan harbor. Minesweepers were called in and went to work, but they were harassed both by enemy fire from the shore and by the mines themselves. Two sweepers were destroyed on impacting Russian-made mines. It would be two weeks and three more damaged sweepers before the field was cleared.

In the meantime the 1st Marine Division was not able to arrive on shore and instead wallowed on board while the Navy moved them in extended patterns. By 25 October, the ROK 3rd Capital Division had already entered the city of Wonsan just two weeks after crossing the 38th. By the time the Marines landed the ROK Capital Division was nearly 50 miles to the north.

The 7th Infantry Division also suffered delays and confusing orders before finally being put ashore at Iwon to the north in the last days of October. The delay was significant and caused considerable concern among Navy personnel, for they realized that for those few days, at least, they had lost control of the sea. Operation Tailboard has also been called **Operation What-the-Hell** and **Operation Yo Yo**.

James A Field, *History of United States Naval Operations: Korea.* Washington, D.C.: GPO, 1962, p. 220–229.

Walter Karig, Malcolm W. Cagle, and Frank A. Manson, *Battle Report: the War in Korea*. New York: Rinehart, 1952, pp. 10–50, 298.

Operation Talons   August–September 1951

General Matthew Ridgway was getting frustrated with the lack of progress at the peace table. He got permission from U.S. President Harry Truman to make a major air strike on Pyongyang and to bomb Rashin (Najin) only a few miles from Vladivostok and the Soviet border. He also approved General James Van Fleet's plan, Operation Talons, to straighten out the Eighth Army line from Kumhwa to Kansong in the central sector. The process would move the line forward from one to fifteen miles. Despite the plan, Operation Talons was never carried out. It had become obvious that such an attack would require numerous casualties, as had been the case at the Battle of Bloody Ridge. The fighting at Bloody

Ridge had displayed the true nature of warfare between forces in which one had deeply entrenched and defended lines of resistance, and the cost seemed unreasonable. General Van Fleet informed Ridgway on 5 September that Operation Talon, a much larger operation than Blood Ridge, was not worth the probable cost in lives.

Tracy D. Connors, "Truckbusters from Dogpatch." *The Combat Diary of the 18 Fighter Bomber Wing in the Korean War.* http://www.truckbustersfromdogpatch.com/index.php?.id=9.

Operation Thunderbolt   25 January 1951

Following **Operation Wolfhound**, all intelligence and reconnaissance efforts suggested that the Chinese were moving north, not south. It was curious but not to be allowed without response. General Matthew Ridgway did not want the conflicting sides to be separated and ordered Operation Thunderbolt,

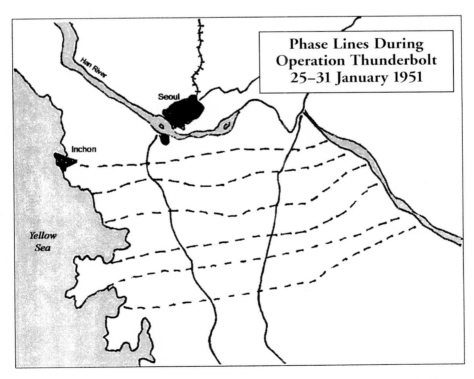

Phase Lines During Operation Thunderbolt 25–31 January 1951

Phase lines during Operation Thunderbolt (courtesy the Center for the Study of the Korean War).

designed to push the Communists all the way back to the Han River. It was to be a serious operation and was mounted by the American I and IX Corps and supporting ROK troops who had pushed into the area bounded by the Han River and the Suwon-Inchon-Yoju Road. They moved out on the 25th of January and by the end of the month had reached the city of Suwon, where there was some heavy fighting. Generally the Communists broke and moved back, abandoning Inchon without a struggle and allowing the Air Force back onto Kimpo Airbase. During the fight, and in response to several attempts at counterattacks, naval bombardment and air strikes seemed to stop the enemy before they got started. Careful attention was given to wiping out any Communist forces located in pockets within the Han River area.

At this point Ridgway informed General Douglas MacArthur that he would move to the Han River and defend it. He saw little military advantage to moving beyond the Han at this time. General Ridgway was never one for seeking much ground, believing that it was not as important as destroying as many of the Chinese forces as possible while leaving no guerrilla activity behind. The idea, known to the Army as "meat grinding," was to keep the battlefield tidy and the opposing forces connected. Therefore Ridgway defined his mission as less the restoration of the city of Seoul then "the destruction of the forces that opposed him." By the end of the second week in February the drive simply wore down. The success of Operation Thunderbolt was in keeping the enemy under pressure. The effort was extended in a follow up exercise called **Operation Roundup.**

Richard Dean Burns, "Operation Thunderbolt," in James I. Matray, *Historical Dictionary of the Korean War.* Westport, CT: Greenwood Press, 1991, pp. 360–362.
Lynn Montross, Hubard D. Kuokka, and Norman W. Hicks, *U.S. Marine Operations in Korea.* Volume IV. Washington, D.C.: Historical Branch G-3, Headquarters U.S. Marine Corps, 1962, pp. 250–51.

James L. Stokesbury, *A Short History of the Korean War.* New York: William Morrow, 1988, p. 120.

Operation Tomahawk   23 March 1951

General Matthew Ridgway decided to include the 187th Airborne Combat Team into his plan to advance General "Shrimp" Milburn's I Corps from Line Lincoln to the Imjin River. He named this drop Operation Tomahawk, and it was carried out on 23 March 1951. The plan was for the 187th to jump at Munsan to capture it and to establish a blockade that would trap the North Korean I Corps, which was retreating and could, he believed, be pushed into a trap. Two armored units would strike from Line Lincoln and link up with the paratroopers.

This was the second airborne operation of the Korean War. It involved 120 C-119s, C-46s of the 314 TCG (Troop Carrier Group), 437 TCW (Troop Carrier Wing), and sixteen escorts of F-51s that were to take the airborne troops from Taegu to Munsan-ni, some twenty miles northwest of Seoul and well behind the enemy lines. Those dropping included the 187th Airborne Regimental Combat Team, 2nd and 4th Ranger Companies, (3,400 men) and 220 tons of supplies. Prior to the drop the area was raided by five AD fighters. During the exercise there was one hit on a C-119, which crashed on its return trip. Helicopters were on hand to evacuate wounded from the drop zone. Operation Tomahawk was designed to catch the enemy off guard and hopefully to retake some American prisoners of war who intelligence had said were being moved with the retreat forces. From 24 to 27 March, fifty C-119s and C-46s dropped another 264 tons of supplies for troops fighting near Munsan-ni.

Tomahawk provided mix blessings. It did bring I Corps forward to the Imjin River as desired, but it failed to trap any of the North Korean I Corps that it was seeking. The historian for the 187th said, "It appeared the enemy was forewarned of a possible airborne assault" (Blair). With this preparation the Communists had withdrawn north of the Imjin River, leaving only elements of their 19th Division as a last guard.

Clay Blair, *The Forgotten War: America in Korea 1950–1953.* New York, Times Books, 1987, p. 766.

Operation Touchdown was about getting supplies here to Heartbreak Ridge (Center for the Study of the Korean War).

Operation Touchdown   5 October 1951

The battle for Heartbreak Ridge was consistent with the name used to identify it. By late September the 2nd Infantry Division of the United Nations Command on the west and the 1st Marine Division had to pull back for some regrouping in preparation to try it again. The supply lines were drained and clogged with ammunition and supplies going up and stretcher bearers going down. The second phase to take Heartbreak Ridge was called Operation Touchdown. This time the artillery support was increased and more tank units were included in the attack force. All the regiments of the 2nd Division, as well as the French Battalion attached, were involved. On the afternoon of 5 October, with heavy support from the Marine Corsairs, the 2nd began to move up the slopes. The plan called for a series of small raids against the North Korean outposts in order to spread out the defense, but the heart of Operation Touchdown was Hill 1220 located at the end of the Kim Il Sung Range. Mobile support was provided by M-4 tanks that arrived on a road specially constructed by men of the 2nd Combat Engineers. The North Korean soldiers, just as exhausted from continuous fighting as were the

UN troops, were moving back slowly but they still gave a good account of themselves. As the fight continued, the commanding peaks were taken one by one, and a tank breakthrough in the western valley took the town of Mundunni and cut off supplies to the enemy on Heartbreak Ridge. Nevertheless, it took until 15 October, fighting with grenades. Flamethrowers, and even bayonets for the enemy to be routed. On that day the 1st Battalion of the 38th Infantry Regiment, supported by the French Battalion, pushed down the Kim Il Sung Range and captured Hill 1220. Operation Touchdown was declared successful and the battle for Heartbreak Ridge was over. The cost had been high. For this readjustment in the line, the 2nd Division had suffered 3,700 casualties and the Communists an estimated 25,000.

Richard Dean Burns, "Battle of Heart Break Ridge," in James I. Matray, *Historical Dictionary of the Korean War.* Westport, CT: Greenwood Press, 1991, p. 36.

Operation Touchy   9–10 November 1951

Operation Touchy was a raid mounted by the Canadians on Hill 166, held by Chinese

Forces, on the night of 9–10 November. It involved two platoons of C Company and the Scout Platoon of the Australian Royal 22e Regiment. The raiders left on their mission at 2100 hours. Platoon No. 8 moved directly north to the objective. Platoon No. 7 tried to move on the objective from the left in what was designed as a textbook maneuver assault without artillery or tank preparation. Platoon No. 8 came under fire about 75 meters short of the objective, a knoll just below the summit of Hill 166. The platoon leader called in heavy

mortars and 25 pounders while the platoon advanced throwing grenades. Platoon No. 7 was also hit. The commander decided to go up the middle and the Canadians, firing and throwing grenades, reached their objective about 0100 hours. The Scout Platoon came under heavy Chinese fire and was forced to take cover. The three platoons consolidated and were waiting for the final assault when one platoon commander reported that Chinese infantry had infiltrated his position, making it impossible to bring down tank fire on

Operation Touchy: Chinese-held Hill 166 was the operational mission (Center for the Study of the Korean War).

previously registered targets. Under the circumstances Lt. Colonel Jacques Dextrze ordered a general withdrawal. Pulling back under fire, the raiders returned to their forward defensive position by 0315 hours. Two men were missing and four wounded.

Paul Wolfgeher, "The Battle Hills, Outposts, Operations and Battle Lines of the Korean War." Unpublished manuscript in the Wolfgeher Collection at the Center for the Study of the Korean War.

Operation Westminster April 1952)

During April of 1952 the activities initiated by the Chinese forces slackened a bit and the United Nations Command was able to do some adjustments. Two rifle companies of 1st Royal Canadian Regiment and 1st R22eR had reached Pusan on 10 and 11 April and had gone on line. Word was received for a shift of divisional boundaries so that the Canadians would turn over the Hook defenses west of the Samichon to the 1st Marine Division. They would then take responsibility for the defense of Hill 355 (Little Gibraltar) on the west, a dominant terrain feature in the Canadian sector of Jamestown Line. The shift to the right was identified as Operation Westminster and was completed on 19 April as the Commonwealth Division reoccupied much of the same positions originally captured during **Operation Commando.**

Norman O. Nelson, "Battles, Operations, and Outposts Found in the Korean War." Unpublished manuscript in the Nelson Collection, Center for the Study of the Korean War.

Operation What-the-Hell
19 October 1950

This was another name given to **Operation Tailboard,** the landing of a portion of X Corps at Wonsan, North Korea, in order to establish a second front. The operation did not go well and this, the second amphibious operation of the war, scheduled to occur on 20 October 1950, was delayed nearly a week because of the presence of Communist mines in Wonsan Harbor. While the minesweepers worked to clear a path to the beach and the Republic of Korea Army staged a successful ground attack against the city, the Marines sailed around and around at eight knots, waiting to get in. Pools were made up as to when the course traveled would be reversed, food became scarce, and sickness spread throughout the troops' ships. Finally, on 26–27 October, 27 transports and 15 LSTs began landing the Marines. The exercise was also known as **Operation Yo Yo.**

Walter Karig, Malcolm W. Cagle, and Frank A. Manson, *Battle Report: the War in Korea.* New York: Rinehart, 1952, pp. 331–332.

Operation Wolfhound
15 January 1951

In what the Chinese called their "third phase offensive," the enemy had advanced along the entire front to a distance of about fifty miles and had captured, for the second time, the South Korean capital of Seoul. Intelligence reports were suggesting that North Korean and Chinese Communist forces were gathering near the southern bank of the Han River. It appeared to be a total victory for the Chinese but it was limited by the fact that had lost casualties at a ratio of three to one, and had extended their supply line farther than it could be maintained. General Matthew Ridgway responded with Operation Wolfhound, a powerful force heavily supported by armor. It was named after the primary regiment involved, the 27th Infantry Regiment, 25th Infantry Division, known throughout the service as the Wolfhound Regiment. In addition to John Michaelis' 27th Infantry, there were Lt. Colonel Welborn G. "Tom" Dolvin's 89th Tank Battalion, Gus Terry's 8th Field Artillery Battalion, and James V. Sanden's 90th Field Artillery Battalion. The operation also included two battalions of the 3rd Division, Herman

Dammer's 2nd of the 65th, and Julius Levy's 1st of the 15th. They were backed up by the guns and armor of Walter "Bing" Downing's 10th and Robert Neely's 39th Field Artillery.

The force consisted of nearly 6,000 men, 150 tanks, and elements of three artillery battalions. It was preceded by an attack of 24 B-26 bombers and 126 fighter planes that provided 107 sorties. It was to be a limited reconnaissance two-day operation and it began at 0700 hours on 15 January and concluded after dark on 17 January. It jumped off on schedule. The operation had several purposes, one of which was Ridgway's belief that Eighth Army should not lose contact with the enemy, preferring to keep an active front line. The flanks of the operation were protected by ROK divisions. As a secondary purpose the operation was to determine if the Chinese Communist Forces were collecting men and supplies in preparation of an overall attack as some believed. But it was also General Ridgway's intention that as many of the enemy as possible be killed.

The attack toward Osan and Suwon was under the command of Colonel John Michaelis. Blown bridges and evidence of large civilian casualties delayed the event, but there was no enemy contact the first day. On the second day air strikes were called in on suspected enemy positions. On reaching Suwon, Operation Wolfhound found the enemy, suspecting no attack, nevertheless quick to respond, running to prepared defenses along the ridges of the southeast and southwest of the town. The operation suffered light casualties. On 17 January, following orders from the previous evening, the task force withdrew to its former position on Line D, north of Sojonni. It was considered to be Eighth Army's first counterstrike in reply to the enemy's January offensive. Perhaps more important was that it brought an end to discussions of withdrawal from Korea, and proved that Ridgway's Eighth Army could "take care of itself in the current situation" (Schnabel).

In retrospect, Operation Wolfhound did not accomplish its purpose of achieving maximum damage on the enemy. In fact, according to Clay Blair, "It scarcely touched the CCF. But its intangible benefits were remarkable," not the least of which was a profound psychological uplift. This operation was followed up by a three corps offensive that began on the 25 of January 1951, code named **Operation Thunderbolt**.

Clay Blair, *The Forgotten War*. New York: Times Books, 1987, pp. 637, 642.
Richard Dean Burns, "Operation Wolfhound," in James I. Matray, *Historical Dictionary of the Korean War*. Westport, CT: Greenwood Press, 1991, p. 362.
Lynn Montross, Hubard D. Kuokka, and Norman W. Hicks, *U.S. Marine Operations in Korea*. Volume IV. Washington, D.C.: Historical Branch G-3, Headquarters U.S. Marine Corps, 1962, p. 41.
James Schnebel, *Policy and Direction: The First Year*. Washington, D.C.: Office of the Chief of Military History, United States Army, 1972, p. 326.

Operation Wrangler   15 October 1952

Just how successfully amphibious landings served the cause in Korea is still up for discussion, but there were several planned and a few executed. There is little doubt about the success of **Operation Chromite** and the landing at Inchon, so the possibility of other landings was often on the minds of the military planners. For more than a year a proposed end-round landing on Korea's east coast near Kojo had been under consideration. The plan was proposed by Rear Admiral T. B. Hill while he was chief of staff to the commander in chief, Pacific Fleet. Once they had landed at Kojo, or somewhere near there, they could link up with Eighth Army and cut off the North Korean supplies coming from China. Vice Admiral J. J. Clark proposed a plan that he called Operation Wrangler and believed it had every chance of success. The plan had the approval of General Matthew Ridgway as well as General James Van Fleet, but it was disapproved by General Omar Bradley, chairman of the Joint

Chiefs of Staff, with the suggestion, "We want no more of the enemy's real estate."

In October 1952, however, Vice Admiral Robert P. Briscoe proposed that a feinting operation of this type be used to relieve pressure on the ground troops. It was never his intention to land any troops, but it was the hope that the enemy would react by sending troops to defend Kojo, and then the Navy and the Air Force could destroy much of the enemy while they were on the move. General Mark Clark approved the idea and assigned Joint Amphibious Task Force 7 to the job. The assemblage included elements from the XVI Corps (40th and 45th Infantry Divisions), the 1st Cavalry Division, and the 118th Regimental Combat Team. Major General Anthony Trudeau was to command the troops and Rear Admiral Francis X. McInerney the amphibious force.

The feint called Operation Wrangler was set for 15 October. Troops from Hokkaido were boarded and off shore waiting for the conclusion of the two day bombardment. When the time came the troops were off-loaded onto the assault boats, at about 23,000 yards, and headed for shore. At the time the sea was calm. At about 5,000 yards as the boats were getting ready to turn back, the wind picked up and before the operation was completed it had turned into a gale. Four boats were destroyed during the recovery operation. Bombardment in the area continued after the exercise as the troops returned to Pohang-dong.

The feint plan directed that "knowledge of the demonstration aspect was confined to only the highest echelons of command" (Cagle and Manson). The individual subordinate commanders were totally unaware that the operation was designed for display purposes only. Later reports suggested that in the three months after the Kojo feint the Communists relocated troops from the interior to coastal regions around Kojo and Wonsan.

Clay Blair, *The Forgotten War: American in Korea 1950–1953*. Berryville, VA: Time Books, 1987, pp. 946–7.

Malcolm W. Cagle and Frank A. Manson, *The Sea War in Korea*. Annapolis, MD: United States Naval Institute, 1957, pp. 391–92.

Operation Yalu

There appears to be no specific operation with this title but the phrase is used in many histories to reflect the move across the 38th parallel in the drive toward the Yalu River. Specifically, it refers to the activities of the 5th and 7th Marine Regiments as they moved north through the mountains toward the Yalu River in November and December of 1950. Whatever the intentions, however, both regiments soon discovered that they had been encircled by three Chinese divisions, a total of about 30,000 men, and it was quickly determined that it was no longer possible to continue the advance north. Operation Yalu was cancelled; the two regiments combined in mutual defense and were told to attack south instead.

Walter Karig, Malcolm W. Cagle, and Frank A. Munson, *Battle Report: The War. in Korea*. New York: Rinehart, 1952, p. 407.

Operation Yo Yo   20 October 1950

Officially the event was called **Operation Tailboard**, but the Marines, never inclined to bypass the pessimistic nature of their situation, named it Operation Yo Yo. The mission was to transport Marines from Inchon to Wonsan where they would conduct an amphibious landing and establish a second front, and then lead the attack north toward the Yalu. On 15 October 1950 Marines fresh from victory at Inchon and Seoul boarded transports. On 19 October they arrived at Wonsan Harbor but due to the Communist mines discovered in the harbor, they were not able to land. Rather the ships of the tractor and transport group began to sail southward. It took the little minesweepers several days to clear a path for the fleet. During this time the Marines, packed like olives in a bottle, sat aboard their troopships steaming for 12 hours in one direction and then 12 hours in another. The conditions on ship were not good; they were short of food and dysentery swept through the crowded transports. The *Marine Phoenix* alone reported 750 men on sick call.

Finally, on 25 October, an administrative landing began on yellow and blue beach, and most of the Marines were ashore the next day.

Most depressing was that the ROK troops had taken the city of Wonsan on 22 October, and Bob Hope and Marilyn Maxwell, who came to entertain the troops, put on a show in which comments about the still waiting Marines were popular.

Lynn Montross and Nicholas A. Canzona, *U.S. Marine Operations in Korea 1950–1953: The Chosin Reservoir Campaign.* Washington, D.C.: Historical Branch, G-3, Headquarters, U.S. Marine Corps, 1954, pp. 30–31.

II. Primarily Air Operations

In the Korean War there was a constant overlapping between the control of air space and its relation to the war on the ground. The air responsibility was to provide tactical support for ground troops, to engage in strategic bombing and air interdiction and to maintain superiority in the air. These assignments, though not in any particular order of importance or need, were, as much as it can be determined, done well, though air power (air pressure, as it was usually referred to during the war) was not as conclusive or dramatic as at first anticipated.

As far as the man on the ground was concerned, the primary role of the air force was to provide air-ground support; that is, to serve as airborne artillery in support of ground actions when it was needed. Such support was in rather constant demand and providing it was a matter of having both the equipment needed and working through the considerable controversy that raged over its control. Part of the problem was that the Air Force was tactically directed toward jets, and yet many commanders believed that jets were unsuitable for tactical ground support — they were too fast to deliver what was needed and to strike fairly small locations without endangering friendly troops. Besides, most of the experience in such support had come in the propeller driven planes of World War II. But perhaps more important was the necessity of being on call, the ability to appear at a designated target on time, and then to hit the enemy in such a

manner as to support the ground action. In time both pilots and some planes, like the AD Skyraider, became amazingly adept in providing this support. It has been estimated that the United Nations flew more than 100,000 tactical air support sorties divided somewhat in half between Navy (including Marine) and Air Force units.

A second assignment, to achieve and maintain superiority in the air, was won quickly, though not as quickly or as completely as is often portrayed by the United Nations. While the protection of Manchuria was available to the Communist air force and is often seen as a deterrent to a more complete victory, the Communists also operated under limitations, primarily designed to protect the secrets of the MiG. There were for a time some rather significant air battles between the United Nations pilots and those of the North Korean and Chinese forces (as well as Soviet pilots). By May 1951 the UN had its first jet ace of the war, Captain James Jabara, and by September Captains Richard Becker and Ralph Gibson had joined him. Allied victories were adding up, but even then there were at least two brief times toward the middle months of the war when the Communists came close to reaching moments of superiority.

In contrast to the combat in the skies, and more in keeping with the policies of the newly organized Air Force, were the campaigns of strategic bombing. This was accomplished by sending bombers (B-29s primarily) against

Damaged T-6 Mosquito after spotting artillery for I Corps, June 1951 (Center for the Study of the Korean War).

landmarks of Korean industrialization. The delivery was slowed by the Communist placement of anti-aircraft weapons and dogged interference by the Communist pilots. Nevertheless, well-planned and executed efforts managed to hit industrial and military targets in areas around Wonsan, Hungnam, Chogjin, and even as far north as Rashin. But this was of questionable value for two reasons: the wiping out of every industrial target in North Korea was not going to bring an end to the war, and the anticipation that they could destroy the enemy's ability to produce the machinery of war was unrealistic, for much of what was coming in came from China and the Soviet Union, both of which were out of bounds for UN air offensives. Even with these limitations, the harshest problem was that the war had not progressed very far before the Air Force had quite honestly run out of significant industrial targets.

Perhaps the most significant mission, though there is still argument about this, was the role in intervention; that is, in missions of interdiction against enemy communications, transportation, and supply. A good portion of the air reserves were directed toward the highly dangerous attacks on the same railroads, switches, highways, bridges, tunnel entrances, and highway junctions in an all-out effort to reduce the enemy's ability to supply itself. This part of the war began almost at once and was successful in taking some of the steam out of the Communist advance. In one form or the other the effort continued throughout the war.

General Otto P. Weyland, commander of the Far East Air Force, believed that interdiction might be used as an independent campaign to encourage the Communists to the negotiation table. Such was the view behind operations **Strangle** and **Saturate**. All the while the United Nations Command had to weigh the costs involved; risking million dollar airplanes and highly trained pilots to blow up a bridge or cut a railway line that might well be repaired in two hours' time. Historian Max Hastings felt strongly about the limited success of these efforts: "There is little doubt that in the first months of the war, thousands of the interdiction missions flown by the Air Force were valueless because of inadequate targeting."

While almost every ground action that took place in the Korean War called on, and received, highly successful air support, some operations were primarily the work of the air services: 5th Air Force, the Marine Air Wing, the planes of the Naval Task Forces, and ROK Air Force planes, including assigned units from many of the participating United Nations forces. The air operations tended to be directed to interdiction, with ground-support offered in connection with other services. Many of the air operations were joint efforts, but some, like **Operation Saturate**, were primarily the initiative and execution of the air forces.

Of the many questions coming out of the Korean War, the evaluation of air operations remains high. It is hard not to acknowledge what was accomplished by the pilots and their crews. And, in the overall picture, there are many who would suggest that the war could not have been conducted, let alone successfully, without the impact of air support. On the other hand, others point out that air interdiction in Korea was a matter of overkill with far too many raids and far too few targets to justify what had been done. Somewhere between those views, perhaps, a more cautious analysis can be made. But there can be no

doubt that the various air operations considered here were examples of careful planning and successful implementation.

The support for interdiction was not universal, certainly, and Vice Admiral J. J. Clark, at one time the commander of the Seventh Fleet during the war, was even harsher in his assessment as it was recorded by B. C. Mossman: "The interdiction program was a failure. It did not interdict. The Communists got the supplies through; and for the kind of a war they were fighting, they not only fought the war they could even launch an offensive."

One of the most dramatic tactical innovations of the war was the use of the helicopter, primarily by the Marine Corps. Before the war and during the early stages, the U.S. Army saw the helicopter primarily as a successor to the truck and the Air Force saw it as a rescue element. During the war, however, Marine combat experience and operations with these vertical-lift aircraft proved their value, and throughout the war tactical operations were worked on and lift techniques expanded. Many of the operations in which helicopter training or evaluation took a primary role are listed in section IV.

In the three years of aerial combat against the Communist Forces in Korea, Far East Air Force flew an astonishing 700,000 or more sorties, and in retrospect it would be hard not to credit them with an amazing accomplishment.

Max Hastings, *The Korean War*. New York: Simon and Schuster, 1987, p. 255.

B. C. Mossman, *The Effectiveness of Air Interdiction During the Korean War*. OCMH Study [2-3-7-AD.H] Histories Division, Office of the Chief of Military History, March 1966, p. 23.

Operation Doorstop 5 February 1953

Air Force General Glenn O. Barcus became gravely concerned about the possibility of a

Communist attack on 5th Air Force bases. After renewing the limited efforts of the early warning radar, it was determined that an initial attack on Kimpo and Suwon air fields could be quick and devastating. The Fifth Air Force's director of intelligence, Colonel John V. Hearn, Jr., warned that "an initial uninterrupted strike on the crowded airdromes at Kimpo and Suwon could destroy more than half of the F-86s in Korea" (Futrell). On 28 November 1952, General Barcus issued a call for the permanent deployment of two Sabre squadrons at Pusan Airfield (K-1).

The dispersal was not made, however, and it was not until 23 January 1953 that General Barcus announced Operation Doorstop. As a result the 5th Air Force was to provide emergency servicing and replenishing for Sabres at Pusan, Taegu, Pohang, Pyongtaek, and Osanni airfields, and would keep half their available pilots and planes on alert. Operation Doorstop was formally implemented in an operational order on 5 February 1953. Lieutenant General B. C. Clark reinforced these protective measures by announcing that additional automatic-weapons battalions were needed at Kimpo, Suwon, and Osan, where no antiaircraft artillery defense existed. Eventually several "quad 50" batteries were installed. The operational orders also included plans to evacuate all 5th Air Force personnel from Seoul on short notice.

Further concern led to a similar operation called **Operation Fast Shuffle,** which was initiated in April 1953.

Robert F. Futrell, *The United States Air Force in Korea 1950–1953*. Air Force History and Museums Program, 2000, pp. 661–662.

Operation Fast Shuffle   12 April 1953

In his increasing concern for the safety of 5th Air Force bases, General Glen O. Barcus expanded on an earlier defensive plan, **Operation Doorstop**, and in April 1953 replaced it was Operation Fast Shuffle. This was a similar plan that directed all four Sabre Wings to be prepared to deploy to alternate bases on short notice. This dispersal plan was never

needed, but the Sabre wings periodically diverted their squadrons on practice bug-out operations to other fields. The plan was extended to include preparation by all air base personnel to evacuate in case of a Communist ground attack. General Barcus told his commanders to "implement every measure both active and passive, consistent with efficient conduct of operations, which will tend to minimize the adverse effects of enemy air activity" (Futrell). Most base commanders went so far as to build revetments, camouflage fuel tanks and provide personnel shelters for their men in case of attack. In the last significant air event of the war, on 27 July 1953, the 4th, 8th and 51st Sabre wings executed an Operation Fast Shuffle deployment with half of their Sabres taken to alternate bases just in case there was a last minute Communist attack.

Robert F. Futrell, *The United States Air Force in Korea 1950–1953*. Washington, D.C.: Office of Air Force History, United States Air Force, 1983, p. 686.

Operation Firefly   29 June 1951

In late June 1951 a unique mission called Operation Firefly was assigned to the patrol squadrons. This plan called for the coordination of flare ships and attack aircraft in a new application of air-ground support, to provide illumination for Marine Corps night fighters. The problem facing the UN Command at this time was that despite control of the sea lanes and dominance in the air, the enemy continued to move supplies and reinforcements with little or no hindrance. This was particularly true at night. Admiral A.W. Radford recommended the use of P4Y2 Privateer aircraft to serve as flare dropping planes. P4Y2 aircraft and their crews from VP-772 were assigned to the Marine Aircraft Wing. The gasoline tanks usually stored in the bomb bay section were removed and the planes departed after sunset, each with a two-ton load of flares, up to 250 flares at a time. The trial flight proved very effective. As a result flare missions started on 29 June 1951 in conjunction with the Marine night-intruder aircraft. The joint exercise required excellent teamwork. The P4Y2s, which were called "Lamp Lighters," had to locate the targets and then fly low over the targets in order to drop flares and illuminate the area. The attack planes would then rush in to push the attack, often calling for another round of flares in order to make a second run. The operation was continued on a limited scale throughout the war.

Michael D. Roberts, *Dictionary of Aviation Naval History.* Volume II. Washington, D.C.: Naval History Center, Department of the Navy, 2000, p. 166.

Operation Get Ready

2 September 1952

When Colonel Maurice F. Casey, Jr., took command of the 403 Wing on 15 May 1952, he found the unit's operational capabilities were not up to his standards and moved quickly to improve them. The problem was that only 28 out of the assigned C-119 "Boxcars" were considered to be safe enough for flying. The difficulty had been a long time in the making and required remedial action. The first step was to get the U.S. Air Force Materiel Command to pressure manufacturers to do a better job of delivering parts, and some of the newer model C-119s, those considered to be maintenance hogs, were returned to Birmingham, Alabama, for complete reconditioning. Then on 2 September 1952, Colonel Casey announced Operation Get Ready and set a standard that required 75 percent of the Wing's planes to be in commission. Encouraged by Operation Get Ready, the 403rd Wing got its commission rate up to 60.2 percent in September. The commission rate continued to grow and allowed the 403rd to participate in the airborne feint that was being put together off Korea's eastern coast.

Robert Futrell, *The United States Air Force in Korea.* Washington, D.C.: Air Force History and Museums Program, 2000, p. 564.

Operation Hawk   27 July 1950

When Canada decided to join with the United Nations in the Korean War, their contingent included the planes and pilots of the Canadian 426th Squadron, a transportation unit flying the North Star. In Operation Hawk, at 1945 hours on 27 July 1950, less than 48 hours after the first arrival, Squadron Leader Harry Lewis and crew took off for Tokyo with a full load of U.S. Army reinforcements. During Operation Hawk, the 426th Squadron flew nearly 600 round trips between McChord Air Force Base in Tacoma, Washington, to Haneda Airfield in Tokyo. The 426th Squadron was the only Royal Canadian Air Force unit to participate in the Korean War under its own command. Canadian fighter pilots fought in USAF squadrons.

Les Peate, *The War That Wasn't: Canadians in Korea.* Ottawa, Canada: Esprit de Corps Books, 2005, pp. 17, 34.

Operation Hawk   20 March 1951

Operation Hawk was a planned parachute jump by members of the 187th, Airborne Regimental Combat Team under Brigadier General Frank Bowen. They were to drop north of the Chunchon road junction. Once on the ground, they were to link up with the 1st Cavalry Division and take the town of Chunchou. Operation Hawk, planned on 18 March 1951, was to drop the 187th, supported by men from the 2nd and 4th Ranger companies, north of town on 22 March. The point was to force the enemy off the main roads and onto more rugged secondary roads to transport its supplies. The move would also provide the UN Command with a logistical hub, and at the same time would flank the enemy forces around Seoul. However, as the men were ready for the drop, General Matthew Ridgway called it off, as the hard hitting 1st Cavalry Division had moved faster than anticipated and had taken the city unopposed. Ridgway quickly reorganized the drop as a part of

Operation Tomahawk that took place on 23 March 1951.

Clay Blair, *The Forgotten War: America in Korea 1950–1953*. New York: Times Books, 1987, pp. 757–58.

Operation Insomnia   13 May 1952

In the continuing struggle to stop, or at least slow down, the enemy supply movements, Far East Air Force committed many planes and pilots. Soon, however, the planners realized that the Communists were timing their efforts to meet those of the United Nations Command attacks. It seemed to some of the more experienced pilots that numerous trucks and trains were starting out just after the planes were finishing a bombing run. Command acknowledged that the enemy was hiding and waiting until the bombardment group had passed, and then moving on again. Operation Insomnia was an effort to catch them at their own game. Beginning on 13 May 1952 the United States Air Force launched varied nocturnal flights to confuse the Communists and to set them up for a second flight that would catch them pulling out. One flight would head out about midnight and the second about 0200 in order to put planes above the targets at break of day. The operation was successful at first, but it ended on 9 June 1952 because command acknowledged that Operation Insomnia was not really making all that much difference.

James A. Field, *History of the U.S. Naval Operations in Korea*. Washington, D.C.: Naval History Division, 1962, p. 436.

Operation Moonlight Sonata
1 January 1952

In January of 1952 the UN negotiators proposed the idea of voluntary repatriation of all POWs, setting the stage for one of the more difficult agenda items. Also, the second phase of **Operation Ratkiller** was in full swing. New efforts to restrict the enemy supply trains from moving were under consideration. Throughout the war many efforts were made to make interdiction raids more successful, and Operation Moonlight Sonata was just one more attempt. The operation was an effort to improve the efficiency of the raids by setting up harassing and heckling night operations focused on the railroads. It was designed to take advantage of the winter snowfall and the moonlight. Because of these conditions, the Korean hills, roads, and railroads stood out in bold relief and were easy to spot and, it was believed, to hit. The idea was to bomb railway tracks both in front and back of a train during the night and then in the daylight to attack with low-flying bombers that could hit the delayed trains. Because of the bad weather conditions in North Korea the operation was limited to those "good days," but the raids were considered partly successful and resulted in the destruction of five locomotives.

History of the USS Halsey Powell *(DD 686)*, Jake Huffaker, "A Cryptologist Remembers." http://www.koreanwar-educator.org/memoirs.

Operation Nannie Able   30 July 1950

As the first month of the war concluded, North Korean units had flanked the 2nd Battalion of the 19th Infantry and the 24th Infantry Regiment was withdrawing to the last high ground about three miles west of Sangju. In the air war the Communist chemical complex, located at and near Hungnam, was considered a particularly important target by the military, and on 21 July 1950 orders were given to prepare a strike. The missions were to be flown by the 22nd Bombardment Group (Medium) and the 92nd Bombardment Group (Medium) and were to be conducted against three targets on three different days. The first of these was Operation Nannie Able and it was scheduled to be executed against the facilities at the Chosen Nitrogen Explosive Factory. Bombing began at 0945 hours on 30 July 1950 as 47 B-29s hit the target. The area was cloudy and the runs were made with the use of APQ-13 radar. All the bombs fell within the targeted area and resulted in an estimated 40 percent of the factory being destroyed.

Robert F. Futrell, *The United States Air Force in Korea 1950–1953* (Revised). Washington, D.C.: Officer of Air Force History, United States Air Force, 1983, p. 190.

Operation Nannie Baker
1 August 1950

The Battle of the Notch had begun with the 1st Battalion, 19th Regiment, holding its ground and then moving into a blocking position on the Masan road near Chindong-ni, when the second of three planned raids against the Communist chemical complex near Hungnam was launched. Operation Nannie Baker, flown by B-29s of the 22nd Bombardment Group (Medium) and 92nd Bombardment Group (Medium) Group, was executed on 1 August 1950. Over target the weather was clear, giving all but the last flight, blinded somewhat by smoke from the fires, the chance to bomb visually. The 46 B-29s that attacked the Chosen Nitrogen Fertilizer Factory with 500 pound bombs caused considerable damage to the factory.

Robert F. Futrell, *The United States Air Force in Korea 1950–1953* (Revised). Washington, D.C.: Officer of Air Force History, United States Air Force, 1983, p. 190.

Operation Nannie Charles
3 August 1950

As the understrength 2nd Infantry Division and the 5th Regimental Combat Team were landing at Pusan, the third in a three-pronged aerial attack against the Communist chemical complex at Hungnam was executed. Following up on **Operation Nannie Alpha** and **Operation Nannie Baker,** Operation Nannie Charles was directed toward the Bogun Chemical Plant. Attacking this time with only 39

B-29s, the 22nd Bombardment Group (Medium) and 92nd Bombardment Group (Medium) bombed through clouds; nevertheless, the results were excellent. As a result of this operation and the previous two, General George Stratemeyer announced that the chemical centers should "no longer be considered a major factor in the Korean War" (Futrell).

Robert F. Futrell, *The United States Air Force in Korea 1950–1953* (Revised).Washington, D.C.: Officer of Air Force History, United States Air Force, 1983, p. 190.

Operation No Doze   June–July
1953

Few night carrier operations were conducted during the Korean War. However, there was a plan called Operation No Doze that was formulated and briefly put into operation during the final weeks of the war. The USS *Princeton* was selected and was given a three-destroyer plane guard. In addition, all the night fighter aircraft of TF 77 were to be transferred to the carrier. The idea was to strike significant targets with delayed fuse bombs so that the morning flight would have more lucrative targets. When the *Princeton* was required to return to Yokosuka for boiler repairs, the operation was postponed. There were a lot of reasons for using night carriers; the most impressive probably was that it relieved the burden imposed on air crews and ship crews during the day. A second reason was the realization that during the night most of the destruction caused during the day was being repaired by the Communists. At night, it was believed, the target area crawled with activity. Nevertheless the debate continued throughout the war and despite the organization of Operation No Doze, little of it was carried out.

Malcolm W. Cagle and Frank A. Manson, *The Sea War in Korea*. Annapolis, MD: Naval Institute Press, 1957, p. 261.

Operation Paralysis 9 January 1953

The United Nations Command had gone on full alert when North Korea threatened to interfere with the release of 22,500 anticommunist POWs taken during the war. At the same time, and in continuing operations, Operation Paralysis was established as a part of the air campaign against the Sinanju communications complex. Marine and Air Force jet squadrons flew flack suppression and interdiction missions, focusing on knocking out ground based air defense weapons and destroying bridges and rails. The joint operation was set up to strike the rail system at Sinanju, 45 miles north of the enemy capital. At night Far East Air Force Bomber Command's B-29s, with Flying Nightmare escorts, worked over the communication nets and during the day fighter-bombers attacked marshaling yards. Operation evaluation showed that enemy rail lines were inoperative for sixteen days. The cost was the loss of seven fighter-bombers.

Pat Meid and James M. Yingling, *U.S. Marine Operations in Korea, Volume V: Operations in West Korea.* Washington, D.C.: Historical Division, Headquarters, U.S. Marine Corps, 1972, p. 243.

Operation Plan Blast

28 September 1952

In the late summer of 1952 the Korean War had dragged into a stalemate with opposing forces locked into lines running along the 38th parallel. Negotiations were stalling and the United Nations had proposed three alternatives in an effort to solve the stalemate over the voluntary repatriation of prisoners. The message to General Mark Clark, commanding Eighth Army, was clear: "Maintain unrelenting military pressure on the enemy, particularly through air action. No major ground action should be contemplated at this time" (Joint Chiefs of Staff). The pressure was designed to try and force the Chinese Communists into a settlement at Panmunjom. But

General Clark had also given instructions in Operation Plan Blast to warn North Korean civilians that the bombings were coming.

One or two days prior to the arrival of the bombing force, according to Clark's orders, leaflets were to be dropped in and around supply depots, railway yards, and other potential targets in order to reduce civilian casualties. The leaflet operation proved to be very useful against the North Korean population. With little availability of radio, there was a susceptibility to messages that were directed toward a particular people or place. Operation Plan Blast missions served a less humanitarian role, however, for it was the intention to cause a disruption of industrial materials produced and the blocking of military roads as civilians tried to avoid the bombing. There was a tendency, as well, to overdo this operation on the American philosophy of more is better, but there is still considerable evidence that the North Korean population, as well as Communist soldiers, often took the information seriously.

In an effort to expand the effect of the leaflet-dropping operation, Lieutenant General Glenn O. Barcus, commander of the 5th Air Force, released to the media the identity of multiple targets. In some respects this plan back fired, as the State Department became afraid the Communists would use the target list as propaganda. And, in fact they did, suggesting it was a plan to annihilate the civilian populations. The leaflet drops were discontinued but the raids continued.

William B. Breuer, *Shadow Warriors: The Covert War in Korea.* New York: John Wiley and Sons, 1996, p. 209.
Joint Chiefs of Staff to Mark Clark, 28 September 1952, National Archives, Washington, D.C.
Michael Haas, *In the Devil's Shadow: U.N. Special Operations During the Korean War.* Annapolis, MD: Naval Institute Press, 2000, p. 72.

Operation Pressure 23 June 1952

This operation represented a change in strategy that reduced the emphasis on interdiction and increased aerial attacks on major industrial targets. It was concluded that these targets were of greater value to the North Koreans and thus a greater loss to the economy. While this was probably true, it was not just that. The interdiction campaign had suffered some significant losses due to the increasing accuracy of Communist anti-aircraft ground weapons.

Two other considerations were involved, however. One was General Mark W. Clark's determination to bring the Communists to an armistice and the second was the Defense Department's removal of the North Korean hydroelectric facility from the restricted bomb list. The plant under consideration was at Suiho and was the fourth largest in the world.

Pressure strikes carried on from 23 to 27 June and were highly successful. Combined Marine, Navy and Air Force planes flew 1,652 sorties, attacking thirteen of the identified targets. Eleven of the planes were put out of commission and two were badly damaged. Only two aircraft were downed and rescue aircraft successfully picked up the pilots.

Pat Meid and James M. Yingling, *U.S. Marine Operations in Korea, Volume V: Operations in West Korea.* Washington, D.C.: Historical Division, Headquarters, U.S. Marine Corps, 1972, pp. 64, 227.

Operation Pressure Pump
11 July 1952

Operation Homecoming, the release of 27,000 civilian internees, had begun and the battle for Outpost Yoke was turning out to be one of the most desperate small actions of the war. In the continuing effort to bring pressure against the Communists, air action was increased through a series of United Nations raids on the North Korean capital of Pyongyang. They were timed to coincide with the Moscow visitation of Chinese Premier Cho En Lai and a large delegation. The operation ran through July and August 1952, with the heaviest bombardment conducted on 11 July

and 26 August. The units involved included the ROK Air Force, which flew against all of the thirty identified targets as well as the Australian and the South African No. 2 Squadron.

Operation Pressure Pump had several goals. One was to focus on the sources providing electrical power, another to bring pressure on the North Korean and Chinese delegates at Panmunjom, and a third to draw attention to the Communists' vulnerability and embarrass the delegation in Moscow. In anticipation of the strikes, General Mark Clark instructed that leaflets be dropped warning civilians of the coming attacks. The plan was for the attacks to be carried out on a twenty-four hour schedule, three separate raids during each day, and one at night. These were difficult targets, for the Communists had reported setting up more than 48 guns and a hundred automatic anti-aircraft weapons at the location. At the height of the strikes Operation Pressure Pump flew 1,254 sorties.

The blow leveled by Operation Pressure Pump was successful and destroyed command posts, supply depots, factories, troop encampments, railway facilities, and gun positions. At least three of the thirty identified targets were completely destroyed and all but two were damaged to some degree. More than 6,000 died in the raids, including, unfortunately, some American POWs being held in the area. Losses for the UNC included two Navy planes, a Thunderjet and eight 5th Air Force planes, and 38 planes were damaged. When the raids were over additional leaflets were dropped, this time saying, "I told you so."

Robert F. Futrell, *The United States Air Force in Korea 1950–1953.* Air Force History and Museums Program, 2000, p. 517.
Pat Meid and James M. Yingling, *U.S. Marine Operations in Korea, Volume V: Operations in West Korea.* Washington, D.C.: Historical Division, Headquarters, U.S. Marine Corps, 1972, pp. 170–173.

Operation Red Cow   8 October 1952

At the negotiation table UN delegate Lieutenant General William Harrison informed the Communist delegates that the United States was no longer willing to consider discussions unless some tangible progress could be made. As a part of the effort to get things going again, air activity was increased. The Far East Command engaged in amphibious demonstrations in early October 1952 and the 5th Air Force combined with Task Force 77 to provide front line attacks that delivered air support and close air-ground support. Operation Red Cow was a joint Navy-Air Force mission with Navy Banshees and Air Force B-29s that attacked positions near Kaesong. The operation targeted Communist troops who had been safe from previous air attacks because of their locations near the neutral positions at Kaesong. Flying between 8 and 25 October, Mosquito controllers directed 105 fighter-bomber sorties from the USS *Kearsarg* and ten B-29 Superfortresses against 24 enemy troops and artillery targets, very close to the main line of resistance and the fringes of the neutral zone. It was the first such operation since August 1951.

Paul M. Edwards, *Korean War Almanac*. New York: Facts on File, 2006, p. 341.

Operation Spotlight   1951–1953

On several occasions during the war, exercises were held to test the validity of using spotlights attached to bombers making night raids. Test raids were also conducted during exercises supported by the 6167th Air Base Group, which dropped flares during dark phases of the moon in order to catch enemy transportation units — particularly trains — at night. All of these operations seem to be referred to as Operation Spotlight. On 30 December 1952, however, a rather specific effort was identified as Operation Spotlight, and involved RB-26s (converted Douglas B-26 light

bombers) from the 12th Tactical Reconnaissance Squadron, which pulled such a raid with mounted spotlights that allowed them to attack a marshaling yard and destroy four train cars and damage a fifth engine. This method, though tried several times, did not prove all that helpful, as the amount of time airmen could maintain the light was limited.

Norman O. Norman, "Battles, Operations, and Outposts Found in the Korean War." Unpublished manuscript in the Nelson Collection, Center for the Study of the Korean War.

Operation Spring Thaw   21–22 March 1953

Once again, as talks slowed down at the negotiation table in March of 1953, the UN Command's air strategy was aimed at destroying targets that would curtail the flow of supplies to troops on the front lines. There was evidence that the Chinese were planning an offensive designed to seize as much territory as they could prior to any negotiated agreement. In Operation Spring Thaw, the Air Force entered into a brief but intense interdiction campaign designed to cut off these massing troops. Far East Air Forces sent medium bombers against bridges in an effort to create choke points, and then fighter-bombers hit along the roads leading to the bridges in order to destroy traffic that had been backed up. Operation Spring Thaw began officially on 21 March when eighteen medium bombers knocked out the two principal bridges at Yonggmi-dong. Bad weather reduced the effectiveness of the plan, but it did slow the arrival of supplies by forcing enemy vehicular traffic onto secondary roads and across makeshift bridges.

A part of the campaign was to lure the Communists up to fight, but engagements had been less than usual. The 5th Air Force combat crews began dropping leaflets asking, "Where is the Communist Air Force?"

Paul Wolfgeher, "The Battle Hills, Outposts, Operations and Battle Lines of the Korean War." Unpublished manuscript in the Wolfgeher Collection at the Center for the Study of the Korean War.

Operation Strangle May 1951–
September 1951

While interdiction campaigns were a regular part of the early phases of the Korean War, it was not until the peace negotiations got underway in 1951 that they began to take on a different role. It was General Otto P. Weyland, the new commander of the Far East Air Force, who suggested that interdiction might well be viewed as an independent campaign. He believed that because the front line had become primarily a stalemate, and the movement of troops limited to reasonably small encounters, an increase in the focus of air power might be the best way to keep the Communists' minds focused on the negotiation table. The idea took some time to catch on, but by May 1951 it had been formalized by setting up Operation Strangle. It was well into August before it was set in motion.

The plan was to break down the Communist transportation system within a hundred miles of the front line. In order to do this, day and night attacks were set up by the Air Force. If they could limit the enemy's ability to supply themselves by focusing the bombing effort, they might be able to produce more success at the negotiation table. Target analysis suggested that this effort would be even more effective if it were launched primarily against railways.

To make this work, a one degree strip of latitude across the narrow neck of North Korea was identified from 38.15 N to 39.15 N, which lay just beyond the battle line. Each of these strips was divided into eight routes. The 5th Air Force would take the three western routes, the 1st Marine Air Wing the three eastern routes and the central routes would be covered by the carrier planes of Task Force 77. Strangle points were identified, thus the name,

along each route as well as bridges, tunnels, and other vulnerable areas that might be considered targets. Night bombings increased. Fifth Air Force divided the runs in Korea between the two B-26 wings stationed at Kunsan Airfield and a third flying from Pusan East airfield that was responsible for covering the main supply routes.

The daylight attacks managed to successfully interdict many of the Communist railway lines in North Korea, especially during August 1951, when pilots reported they had never seen so many vehicles on the road at one time. Between late August and the middle of September, the 52nd Wing claimed 4,959, vehicles destroyed or damaged.

The effectiveness of the plan declined, however, as the Air Force and other involved units simply could not create enough trouble to increase pressure on the negotiators. Perhaps a far more realistic reason was that the operation was not effective. Despite the fact that rails were bombed, bridges blown up, and tunnels collapsed, the traffic was still moving. Portable bridges were constructed and moved in after an attack; in some cases bridges were built under water where they could not be seen. Rail breaks were being repaired in hours rather than several days, as had been anticipated. An additional problem was that the Communists had brought in considerable anti-aircraft artillery and grew very proficient in its use. One approach often used resulted in so many hits that the area where it was deployed became known as Death Valley. It soon was seen as less and less wise to risk a million dollar plane and its pilot to delay railway traffic for what was often less than an hour.

By late summer 1951 it was apparent that Operation Strangle had failed in its intent. The reasons were simple: not only did the enemy repair damages quickly, but redirected transportation onto smaller less traveled roads, often compensating faster than the Air Force could destroy.

Some after-the-fact analysis suggests that if

the night-intruder aircraft had possessed electronic equipment designed to identify hostile vehicular targets at night and in all kinds of weather, it might have been more effective. Air Force historian Robert F. Futrell concludes: "United Nations airmen achieved the stated purposes of the railway-interdiction campaign but did not measure up to the idea inherent in the code name 'Strangle.'"

General Vandenberg, Air Force chief of staff, saw the effort in a different manner. "An effort like Operation Strangle will not stop the enemy dead in his tracks. As long as he is willing to pay the price in transport vehicles and equipment destroyed, he may be able to maintain his armies in some degree of operational effectiveness at the front line." Far East Air Force finally agreed, however, that "Operation Strangle was not successful ... due to the flexibility of the Communist logistic system" (Mossman).

Robert F. Futrell, *The United States Air Force in Korea 1950–1953*. Washington, D.C.: Air Force History and Museums Program, 2000, p. 703.
Callum A. MacDonald, "Operation Strangle," in James Matray, *Historical Dictionary of the Korean War*. Westport, CT: Greenwood Press, 1991, pp. 297, 360.
B. C. Mossman, *The Effectiveness of Air Interdiction During the Korean War*. OCHGH Study [2-3-7-AD.H], Histories Division, Office of the Chief of Military History, March 1966, p. 15.
Rod Paschall, *Witness to War: Korea*. New York: Berkeley, 1995, p. 106.

Operation Tack   4 February 1951

This was an idea generated by the 3rd Bomber Wing as a means of stopping the truck traffic that delivered arms and reinforcements to the Communist troops. It suggested that night flying C-47s ought to fly low over enemy held roads and drop tacks along the length of the road. On the night of 4 February several C-47s flew at heights of no more than ten or twenty feet scatting eight tons of roofing nails along four twisting highways south of Pyongyang. The planes were flying so low that one pilot, Major Robert Spencer, nearly collided with three Communist tanks. When daylight arrived, scores of 5th Air Force fighters flew over the targeted highways and destroyed twenty-eight trucks that had been halted by the punctures in their tires.

At the 3rd Bomber Wing's request, Far East Air Materials Command fashioned some hollow tire puncturing barbs. These tetrahedrons were so constructed that they would provide an upward spike no matter how they landed. These were dropped at low altitudes along well used highways. William Breuer reports one additional bonus of this effort is that Chinese Communist convoys were often slowed down as one man was assigned to walk in front of them to warn of tetrahedrons. Weather prevented the planned follow up raid so the success of Operation Tack was never evaluated.

William B. Breuer, *Shadow Warriors: The Covert War in Korea*. New York: John Wiley and Sons, 1996, p. 146.

III. Primarily Naval Operations

The conflict in Korea was very much a ground war in which thousands of foot soldiers slugged it out among the humid valleys and frozen hills of the divided Korea, but it is also important to acknowledge the highly significant role played by the U.S. and UN Navy. The transportation, delivery, supply, support, and withdrawal of United Nations forces were to a large degree dependent on the Navy, not only for the movement itself, but because any such movement would have been impossible without freedom of the sea. Because the Navy was able to establish control over the sea lanes, ships sailing from America to Korea with men and equipment traveled without hesitation or fear of interference. Men fighting on the shores were free from concern about enemy naval bombardment, and complicated ground movements were never long curtailed because of the inability to move troops. For more than three years, the United Nations enforced a naval blockade of Korea, while it maintained one of the longest naval sieges in history at the port of Wonsan.

During the brief peace between World War II and Korea, some consideration was given to the idea that because of the newly organized and effectively equipped Air Force, and the possession of the atomic bomb — as well as ballistic missiles — the role of the Navy had been overshadowed, perhaps had even outlasted its usefulness. As it turned out, of course, the disruption in Korea served to discount such thinking, as the UN fought out the first of many twenty and twenty-first century wars against nontraditional enemies. Despite the disagreements and the cutbacks, when the war broke out in 1950, the United States Navy was still the most powerful fleet available.

The U.S. did not have a lot of naval presence in Korean waters, however, for there was present only one cruiser, four destroyers, and a few outdated minesweepers active in the Sea of Japan. Yet it was understood from the beginning that control of the sea was a necessity if the U.S. was to be involved in a war halfway across the world, and one of the first moves by President Harry Truman was alerting the 7th Fleet. Dealing with a nation that possessed an elongated coast line, and for which water was a primary means of transportation, the Navy was destined to play a significant role.

A major factor in the outcome of the war was that the naval forces of the United Nations Command prevented any participation by the Chinese Communist and Soviet navies. While the North Korean Navy was small and would not have been a major factor, both the Chinese and Soviet navies could have posed serious threats to the United Nations effort. No one is exactly sure why these two powers made the decision not to get involved in the naval war, but their presence never went away and one constant pressure was the need to remain on the alert for such possibilities. Soviet submarines operating near the UN fleet were anticipated and often acknowledged as a

USS *Philippine Sea* **prepares for refueling during naval operations (Center for the Study of the Korean War).**

factor though it has never been correctly understood to what degree.

This also meant that the presence of UN ships prevented, or at least greatly limited, the Communists' ability to attack from the sea, denying them much of the rapid movement that sea transport might have provided, and denying them the opportunity for any serious reinforcement or supply from the sea. At the same time, the threat of sea bombardment against UN troops was nonexistent and made movement not only considerably easier but with a great deal less risk.

The naval force launched hundreds of air strikes in support of ground action and participated in saturation and interdiction bombing. It provided transportation and support for the men and equipment used to fight the war. And, it allowed the United Nations forces to be reinforced and supplied through Pusan. It was a vital component in the Inchon invasion, played a heroic role in the evacuation at Hungnam, and served as the core of a series of amphibious landings, evacuations, with the deployment of clandestine commando teams and partisan groups.

While the United States Navy was the core of the United Nations force and provided the larger percentage of the warships to the effort, they were not in it alone. Led by the nations of the Commonwealth (Great Britain, Australia, Canada, and New Zealand) ships from France, Colombia, the Netherlands and Thailand joined with the determined men and women of the Republic of Korea Navy to provide this essential contribution to the war effort.

The only real naval battle took place on 2 July 1950 when the cruiser U.S. *Juneau* and the British cruiser HMS *Jamaica*, along with the British frigate *Black Swan*, took on four North Korean torpedo boats supported by a

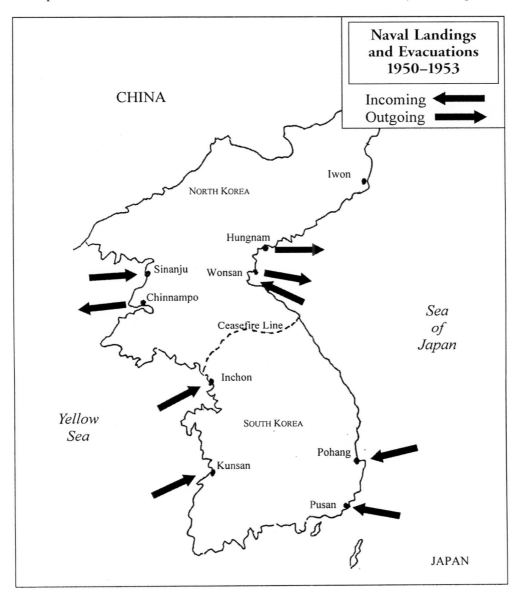

Naval operations (courtesy Paul Wolfgeher Collection, Center for the Study of the Korean War).

gunboat. The North Koreans tried to put up a fight but were quickly outgunned and destroyed. Several other Communist ships were sunk during the war, mostly small ones bringing in supplies or laying mines. In terms of significance to the war, perhaps the most important was an ROK ship which sank a North Korean troop ship heading from Pusan during the first days of the war.

Many of the operations in Korea were joint efforts, and the naval forces were quite often participants in the operations planned by other services. Those listed here were primarily sea operations.

James A. Field, Jr., *History of United States Naval Operations: Korea.* Washington, D.C.: Government Printing Office, 1962.
Edward J. Miralda, ed., *The U.S. Navy in the Korean War.* Annapolis, MD: Naval Institute Press, 2007.

Operation Amphibious Kojo
June 1951

This was an operational plan designed to center on General Paik Sun Yup's Republic of Korea I Corps. He received orders, in June 1951, from General James Van Fleet to prepare for a new operation: an enormous invasion that would involve elements of four UN Command corps. Operation Amphibious Kojo, as it was known, called for the ROK I Corps to attack along the east coast to Kojo, sixteen miles or so from Wonsan, the U.S. 9th Infantry Division at Chorwon to launch their attack northward, the U.S. X Corps to attack through Mundung and follow the Pukhan River, and the U.S. 40th and 45th Infantry Divisions, which at that point comprised XVI Corps in Japan, were to embark and conduct an amphibious assault on Kojo, thereby linking up with the other troops. The point was to destroy enemy positions at the Punchbowl and strengthen Eighth Army's flank. The operation never got off the ground, stymied by General Ridgway, who sent the clear message that while Eighth Army was to remain on the offensive, it was not to mount any significant offensive operations. Another launch into North Korean territory would not, it was believed, help win a truce.

Paik Sun Yup, *From Pusan to Panmunjom*. Dulles, VA: Brassey's, 1992, pp. 159–161.

Operation Ashcan   10 May 1951

HMS *Hawea* set out from Sasebo, Japan, on its first patrol on 10 May 1951. After patrolling off the coast of Inchon, it proceeded north to take part in Operation Ashcan, a demonstration set up by Rear Admiral A. K. Scott-Moncrieff, the British flag officer second in command. He believed that a feint, if properly mounted and publicized, would ease the pressure that was being felt by United Nations forces that were anticipating the second phase of the Chinese Communist spring offensive. What he wanted to do was to suggest to the enemy that the UN forces were about to descend on them with a sweeping attack from the flank. To begin with, rumors were spread throughout the guerrilla forces and minesweeping operations were conducted to give the impression that a sizable force was planning to put ashore on the mainland just opposite Cho-do. The exercise would conclude with a force of Royal Marines actually being landed. As the exercise unfolded the Royal Marines were ashore for about five hours, during which they penetrated several miles inland and burned some deserted villages, but met no serious opposition. They then withdrew and re-embarked. The effect on the Communists seems to have been minimal, however. But, even if it did not alter the disposition of land forces, it did prompt an increase in defensive activity in the area.

Ian McGibbon, *New Zealand and the Korean War: Combat Operations*. Melbourne: Oxford University Press, 1996, pp. 171–172.

Operation Cave Dweller   11 July 1951

As the United Nations stepped up its attacks around Kansong, the Republic of Korea's 1st Division hurled itself against the enemy defenses re-established there, the USS *Blue* (DD-744) and the USS *Evans* (DD 754) were fired on near Yo-do without damage, and Operation Cave Dweller went into effect. This operation sent the USS *New Jersey* (BB-62) under Captain David M. Tyree and the USS *Leonard F. Mason* (DD 852) under the command of Commander J. B. Ferriter to harass enemy troops at the location. On 11 July they approached the bomb-line and opened fire on enemy troop concentrations and supply buildups in around Kansong. Working with shore fire control teams spotting troop buildups, Operation Cave Dweller is reported to have caused 129 enemy deaths

Paul Wolfgeher, "The Battle Hills, Outposts, Operations and Battle Lines of the Korean War." Unpublished manuscript in the Wolfgeher Collection at the Center for the Study of the Korean War.

Operation Chicken Stealer
18 January 1952

In the inland waters along the coast of Korea, the Navy soon discovered a new use for its whaleboats. These small craft worked well when used in the detection of targets along the inlets and harbors, as well as being able to direct ships' gunfire. There had been a change in the earlier efforts at rail cutting, redirecting the attacks from diverse and widely scattered targets to focusing on stretches of a line causing a disruption that ran from 1,500 to 4,000 yards. The hope was to increase the time necessary to repair the line.

They were also invaluable for landing parties sent ashore to capture enemy supply buildups. The USS *Halsey Powell* (DD 686) in Operation Chicken Stealer sent her small boats in close enough to the waterfront areas of Sam-he that her spotting crew could direct the ships guns' to the most desirable targets. With excellent spotters, the *Powell* was able to damage eighteen jetties, riddle several small boats in the harbor with shrapnel, and destroy a warehouse on shore. While on this mission the *Powell* also engaged enemy shore batteries.

History of the USS Halsey Powell *(DD 686)*, Jake Hufaker, "A Cryptologist Remembers." http://www.koreanwar-educator.org/memoirs.

Operation Cigarette   May 1951

This operation, which was activated north of Inchon in the Chinnampo area, was in the British sector and conducted by their forces. Here the British check-swept the coastline where the Chinese were depositing sea mines in order to prevent the landing of UN troops near the road to the capital.

Paul Wolfgeher, "The Battle Hills, Outposts, Operations and Battle Lines of the Korean War." Unpublished manuscript in the Wolfgeher Collection in the Center for the Study of the Korean War.

Operation Counter Punch
13 November 1951

Neither the North Koreans nor the Chinese put much of a fleet in the waters around Korea; in fact there were hardly any naval efforts to counteract the United Nations' fleet at sea. And, for its own reasons, the Soviet Union did not include naval support in its contributions to North Korea. As long as this was true, the biggest fear for the UN naval forces around Korea came from the threat of heavy gun emplacements on shore. It was this danger that led to Operation Counter Punch. The gun emplacements scattered throughout the islands near Kojo had been harassing UN ships moving through the area on assignment. When gunfire began to hit UN ships, Operation Counter Punch was launched. It sent the cruiser *USS Toledo* (CA 133) to bombard the enemy batteries. During the operation three of the gun emplacements were hit and destroyed.

Paul M. Edwards, *Korean War Almanac*. New York: Facts on File, 2006, p. 226.

Operation Derail   January 1952

By this time in the Korean War more than sixty Navy and Marine Corps planes had been lost to enemy anti-aircraft fire. For this reason, as well as concern over the effectiveness of the effort, the interdiction raids were coming under serious question. A good many pilots involved considered the raids no longer cost effective. By now shore bombardment had become the primary business of the surface ship, firing on fixed targets as well as floating ones. Nevertheless, in a continuation of the interdiction efforts, a series of planned raids were set up to be conducted during January 1952, this time by the Navy: **Operation Package** and Operation Derail. Operation Derail was a program of directed naval gunfire on targets in the northeast, while Operation Package allowed naval guns to fire after being zeroed in by spotter planes. The idea was to disrupt the rail traffic and reduce the movement of enemy supplies along the coastline. The strikes focused on those areas considered the most difficult to repair. For Operation Derail this meant their main targets lay along the Chogjin to Hungnam Railroad. The method employed was to fire a defined number of shells into the area every 24 hours. Operation Derail halted railway traffic into Wonsan for weeks, but there were not enough ships available to continue the shelling indefinitely.

Jake Huffaker, "A Cryptologist Remembers." http://www.koreanwar-educator.org/memoirs.

Operation Fireball   April 1951

While the blockade of Wonsan Harbor was primarily a stable action, there were occasions when the siege would be intensified by rocket attacks set out by the Landing Ship, Medium Rocket (LSMR) Division and air strikes from the planes of Task Force 77. In April 1951 an experiment, Operation Fireball, was worked out between the bombarding ships of Task Force 95 and the aircraft of the Twelfth Reconnaissance Squadron. Fifty Air Force planes and several flare dropping P4Y2 Privateers from Fleet Air Wing Six provided target guidance on enemy positions up and down the east coast. This "bombardment at night" exercise was considered very effective. During the exercise the LSMR division fired more than twelve thousand 5-inch rockets between June and September 1951. The heaviest night was 20–21 May when Operation Fireball and two LSMRs (*401* and *403*) fired 4,003 rockets at Wonsan targets in 35 minutes.

Malcolm W. Cagle and Frank A. Manson, *The Sea War in Korea*. Annapolis, MD: United States Naval Institute, 1958, p. 404.

Operation Junket   13 January 1952

The USS *Collett* (DD 730) and USS *Rochester* (CA 124) joined with planes from the USS *Badoeng Strait* (CVE 116) to execute an attack against gun batteries on Amgak Peninsula, an exercise planned and carried out by CTF 95. It was organized to try and stimulate United Nations ships operating in the area to capture small enemy craft. Not only would these captured crews have provided intelligence information, but the vessels themselves would be used for covert operations.

Paul M. Edwards, *Korean War Almanac*. New York: Facts on File, 2006, p. 269.

Operation Kickoff   18 July 1951

The United Nations Command was determined to maintain the blockade at Wonsan Harbor despite the fact that enemy fire from batteries hidden among the hills were harassing UN ships in the harbor. On 18 July 1951 the battleship USS *New Jersey* under Captain David M. Tyree and the destroyer *Leonard F. Mason* (DD 852) under Commander J. B. Ferriter returned to Wonsan Harbor after conducting a bombardment along the bomb-line. The mission had been to initiate an intensified bombardment plan that was known as Operation Kickoff. For weeks thereafter this became standard tactics, as each day ships would fire at known and suspected positions of enemy harbor defenses and gun emplacements in the Wonsan Harbor area, with both delayed bursts and air bursts. The ships continued to sail counterclockwise along the bomb-line at five knots beginning at about 1500 hours and operating until dusk, firing at will. The operation, which directed returning fire at enemy batteries that fired on UN ships in the harbor, continued for some weeks.

Malcolm W. Cagle and Frank A. Manson, *The Sea War in Korea*. Annapolis, MD: United States Naval Institute, 1957, p. 325.

Operation Muffler

Operation Muffler was an ongoing effort carried out by UN naval forces in Wonsan

Harbor to determine if any new mines had been laid by the Communists since the last check sweep.

Jake Huffaker, "A Cryptologist Remembers: Terms." *Korean War Educator.* www.koreanwar-educator. org/memoirs/huffaker/index.htm.

Operation Order 8-50   30 June 1950

Shortly after the Korean War began, Admiral Forrest P. Sherman, chief of naval operations, recommended a blockade of Korea as a component of U.S. strategy. The following day, Operation Order 8-50 was established. It was further defined on 3 July 1950 as detailed plans for the escorting of shipping in the area. The South Korean naval forces (Task Group 96.7) were assigned the coasts south of latitude 37 degrees north. The coast, north of that line, went to East Coast Support Group (Task Group 96.5). The west coast north of the 37th parallel was given to the British ships, designated as West Coast Support Group (Task Group 96.8). All ships were prohibited from operating any farther north than the 41st parallel on the east coast and the 39.30th parallel on the west, in order to prevent any potential confrontation with the Chinese or Soviet navies.

Operation Order 8-50 was in operation, in one form or another, throughout the war. While the South Korean vessels were active and prevented North Koreans from landing additional troops and supplies along the east coast, the limited number of United Nations ships available during the early months made a really effective blockade impossible. International law required that if a blockade was to be considered legal it had to be effective, and while that was questioned in the beginning, it quickly became a fact. After that the U.S. Navy maintained what Rear Admiral Alfred Thayer Mahan would call an "overbearing power on the sea." The one exception to its success, if there was one, would be the mining

of Wonsan Harbor and the delay of **Operation Tailboard**.

Norman O. Nelson, "Battles, Operations, and Outposts Found in the Korean War." Unpublished manuscript in the Nelson Collection, Center for the Study of the Korean War.

Operation Package   11 January 1952

Task Force 77 was given major interdiction responsibility in **Operations Derail** and Package. Reports from Soviet sources claimed six more F-80s had been shot down during raid near Anju. Such losses showed again that while interdiction efforts continued, they did so at a significant cost. Between October and December 1951, sixty-five Navy and Marine Corps planes had been shot down by enemy anti-aircraft fire. And, after every raid the Communists were quick to repair the damage. Many pilots considered the interdiction missions to be very unprofitable. Nevertheless, in January 1952, several interdiction flights were assigned in conjunction with naval force bombardment in Operation Package. Focused on the northeast coast, the operation defined a series of shoreline targets for both ships and planes.

It set up five specific targets along the Songin-Hungnam Railroad, identifying each with a number. The ships, sailing as close as 2,000 yards from the target, began regular bombardment. The hope was that the destruction of key rail points would impede the supplies coming out of Manchuria. The missions were as follows: number 1, a bridge, 3,000 feet long, that carried a single track over a valley between two tunnels; number 2, 220 yards of track between two tunnels; number 3, a 35 foot, two-span bridge across a canal; number 4, tracks at the foot of a mountain at the base of a tunnel; and number 5, a bridge. In addition to the specific bombardment, the ships were to fire a specific number of rounds at irregular intervals every day and night to hamper repair efforts. Like many such missions, the efforts, while somewhat effective, petered out as the demand for ships increased.

Malcolm W. Cagle and Frank A. Manson, *The Sea War in Korea.* Annapolis, MD: United States Naval Institute, 1957, pp. 49–51.

Operation Pronto   5 April 1952

As a part of the 1st Marine Corps' exercises designed to test the combat value of the helicopter, Operation Pronto provided the first major helicopter airlift into the I Corps sector near Field A-17. It combined the shortest notice with the longest distance of any large-scale troop movement by helicopter. It was primarily designed to evaluate the tactical value of immediate helicopter employment. The exercise was conducted on 5 April 1952 when Marine Helicopter Squadron 161 received a call giving it three hours to prepare to move 670 personnel from the 2nd Battalion, 7th Marines, and all their equipment, including 10,000 pounds of rations, from the Munsan-ni area across the Han River to the Kimpo Peninsula. The trip was just over 57 miles from the front line area and required a detour in order for the MHS 161 to stay clear of the demilitarized zone around Munsan-ni. The 99 flights during the day consisted of 81 troop movements, ten cargo lifts, and eight administrative lifts. The transfer took place at a spot where the reserve battalion was to provide a counterattack against a hypothetical enemy landing. It was the longest round-trip distance of a helicopter troop movement up to that time. As far as the military was concerned, this exercise proved a helicopter unit could move a troop organization virtually on call and without the benefit of previous liaison.

Lynn Montross, *Cavalry of the Sky: The Story of the U.S. Marine Combat Helicopters.* New York: Harper and Brothers, 1955, p. 184.

Operation Retribution
3 October 1951

While **Operation Commando** had begun in an effort to push UN lines forward from Line Wyoming, enemy fire from gun emplacements was proving to be a constant problem for the UN forces operating near the coast and rivers. Several attempts were made to neutralize the success of these guns, but few things worked. Several United Nations ships had been hit including, on 18 September 1951, the *JML 302*, and later the HMAS *Murchison,* which at the time had Rear Admiral G. C. Dyer on board. The admiral hastily ordered a more effective response to these attacks. One of the major problems was locating the Communist guns so that they could be silenced.

Operation Retribution was carried out by the Commonwealth destroyer HMS *Black Swan* and thirteen aircraft from United Nations Task Force 95.11. The *Black Swan* made a feint up the Han River's "Sickle Route" to get enemy guns to open up and give away their location. Then, ten minutes after the *Swan* showed up, the aircraft arrived and fire on those emplacements that had given themselves away. The frigate and accompanying aircraft continued this harassment for two days. On 4 October, the HMAS *Rotoiti* did a bombardment run through the navigationally dangerous "Lambeth" channel, and the *Black Swan* replied with one additional series of feints and raids. The result of Operation Retribution was the destruction of several enemy gun batteries and some villages. In response to the *Rotoiti*'s contribution to the effort, Admiral Scott-Moncrieff wrote, "She has made a name for herself in Korea which will be long be remembered" (McGibbon).

Ian McGibbon, *New Zealand and the Korean War.* Melbourne: Oxford University Press, 1996, pp. 186–187.

Operation Roof Lifter   6 March 1952

Units of the East Coast Element 2 (Task Element 95.22), consisting of the HMAS *Warramunga* and the USS *Moore* (DD 747), and with support from the UN Blocking and Escort Force (Task Force 95), spent more than an hour in the inner Songjin Harbor carrying out their phase of Operation Roof Lifter. In this case a steady bombardment was delivered in order to destroy as many buildings as possible. The particular intent of the operation was to start fires and destroy homes in order to deny potential shelter in the area.

Korean War Chronology of U.S. Pacific Fleet Operation, January–April 1952. Washington, D.C.: Naval History and Heritage Command, Navy Historical Center, Department of the Navy.

Operation Sea Dragon   April 1951

North Korean and Chinese controlled sampans and junks were a constant threat to the UN forces. Small, quick, capable of carrying large loads, and well-commanded, they were able to move in close to the coastline, where they could avoid naval ships, and make deliveries or land small harassing forces. In response, Operation Sea Dragon was set up to capture some of these smaller vessels and use the captured junks to track down and destroy enemy sampans that were supplying the Communist troops. The Communist boats had also been seen delivering sea mines that proved to be a constant harassment to UN shipping. In addition, the UN made good use of the captured vessels to conduct covert reconnaissance on the Yalu River Estuary and among the many islands dotting the east coast.

Norman O. Nelson, "Battles, Operations, and Outposts Found in the Korean War." Unpublished manuscript in the Nelson Collection, Center for the Study of the Korean War.

Operation Shoe String   August 1950

This is the name given to the manner in which minesweeping was carried out in the

Operation Sea Dragon was launched to capture this type of motorized sampan.

early months of the war. After the end of World War II many sweepers had been retired or put in mothballs and when needed again were in short supply. Often only two groups were available for sweeping and they worked around the clock. The shortage of sweepers became grossly apparent when mines held up the Marine landing at Wonsan in October 1950.

Jack Huffaker, "A Cryptologist Remembers: Terms." *Korean War Educator.* www.koreanwar-educator. org/memoirs.

Operation Siciro   10 September 1952

On 10 September 1952, the American carrier USS *Sicily* and the gunboat USS *Iroquois* led Operation Siciro, the code name being compounded from the names of the two warships. Set up partially to restore morale after the failure of a raid in August supported by HMCS *Nootka* and *AMC 302*, the operation was designed as an assault by three companies of guerrilla forces (Wolfpack), about 350 strong. They pushed off from the island of Yongmae-do at 0100 hours aboard junks, some steam and some sail, and moved out through the three mile passage across the mud flats to the Shangdong Peninsula. The peninsula was softened by 90 minutes of gunfire from the HMCS *Iroquois*. The bombardment was reported as "a battle of wits between the ship's gunnery officer who wished to have reasonable ammunition expenditure and the spotter who was determined to empty our magazine as rapidly as possible" (Meyers). The USS *Sicily* arrived at 0620 and covered the planned withdrawal of the guerrilla force on the return journey to Yongmae-do. The enemy casualties were estimated at 400 and the destruction of several gun emplacements. The invading force rescued three agents who had been in enemy hands.

According to the commanding officer of the *Iroquois*, Operation Siciro, carried out with

semi-trained troops led by officers commanding through interpreters and with a rather fuzzy aim in mind, did astonishingly well.

Edward C. Meyers, *Thunder in the Morning Calm.* St. Catharines, Ontario: Vanwell, 1991, p. 180.

Operation Squeegee   May 1951

Controlled shore bombardment was an essential part of the naval assignment in Korea, but one specific bridge caught the attention of the Canadian Navy; it had become a personal affront to the crew. The bridge was located two miles south of Sonjin and was called the Rubber Bridge. Despite the constant shelling by the gunners of HMCS *Nookta*, the bridge remained standing. No matter how many times it was hit, the Communists always seemed to have it up and useable the following day. The larger cruisers were unable to reach the target because of the shallow water near the coast, and the Chinese had mined the waters to prevent the destroyers from coming very close. Commander A.B.F. Fraser-Harris, the commanding officer of the *Nootka*, suggested a plan called Operation Squeegee that was accepted by higher command.

In this plan two cutters from the *Nootka*, with an improvised paravane, would sweep the area and as mines came to the surface, destroy them with rifle fire. This action was accomplished without too much difficulty. Enemy soldiers gathered on the beach to watch the operation and, at one point, they moved in an artillery unit to respond, but fire from the *Nootka* was able to silence them. Once clear of the mines, the *Nootka* kept up the shelling, and with aid from the USS *Stickle*, from a range of 1,300 feet, the men rained shells on the surrounding area, destroying marshaling yards and buildings. Then they turned their attention to the bridge — shell after shell was hurled into the structure. The damage was so extensive it was expected that the bridge would fall immediately, but as it turned out, when the ships were called away to

USS *William R. Rush* on screening duty during Operation Squeegee (Center for the Study of the Korean War).

other assignments, the bridge was still standing. However, later reconnaissance showed that the bridge was damaged badly enough to be unusable for at least a little while.

In Malcolm Cagle and Frank A. Manson's *The Sea War in Korea*, the idea is credited to Commander Jesse B. Gay, Jr., but *Nootka's Report of Proceedings*, May 1951, indicates the plan came from Commander Fraser-Harris.

Edward Meyers, *Thunder in the Morning Calm: The Royal Canadian Navy in Korea 1950–1955*. St. Catharines, Ontario: Vanwell, 1991.

Malcolm Cagle and Frank A. Manson, *The Sea War in Korea*. Annapolis, MD: United States Naval Institute, 1957, pp. 322–23.

Operation War Dance

December 1952

This was the operation under which the United States conducted the naval siege maintained by Task Force 95 during the Korean War. More specifically it referred to the December 1952 operation carried out by the USS *Kidd* (DD 661). The *Kidd*, the "Pirate of the Pacific" under the command of Commander Charles A. Bellis, had taken part in the mock invasion near Kojo and had served in a variety of bombardment assignments when it was called on to conduct this operation. It required the USS *Kidd* to cruise at ten knots, sailing around Wonsan Harbor as bait, in order to draw fire from the Communist batteries hidden ashore. When one of the batteries fired, then the *Kidd* was able to identify the source and return fire. During Operation War Dance the *Kidd* silenced several Communist batteries.

Alfred Smith McDonald, *Operation War Dance*. Buffalo, NY: Talking Leave Books, 2008.

Operation Whoomph

Sea mines were one of the most destructive of all the Communist weapons used during the conflict in Korea, and they accounted for all the sinking of UN ships during the war. Because of the extent of the sowed mines and the shortage of sweepers, sooner or later many ships took on the role of minesweeper. In Operation Woomph the Canadian destroyer *Athabaskan* was in a minefield. With no facilities on board for dealing with mines, Commissioned Officer David Hurl of Winnipeg, a mine specialist, came up with a simple but pragmatic solution. He sent out a small party in a motor cutter that was towing a dinghy.

When they spotted a mine, a crew would get in the dinghy and row in next to the floating explosive. There they would attach a demolition charge to the rings on one side of the pear-shaped mines. Leaving it with a five-minute fuse, they world race back to the cutter and away from the area before the geyser could overtake them. When the mine exploded, they moved on to the next mine. Five Russian mines were destroyed in Kunsan harbor in this unusual operation.

Walter Karig, Malcolm W. Cagle, and Frank A. Manson, *Battle Report: The War in Korea*. New York: Rinehart and Company, 1952, p. 342.

IV. Primarily Specialized, Experimental, Training, Feint, and Administrative Operations

Maybe this grouping should be identified as "Miscellaneous Operations," for the operations included are extremely diverse. These efforts varied in size, intent, and accomplishments, and while combat-related, they were not necessarily front-line related activities. These operations often appeared to be isolated from the rest of what was going on, arising to meet a specific need, or to accomplish a rather well-defined task. They usually required special preparation. Several of these Korean War operations were designed to be quick and dirty in order to meet an immediate challenge. Others were to destroy one particular enemy fortification, or to transport civilians or children caught in the cross-fire, or to anticipate a coming need, to retake ground in order to collect the dead or wounded, or to collect a prisoner for interrogation.

Quite a few of the operations were experimental or designed to test procedures. The Korean War saw the first significant use of helicopters. Some, like the YUR-4, were used during World War II, but it was rare. Korea provided the opportunity to test the helicopter's wide potential as a combat weapon, and it was the Marine Corps that took the lead, especially dealing with combat-transportations operations. Other experiments, like the testing of long range fuel replenishment or expanded cargo planes, continued through-

out the war. Most of these were highly productive, identifying combat tactics and equipment for wars yet to come. Some of the operations were simply exercises to train units, like in the case of the South Korean pilots in **Operation Bout One**. Some of these operations were designed to try out, or give the final test, to new equipment being made ready for battle.

During the war the United Nations Command planned several feints designed to confuse the enemy, or cause it to move troops from one location to another for protection of a site, or to hide the developing activities at some other location, illustrated by the much-planned **Operation Decoy**. This tactic was perhaps tried too often and there does not seem to have been a lot of success in drawing the enemy to the point of the feint. Nevertheless, they required careful planning and execution, and sometimes, even lives.

Several operations, for lack of a better grouping, have been identified as "administrative." These, like **Operation Christmas Kiddie Car Lift**, are illustrative of the wide humanitarian role played by many of the United Nations forces. Or, perhaps, the highly important but primarily theoretical **Operation Everready**, designed to remove President Syngman Rhee from office if he could no longer be counted on to serve the best interests of the war effort.

A Navy rescue helicopter waits over the wreckage of a damaged Panther jet (Center for the Study of the Korean War).

Clay Blair, *The Forgotten War: America in Korea 1950–1953*. New York: Times Books, 1987.

James A. Field, Jr., *History of United States Naval Operations in Korea*. Washington, D.C.: Government Printing Office, 1962.

James I. Matray, *Historical Dictionary of the Korean War*. Westport, CT: Greenwood Press, 1991.

Operation Albany   Spring 1951

After the intervention of the Chinese Communist Forces and the United Nations retreat at Chosin, as well as Eighth Army's Christmas withdrawal and reorganization, General Matthew Ridgway's Eighth Army began to move north once again until it finally crossed the 38th parallel. As Ridgway advanced he collected vast numbers of prisoners of war, as Communist soldiers were overrun or surrendered en masse. As it turned out, there were far more prisoners than had been anticipated; by November 1950 the UN held about 137,000 prisoners in makeshift camps. Because this was

unforeseen, arrangements were inadequate to handle the large number, and as a result the prisoners were scattered about in a variety of camps. This dispersion required Ridgway to keep a good many men out of combat just to guard them. The general also expressed great concern about the presence of these enemy troops, even in camps, behind his lines. In response, Eighth Army launched Operation Albany, which was the collection of all prisoners of war and their relocation to the off-shore islands, primarily Koje-do. The island on which the camp was located was about twenty miles off the coast of Pusan. During the several months required to complete the operation, more than a thousand prisoners a day were transported to the island camp. While the immediate advantages were good and released pressure on Eighth Army, the presence of so many prisoners in one or two locations would cause considerable difficulty for the United Nations later in the war.

"UNC POW Administration," in James I. Matray, *Historical Dictionary of the Korean War*. Westport, CT: Greenwood Press, 1991, pp. 503–506.
C. A. MacDonald, *Korea: The War Before Vietnam*. New York: Freepress, 1986.

Operation Amber Liquid
October 1952

In October of 1952 a C–46 landed at K–16 with a delivery for the aviary (special operations) officer. The boxes were delivered to the 8240th AU (Army Unit) orderly room, and then sent on to the mess hall. On opening it was discovered the boxes contained a considerable amount of Kirn beer (Operation Amber Liquid) and several small painted frogs with parachutes (**Operation Red Frog**).

Ed Evanhoe, *Dark Moon: Eighth Army Special Operations in the Korean War*. Annapolis, MD: Naval Institute Press, 1995.

Operation Ascendant 29 January 1951

Intelligence services continued to express the belief that the Chinese Communist Forces were worried about additional amphibious landings to their rear. In light of this, they recommended the UN should either undertake additional landings or, at least, set up some feints designed to confuse the Communists. Admiral A. E. Smith, commander Task Force 95 (West Coast Support Group), came up with the idea of supporting Eighth Army's advance by an amphibious feint in the Kansong-Kosong area, about fifty miles beyond the front line. There, at an expanded coastal plain, a road was cut through the mountains that

made it a logical objective for such an attack. To accomplish Operation Ascendant, CTF 95 borrowed two attack cargo ships (AKAs) and two LSTs, as well as a couple of rocket-ships. With command in the Task Force's flag ship, the USS *Dixie*, the force moved out on 29 January. Heading out to sea, the force reappeared on the morning of the 30th as the bombardment group, the battleship USS *Missouri* and cruiser USS *Manchester*, and their screening group opened fire in the Kansong area. As they did so minesweepers carried out their mission as if cutting a path to the shore. Every effort was made to give the impression that there was an amphibious invasion taking place. However, late on 31 January, the USS *Dixie* finally fired off the last of its 204 rounds and moved on. The operation was unique in that it included a destroyer-tender as a flagship. The effectiveness of this effort, particularly the movement of troops away from the front, has been inaccessible, but other operations like Ascendant were not particularly successful.

James A. Field, Jr., *History of United States Naval Operations in Korea*. Washington, D.C.: Government Printing Office, 1962, p. 323.

Operation Back Door
September 1953

The final signing of the armistice agreement soon brought on new work schedules for the troops who, though somewhat relieved, were still primarily on the alert. The renewed schedules included imposed activities and training missions designed to provide new defensive positions and to prepare for whatever might still be coming. Few believed that the cease-fire would hold. In the immediate post-armistice period, the pilots of Marine Air Group 33 participated in Operation Back Door, a successor to, and very much in the same venue as, **Operation Spyglass**. This September exercise stressed interception flying and working with ground control intercept squadrons. Acting as the aggressors, the Pohang-based airmen would make simulated attacks on various South Korean targets that were defended by Air Force and land-based Marine units. The exercises were to alert them to the dangers that still faced most UN positions, and to prepare them for attacks that many in the military still believed would be forthcoming.

Pat Meid and James M. Yingling, *U.S. Marine Operations in Korea, Volume V: Operations in West Korea.* Washington, D.C.: Historical Division, Headquarters, U.S. Marine Corps, 1972, p. 473.

Operation Beat Up
25–26 November 1952

This was a diversionary exercise fought by the 1 Royal Australian Regiment in support of the Royal Fusiliers in their attack on Hill 227.

Paul Wolfgeher, "The Battle Hills, Outposts, Operations and Battle Lines of the Korean War." Unpublished manuscript in the Wolfgeher Collection at the Center for the Study of the Korean War.

Operation Big Ben   Spring 1951

Operation Big Ben was a program established by Eighth Army during the spring of 1951 to evacuate ammunition in case it became necessary for massive redeployment. The intent was to avoid the losses suffered in the early months of the war. In those cases where it was necessary for ammunition to be evacuated, it was done in good order.

Paul Wolfgeher, "The Battle Hills, Outposts, Operations and Battle Lines of the Korean War." Unpublished manuscript in the Wolfgeher Collection at the Center for the Study of the Korean War.

Operation Big Switch   5 August 1953

The last major unfinished business of the Korean War was the exchange of prisoners of war. Final arrangements for the exchange were reached on 25 May 1953, but even at this late date the proceedings involved were marked with controversy stemming from the voluntary repatriation provision. This issue of forced repatriation of the prisoners had been the primary stumbling block to the conclusion of the negotiations. The U.S. was holding out for the individual's right to determine repatriation, while the Communists were demanding the return of all captured nationalists to the point of their origin. The eventual agreement stated that the UN would establish the Neutral Nations Repatriation Commission (N.N.R.C), chaired by India, to take the responsibility for those prisoners who indicated their preference to remain with their captors. The ten-man commission was from Sweden, Switzerland, Poland and Czechoslovakia. Those individuals who wished to avoid repatriation were held for a 90 days, during which time they would be advised by their home nation, and would complete their choice.

The first Communist truck, a Molotov, arrived at 0856 on 5 August 1953 full of U.S., Turkish, and South Korean soldiers, and moved through Freedom Gate at Panmunjom. During the exchange the United Nations Command returned 75,823 prisoners (70,183 Koreans and 5,640 Chinese); the Communists repatriated 12,772 UN prisoners (7,862 Koreans, 3,597 Americans, including General William Dean, and 946 British). Some 22,600 enemy soldiers refused repatriation, with only 137 changing their minds during the 90 day cooling off period; 357 United Nations personnel preferred to remain with the Communists (333 Koreans, 23 Americans, and 1 Brittan). A total of ten decided during the 90 day period to change their minds. Two late releases on 21 October and 1 January 1954 appear to be reporting errors.

While both the United Nations and the Communists accepted the agreement and were ready to carry it out, South Korean President Syngman Rhee rebelled and threatened to have his soldiers fire on the Indian troops if they tried to enter the Republic of Korea. At this point President Rhee was anxious for the

In Operation Big Switch, Communists strip off UN clothes before going home (Joseph Adams Collection: Center for the Study of the Korean War).

war to continue, since his primary objective, the unification of Korea, remained unrealized. As a result of his threats, the exchange point was created in the Demilitarized Zone at the cost of about eight million dollars, at a place identified as Freedom Village, at Munsan-ni, Korea. The UN prisoners were greeted with a royal welcome and all the comfort and efficiency that the Quartermaster Corps could come up with. The Communist prisoners were so happy to be released that they stripped off their hated capitalist prison uniforms and marched off "singing party-approved songs" (*Time* magazine).

At the conclusion of the exchange, which took thirty-three days, 8,177 prisoners or missing soldiers remained unaccounted for, their whereabouts unknown. General Mark Clark, at first refused to sign the armistice agreement that verified all POWs had been exchanged, but did so after being instructed by President Harry Truman. The government was aware that not all of the prisoners had been accounted for. During the war some 642 men had returned to the service claiming they had been prisoners of war. Whether they were released, escaped, or were never really in captivity is not known. On 17 June 1955 the office of the secretary of defense issued a report, "Recovery of Un-repatriated Prisoners of War," which stated that numerous prisoners of war were still unaccounted for.

Barton Bernstein, "The Struggle over the Korean Armistice: Prisoners of Repatriation?" in Bruce Cumings, *Child of Conflict: The Korean-American Relationship 1943–1953*. Seattle: Washington University Press, 1983.

Clay Blair, *The Forgotten War: America in Korea 1950–1953*. New York: Times Books, 1987, p. 975.

Michael E. Haas, *In the Devil's Shadow: U.N. Special Operations During the Korean War*. Annapolis, MD: Naval Institute Press, 2000, p. 57.

Time magazine, August 17, 1953.

Operation Blackbird

27 September 1951

As the battle for Heartbreak Ridge continued, the Marines provided another test in their ongoing efforts to evaluate the helicopter as a weapon for combat. Operation Blackbird was a night training lift by Marine helicopter transportation that was successfully completed by HMR 161. It was the first night helicopter action in history and was designed to test the ability of the helicopter to provide a night supply landing mission. Despite some difficulties in the landing zone, Operation Blackbird was the beginning of a very successful program. The helicopters from HMR 161 lifted 200 Marines of Easy Company, 2nd Battalion, 1st Marine Regiment, under 2nd Lieutenant William K. Rockey, from Hill 702 northwest to the rim of the Punchbowl area on a dark night with no moon. Hill 702 was in the Marine sector and had been taken after a considerable struggle. The drop was accomplished in just over two hours.

While the venture was not without its problems, it did prove that the movement of troops along with their equipment and supplies through rugged and mountainous terrain was possible as long as they were able to provide daylight reconnaissance to establish a landing zone. The exercise resulted in the suggestion that until some of the kinks could be worked out, the maneuver should only be done in friendly territory. As it turned out, Operation Blackbird, under command of Lt. Colonel F. Brooke F. Nihart, was one of the largest nighttime troop movements of Marines during the war. Shortly after landing, the troops, proceeding on foot to the assembly area, set off a mine and one man was wounded. Since it was discovered the area was covered with mines, the battalion commander abandoned the march.

Lynn Montross, Hubard D. Kuokka, and Norman W. Hicks, *U.S. Marine Operations in Korea.* Volume IV. Washington, D.C.: Historical Branch G-3, Headquarters U.S. Marine Corps, 1962, pp. 211–212.

Operation Boar   July 1951

One of the most significant innovations of the Korean War was the armored jacket, an improvement on the World War II "flack jacket." Forty sets of the prototype jackets were sent to Korea to be distributed among personnel in one Marine and two Army regiments in a test called Operation Boar. The operation was monitored by Lieutenant Commander Frederick Lewis and Commander John Cowan, Navy doctors responsible for the development. During the two month trial more than six thousand soldiers and Marines wore the vests. They were hot, heavy, and inconvenient, but soon proved their efficiency, as chest wounds decreased by 60 percent among those wearing the armor. A month later, a considerably improved vest appeared (M-152 Flack Vest) weighing slightly less than eight pounds and having more flexibility. The vests were quickly adopted by troops whenever available.

Jan K. Herman, *Frozen in Memory: U.S. Navy Medicine in the Korean War.* Booklocker, 2006, p. 147.

Operation Booklift   15 September 1950

The Civil Air Transport Company (CAT) was the private airline of the Central Intelligence Agency. Originally operated as a Chinese air lines, it was created by Claire Chennault and Whiting Willaver in 1946, immediately following the end of World War II, and was set up with military surplus and discharged pilots. It was purchased by the CIA in 1950 and registered as subsidiary to the Airdale Corporation, a privately operated Delaware company. During the Korean War the CAT worked with the United Nations in Operation Booklift. This was a contract with the U.S. Air Force for the airlift of men and supplies between designated points throughout the Far East. The operation began on 25 September 1950 with twenty-two planes assigned. It lasted during the entire Korean War and was primarily involved in the transportation of men and cargo.

During the whole of the war, the CAT flew in excess of 15,000 missions for the United States Combat Cargo Command between Korea and Japan. However, CAT was also involved in the transportation segment of some of the clandestine operations behind enemy lines, including the rescue of downed U.S. airmen. These operations were known as "third force support." They also flew evacuees and partisans to camps for advanced training, and parachuted some into enemy territory for sabotage, interception, and reconnaissance. The CAT made more than 100 hazardous overflights of mainland China, dropping agents and supplies. A good many of the civilian CAT pilots refused to make clandestine runs during the war. After the armistice was signed, Operation Booklift continued, providing operations in Thailand. In 1959 the CAT became Air America.

William Leary, *Perilous Missions: Civil Air Transport and CIA Covert Operations in Asia.* Washington, D.C.: Smithsonian Institution Press, 2003, pp. 117–120.

Operation Bout One   July 1950

The South Korean Air Force proved to be a brave and determined group at the beginning of the war, but it did not have the pilots, or the planes, to compete with the Communist invaders. So when the United States was able to supply some planes, the instruction of new pilots in their use became high priority. In an attempt to meet this need a special group (a squadron with ground support elements) was formally organized in Japan on 27 July 1951 under the command of Major Dean Hess. At this time Hess was in his second war and was a recognized fighter pilot with more than a hundred missions and a lot of experience in air-ground combat. The unit was assigned P-51 fighters and was transferred to Daegu (Taegu), South Korea, where it continued combat training. Designated the 6146th Air Base Unit, the training command was eventually designated as the 51st Provisional Fighter Squadron, Republic of Korea Air Force, but remained under U.S. Air Force Command.

Through the summer and autumn of 1950, Hess's volunteers worked with the new pilots. The units were quickly committed to combat and flew in support of the U.S. 24th Infantry Division that was engaged near Daejon. Operation Bout One got off to a shaky start for several reasons, among them the language problem, but also because some of the ROK pilots were experienced in their own right and were not all that sure they needed additional training for the P-51. But the unit quickly became prepared and the extreme need for fighters called on the Air Force to identify them as available for independent operation. Pilots from the original group were soon called upon to begin additional squadron. In an action dubbed the "Pyongtaek Massacre," Hess and his unit attacked a North Korean armored column bearing down on Daejon.

Major Dean Hess later became well known as the author of *Battle Hymn*, a book that was made into a movie about his life as a fighter pilot in Korea. An ordained minister, he flew his own F-51 emblazoned with *By Faith I Fly*, to complete his 250 missions.

Allan R. Millett, *Their War for Korea.* Washington, D.C.: Brassey's, 2002, pp. 180–185.

Operation Breakup   7 May 1952

One of the more embarrassing incidents of the Korean War was the revolt at the prisoner of war camp at Koje where Brigadier General Francis T. Dodd was the camp commander. There had been serious unrest in the compound with the Chinese organized by Communists who had been deliberately sent into the camp to create trouble. In a surprise and well designed exercise on 7 May 1952, the Communists kidnapped General Dodd and held him for ransom. Brigadier General Charles

F. Colson, next in command, in an effort to save Dodd's life, gave in and assured "humane treatment in this camp" (Jinwung Kim, in Matray, p. 231) in the future. The Communists were quick to pick up on the propaganda value of both the outbreak and the "admission," and the issue was soon being used by the delegates at the peace talk to condemn the UN. General Mark Clark sent combat troops and both Dodd and Colson were court-martialed (reduced to colonel). A new commander, Brigadier General Haydon L. Boatner, was given command and told to restore order. In Operation Breakup he dispersed the Communist compounds into smaller units. On 10 June, in a last defiant action by the Communist prisoners, a bloody fight broke out. More than 150 prisoners were killed and one U.S. soldier was killed and one wounded. The Communist resistance was broken after about an hour.

Callum MacDonald, *Korea: The War Before Vietnam*. New York: Free Press, 1986.
"Boatner, Haydon L.," in James Matray, *Historical Dictionary of the Korean War*. Westport, CT: Greenwood Press, 1991, pp. 55–56.

Operation Bumblebee
11 October 1951

In many ways this was a historical operation that would mark the beginning of large scale troop movement by helicopter. Carried out by the Marine Medium Helicopter Squadron 161, Operation Bumblebee set the stage for what was to become the standard for the Marine Corps use of the helicopter in combat. In this operation the 3rd Battalion of the 7th Marine Regiment was sent to relieve a battalion of the 5th Marines on the main line of resistance. The point of the exercise was twofold, to gain planning experience to determine time factors in a tactical movement, and to speed up the relief process and to reduce the demands placed on motor transportation.

Help had been requested by elements of IV Corps, who found themselves in need of ammunition and casualty evacuation. Lieutenant Colonel William P. Mitchell was called on to lead six HMS-161 units to deliver supplies and recover men and equipment from the top of a 3,000 foot mountain northeast of Yanggu, North Korea, that was identified as Hill 702. It was the first large scale troop transport of the war and was preceded by a full rehearsal of loading and unloading. Beginning at 1000 hours on 11 October 1951, leaving from X-77 field, twelve helicopters engaged in 156 flights that took over 65 hours of flight time. In this time they managed to move 958 Marines and all of their equipment, which was a total weight of 229,920 pounds. This was only the first of many such flights over 35 months, during which they flew a total of 18,607 sorties, lifting a total of 60,046 persons and 7,554,336 pounds of cargo.

Lynn Montross, *Cavalry of the Sky: The Story of the U.S. Marine Combat Helicopters*. New York: Harper and Brothers, 1954, 167–171.
Gary Parker, *A History of Marine Medium Helicopter Squadron 161*. Washington, D.C.: History and Museum Division Headquarters United States Marine Corps. 1978, p. 12.

Operation Butterfly   June 1952

During the period that Eighth Army was involved in **Operation Counter**, commanders were encouraging an increase in reconnaissance and emphasizing the vital need to capture more prisoners. The Marines were still involved in testing the tactical advantages of the helicopter. Operation Butterfly was a Marine Corps exercise involved in the moving of a battalion-sized relief unit across the Han River. While an active combat move, it nevertheless served to test the HMR-161's ability to carry out a troop lift with only a few hours' notice. The operation was successful.

Lynn Montross, *Cavalry of the Sky: The Story of U.S. Marine Combat Helicopters*, New York: Harper and Brothers, 1954, p. 189.

Operation Changie Changie

10 January 1952

Having become frustrated with the lack of action at Panmunjom, the UN delegates rejected further negotiations as long as the North Korean delegates refused to consider a ban on the building of new air bases after an armistice was signed. At sea carrier Task Force 95 was carrying out its responsibility for clearing out all small craft operating in their area. In January the Marines were called on for another effort at troop exchange. In Operation Changie Changie, which is pidgin English used between Americans and Koreans to mean swap or exchange, the swap in question was a battalion relief lift. The flight differed from those of **Operation Bumblebee** in that troops were flown to sites on the company level rather than the battalion level, and to a site only two-hundred yards from the front line. In this case the 2nd Battalion of the 7th Marines under Lieutenant Colonel Edward O. Kurdziel relieved the 1st Battalion, 5th Marines, under Lieutenant Colonel Norton. The helicopters of HMR-161 flew in defilade throughout the approach, landing and return. Because of the artillery and air support given this effort, they were able to take the troops involved to within a few yards of their front line positions.

Lynn Montross, Hubard D. Kuokka, and Norman W. Hicks, *U.S. Marine Operations in Korea 1950– 1953.*Volume IV. Washington, D.C.: Historical Branch, G-3, Headquarters, U.S. Marine Corps, 1962, p. 241.
Lynn Montross, *Cavalry of the Sky: The Story of the U.S. Marine Combat Helicopters.* New York: Harper and Brothers, 1954, pp. 177–8.

Operation Chow Chow June 1950

Operation (sometimes referred to as Plan) Chow Chow was the military response to the problem of civilian evacuation. As the Communists moved rapidly down the peninsula, about 1,500 American civilians were in peril. This group was made up of the families of men and women working in the area, primarily in Seoul, and a sizable number of men who worked with either the Department of State or the Korean Military Advisory Group. The evacuation plan had been drawn up in early July 1949 when the commanding general of Eighth Army was assigned the responsibility (along with the commanding general of Far East Command and the commander of Naval Forces Far East) for the protection and evacuation of all American civilians. The plan was based on the assumption that it would take the North Korean forces at least ninety-six hours to reach Seoul after crossing the 38th parallel. During the early morning hours of 25 June (Korean time), Ambassador John J. Muccio, well aware that the Communists were moving south much faster than anticipated, ordered all dependents of military and governmental personnel evacuated.

The evacuation was an inter-service activity. Two American destroyers, the USS *Mansfield* and *DE Haven*, were sent steaming west to provide protection for those who were leaving the country from Inchon. Air Force fighter planes hovered over the port of Pusan while evacuees were moving out, and at the same time Far East Air Force transports were moving personnel out of the capital's airfield at Kimpo. A significant number of dependents were taken out on the Norwegian freighter SS *Reinholt,* while others were flown out on commercial and military aircraft. Eventually more than 1,500 were evacuated to Japan, 932 by air. The first artillery fire struck the capital city, Seoul, around 0600 on 28 June 1950 and by dusk the city had fallen.

Laurence Oglethorpe memoirs, Center for the Study of the Korean War.

Operation Christmas Kidlift

20 December 1950

For many United Nations servicemen in Korea the plight of young people caught up in the war was a concern. The war had produced thousands of young boys and girls who, having lost their parents, were at the mercy of the ever-present ravages. Two Air Force chaplains, Colonel Wallace I. Wolverton and Lt. Colonel Russell L. Blaisdell, went to great pains to respond to the needs of many of these children. Near the end of 1950, fearing what would happen to the children when the advancing Chinese Communist forces arrived at Seoul, Chaplain Blaisdell appealed to General Turner for an airlift. In Operation Christmas Kidlift, on 20 December, Turner dispatched twelve C-54s from 61st Group to Kimpo Airfield near Seoul. There, in the midst of a driving snowstorm, as many as 128 children were loaded onto a plane and a total of 989 children were air lifted to the safety of Cheju-do Island. There, off the southern coasts of Korea, the orphans were made at home and cared for. The following year, airmen returned to Cheju-do with Christmas gifts and the men of the 5th Air Force continued to provide money for operation and expansion of the facilities. See **Operation Kiddie Car, Kiddie Car Lift, Santa Claus**, and **Little Orphan Annie**.

George Drake, "Hess: Fraudulent Hero." *McCormic Speaking*, Volume VI, December 1952, No. 3, Korean War Children's Memorial. Dean Hess, *Battle Hymn*. New York: McGraw Hill, 1956.

Operation Circus 23 April 1952

Operation Circus was one of three operations, the others **Operation Leapfrog** and **Operation Pronto**, designed to test the value of helicopter transportation. This time the concern was transportation over water. Helicopter transportation was becoming fairly common at this point, but there was still a great deal to be learned about any large-scale troop employment. In this case Marine Helicopter Squadron 161 moved the 1st Battalion, 7th Marine Regiment, plus its headquarters and supply company, across the Imjin River to areas to the rear of the secondary defense,

Line Wyoming forward. The river was a key point with more than 35,000 meters of front divided by the Han, Sachon, and Imjin rivers.

It was necessary to prepared four loading zones for the helicopters that first took off at 0830 on 23 April 1952. The sites varied in distance from 850 meters to more than 1,600. Ten helicopters carried more than 1,185 Marines over the river to a blocking position in less than 90 minutes. The exercise was considered a success but demonstrated the need to have a minimum distance between loading and unloading sites. The operation was conducted just three days before all HRS aircraft were grounded because of a defect discovered in the tail rotors.

Lynn Montross, *Cavalry of the Sky: The Story of the U.S. Marine Combat Helicopters*. New York: Harper and Brothers, 1954.

Operation Clambake 3 February 1953

All of the units of the 5th Marine Regiment were to be involved in Operation Clambake. This was to be a tank-artillery feint against several Chinese Communist Forces positions, including Hill 104, Kumgok, and Red Hill. The two hills were to be assaulted by platoons from Company A of the reserve battalion. The operation was planned and rehearsed for five weeks with final rehearsals on 1 February. Four air support strikes were made that day. On the morning of 3 February, three tanks moved out and heavy artillery from the 11th Marines was sent striking on the enemy hills. Communist forces defending the area made three counterattack attempts, stopped each time by the infantry and friendly air support. An estimated 390 Chinese casualties were inflicted, and caves, bunkers, and weapons were destroyed. The Marines lost 14 killed and 91 wounded.

Pat Meid and James M. Yingling, *U.S. Marine Operations in Korea, Volume V: Operations in West Korea*. Washington, D.C.: Historical Division, Headquarters, U.S. Marine Corps, 1972, pp. 255–257, 259.

Operation Comeback

October–November 1950

The Canadian Navy was given much of the responsibility for clearing out enemy troops who, as the UN forces moved north in October and November of 1950, had sought haven among the small offshore islands. It was during this activity that Captain J. V. Brock, Canadian commander, Destroyers Pacific, took note of the hardships imposed on the villagers there. When possible the destroyer crews shared food and supplies with them, but it was soon obvious that it was not enough. Brock believed that if the villagers whose livelihood had been upset were restored to some sort of normality by the issuance of food and basic needs, they world be more favorable to the United Nations cause. Thus Operation Comeback was established and the Canadian destroyers HMCS *Sioux* and *Cayuga* were assigned, along with some ROKN vessels, to move among the islands providing what help they could. The first step was setting up a fishing sanctuary for the islanders, whose normal occupations had been denied by the UN blockade. As far as it went Operation Comeback was successful. The supply and administrative personnel within the Royal Canadian ships arranged for the transfer of goods with a minimum of difficulty. Unfortunately for the program, the need for the Canadian destroyers elsewhere became paramount and the project was turned over to the ROKN to do the best it could.

Edward C. Meyers, *Thunder in the Morning Calm*. St. Catharines, Ontario: Vanwell, 1991, pp. 77–78.

Operation Decoy   15 October 1952

This operation was set up by the commander, Joint Amphibious Task Force 7, to create a diversion in the Kojo area. Operation Decoy was designed to assault, occupy and defend a beachhead in the Kojo sector with the 1st Cavalry Division's 8th Cavalry Regimental Combat Team. The aim was to create a psychological reaction that would cause the enemy to withdraw combat troops from the area. The one thing that was not stated in the operational order was that it was all a ploy. Since it was for deception purposes, Admiral Joseph J. "Jacko" Clark had directed that "knowledge of the demonstration aspects was confined to only the highest echelons of command" (Cagle and Manson). None of Clark's subordinate commanders, not even the carrier commanders, were informed.

Throughout the war the United Nations maintained a tight blockade of North Korean waters. This control not only prevented the supplying of troops and materials, it also allowed the UN to threaten more amphibious assaults of the type accomplished at Inchon. It was believed, though never fully proven, that such action could be used to tie down Communist troops, or even get the enemy to move troops already involved in combat, to those areas that might be threatened.

In the case of Operation Decoy, a pre-invasion barrage was leveled on 14 October by Admiral Clark's flagship, the USS *Iowa*, and the accompanying cruisers and destroyers, which shelled the beaches all night. During the night minesweepers that were operating within visual range of enemy gunners received considerable counter battery fire. On the morning of D-day, troop transports of Task Group 76.4 (ComTrans Div-14) held reveille at 0300 hours. Heavy fog delayed the launch until 1400 hours. At that time the troop ships began to lower boats for embarking. The boats headed for the beach until they reached the pre-determined turn away-line — about 5,000 yards from the beach — and headed back to the ship. The enemy had lobbed a few shells at the incoming boats without causing any damage. Once all the troops were back aboard, the transport group departed for Pohang-dong to disembark. As they did so the naval and navy air bombardment continued through the rest of the day. At 1900 on 16 October, Joint

Amphibious Force Seven was dissolved and all naval units were returned to their usual assignments.

Malcolm W. Cagle and Frank A. Manson, *The Sea War in Korea.* Annapolis, MD: United States Naval Institute, 1957, p. 392.

Operation Defrost   24 November 1950

As Eighth Army moved slowly toward the Yalu River and talk of General MacArthur's "Home by Christmas" suggestion was moving through the command, the Commonwealth Brigade was pulled off line and sent into Operation Defrost. It had previously been involved in chasing stragglers from the Battle of Pakchon. Then the brigade moved about a thousand meters north of Pakchon, where the men were to be billeted and given a chance to rest. However, they had hardly begun to relax when, on 25 November, the Chinese Communist Forces began their second phase offensive and attacked IX Corps in the Kunu-ri area. On the morning of the 27th, the Commonwealth Brigade was ordered out of the rest area, put into support of IX Corps, and moved to make a stand in a creek bed in Kunu-ri. With this movement Operation Defrost was over before it began.

Ben O'Dowd, *In Valiant Company: Diggers in Battle-Korea 1950–1951.* Australia: University of Queensland, 2000, pp. 47–48.

Operation Eveready   June 1952

This operation was another in a series of test exercises carried out in a combat situation, which involved the movement of a Marine battalion in relief across the Han River. The plan was to evaluate HMR 161's ability to carry out a troop lift with only a few hours' notice. The operation was successful.

Lynn Montross, *Cavalry of the Sky: The Story of U.S. Marine Combat Helicopters.* New York: Harper and Brothers, 1954, p. 189.

Operation Everready   June 1952

The relationship between the military and Korean President Syngman Rhee had not always been cordial, and on several occasions it seemed wise to consider replacing him. With this in mind Eighth Army prepared a plan called Operation Everready in which a specific response was to be executed in case there was an emergency. The plan called for the UN to disarm ROK forces and restrict the movement of the civilian population. In the extreme case, Operation Everready would call for a coup and the removal of President Rhee from power. General Mark Clark was aware that such a removal might create considerably more chaos.

After an assassination attempt on President Rhee on 25 June 1952 that may well have been a hoax, Rhee was re-elected president in August in an election with widespread repression of political opponents. U.S. President Harry Truman and later President Dwight Eisenhower contemplated implementing Operation Everready because of Rhee's behavior at the time, but no action was taken. In 1952 General Clark felt that such action should not be taken unless the situation deteriorated so far that it put the military in danger. He did not have the troops necessary to deal with the civil unrest he expected would be the result of such a move.

The question arose again in 1953 when, in violation of the discussions going on at the truce table, President Rhee released prisoners of war and announced that he intended to fight on, even if an armistice was signed. At this point, while still considering Operation Everready, President Eisenhower sent Walter S. Robinson, assistant secretary of state, to talk to Rhee. If the South Korean president did not give in to the United Nations demands, General Mark Clark, with Robinson's concurrence, was willing to implement Operation Everready and replace Rhee with Prime Minister Chang T'aek-sang.

Some historians today continue to question if Operation Everready was a legitimate idea worth serious consideration, or simply wishful thinking. General Paik Sun Yup of the ROK Army suggested there is no way to know so long after the fact if this was a worst-case scenario or if Washington was actually looking for an excuse to remove Rhee.

Bradford A. Wineman, *Encyclopedia of the Korean War*. Volume I, Santa Barbara, CA: ABC-CLIO, 2000, p. 210.

Paik Sun Yup, *From Pusan to Panmunjom*. Dulles, VA: Brassey's, 1999, p. 234.

Stanley Sandler, *The Korean War: No Victors, No Vanquished*. London: University College London, 1999, p. 259.

Operation Farewell
19–20 December 1951

As the war moved into its second year, the Marine Corps' use of combat helicopters was increasing both in number and in the variety of missions. During this time Marine patrols went out almost nightly, manning outposts called "duck blinds," which were met with little opposition.

Operation Farewell was a large scale troop deployment on Hill 884, where the 1st Battalion of the 5th Marines was transported by HMR 161 from an assembly area to the front lines on 19–20 December for the relief of 2nd Battalion, 5th Marines. It was the final flight for George Herring, the squadron's first commander, who recalled later, "The cold weather and wind velocity assisted performance; the altitude worked against it slightly. Few pilots had experienced such conditions prior to Korea."

In support of the 1st Marine Division, Marine Helicopter Squadron 161 provided maximum service. Operation Farewell was both an experiment and a combat exchange. In this case a Marine battalion from the 7th Regiment was lifted from the reserve area and dropped in place to relieve a battalion that was in defense on Hill 884. On the return trip they brought with them the exhausted troops and returned them to the reserve area. The relief was by

Lieutenant Colonel Norton's 1/5 helicopters. The support of men on Hill 884 by this medium helicopter squadron was seem as so extraordinary that the area was soon called Helicopter Hill.

Lynn Montross, *Cavalry of the Sky: The Story of U.S. Marine Combat Helicopters*. New York: Harper and Brothers, 1954, p. 176.

Lynn Montross, Hubard D. Kuokka, and Norman W. Hicks, *U.S. Marine Operation in Korea 1950–1953*. Volume IV. Washington, D.C.: Historical Branch, G-3, Headquarters U.S. Marine Corps, 1962, p. 223.

Operation Farmer   Summer 1951

Operation Farmer was a strategy designed to further disrupt the North Korean agricultural community. Things were already bad for the North Korean farmer since the majority of land capable of being used for farming was in the southern section of the country. When war broke out it was necessary for northern farmers to provide much of what was needed, to compensate for the loss of significant influx from the south. Many of them rebelled against large amounts of their crops being taken for use by the military. When the United States became aware of this situation, they instigated Operation Farmer to take advantage of the unrest. Planes dropped millions of leaflets over the agricultural regions suggesting that the farmers rebel against the harshness of the Communists' treatment by hiding significant segments of their crops for the family, or even selling some of the produce to the ever-thriving black market. The hope was to keep as much produce as possible out of the hands of the military.

William B. Breuer, *Shadow Warriors: The Covert War in Korea*. New York: John Wiley & Sons, Inc., 1996, p. 177.

Alfred Paddock, "No More Tactical Information Detachment: U.S. Military Psychological Operations in Transition," in Frank Goldstein and Benjamin Findley, *Psychological Operation: Principles and Case Studies*. Maxwell Air Force Base: Air University Press, 1996, p. 82.

Operation Feint   12 October 1952

The operation took place in conjunction with a six week battle near Kumhwa for an area that included Triangle Hill and Sniper Hill, called **Operation Showdown**. Operation Feint, however, was set in motion as a mock invasion to relieve some pressure and was staged at Kojo on 12 October 1952, by land, sea, and naval forces, including the American destroyer USS *O'Brien IV* (DD 725), which received enemy fire. More than 100 ships were involved, as well as elements of the 315th Air Division, the 187th Regimental Airborne Combat Team, and the 403rd Transportation Wing. The plan was an attempt by the United Nations forces to lure the enemy out into the open, and to cause them to withdraw troops from other defensive positions, and thus weaken the number of Communist troops addressing Eighth Army. Once launched, Operation Feint continued for several days, but was only moderately successful. Despite that, it is often referred to as "the greatest hoax of the war."

Paul M. Edwards, *Korean War Almanac*. New York: Facts on File, 2006, p. 343.

Operation Ferret   18 April 1952

UN troops, constantly harassed by enemy agents as well as the sometimes overwhelming appearance of refugees, sought some relief in the introduction of Operation Ferret. It was conducted in April 1952 and was designed to search out and remove all unauthorized persons in the 45th Division Sector.

Paul Wolfgeher, "The Battle Hills, Outposts, Operations and Battle Lines of the Korean War." Unpublished manuscript in the Wolfgeher Collection at the Center for the Study of the Korean War.

Operation Firecracker   4 July 1952

An ceremony to celebrate Independence Day was set up in Operation Firecracker. I

Corps called on each division to select the most lucrative target in their area and, on 4 July, to fire simultaneously for a one-minute period. The men used the technique called Time on Target (TOT). This system had participating units timing their initial volleys to ensure that their shells would arrive on the target at the same time. The firing display used 3,202 rounds in the Marine sector alone. The mortar battalions of the 11th Marines destroyed numerous enemy trenches in the process. It is estimated that the firing accounted for 44 Chinese Communist casualties.

Pat Meid and James M. Yingling, *U.S. Marine Operations in Korea, Volume V: Operations in West Korea.* Washington, D.C.: Historical Division, Headquarters, U.S. Marine Corps, 1972, p. 93.

Operation Fishnet   April–September 1952

Eighth Army high command believed that the difficulty of supplying Communist forces could be made even more difficult by interfering with North Korea's ability to feed itself. Operation Fishnet was set up as a strategic initiative designed to drive the North Koreans into submission by destroying their ability to fish, thus making additional demands on their supply system. A major reduction in their fishing operations could be brought about by the destruction of nets and the sinking of smaller fishing boats, and it would provide even greater pressure on the military supply routes. Both American and British ships were involved as well as several members of the Navy Underwater Demolition Teams. The primary targets were addressed when the USS *Douglas H. Fox* (DD 779) conducted raids that took over a small rock island in Hungham harbor that the North Koreans used as a fishing base. Divers were sent down to destroy the fishing nets. The HMS *Charity* (R29) provided harassment among fishermen off the coast of North Korean, and the USS *Ptarmigan* (AM 376) and the USS *Toucan* (AM 387) conducted night raids near the fishing community at Sinchang; all of which added to the limited success of the operation.

James Berry, "Operation Fishnet." *Proceedings* 116:12 (December 1990) pp. 107–108.

Operation Flush Out   July–August 1950

There were few American reserves to meet the needs imposed by the outbreak of war in Korea. The concern was aggravated by the belief that this might well be the opening salvo of a larger, more inclusive war and would require troops and equipment in a much wider scale. Nevertheless, General Walton Walker faced the fact that he needed immediate reinforcements. First of all, he wanted to build up the ROK Army, which in August had a total of about 85,000 men but was not particularly strong. Walker intended to add five divisions to the ROK standing army. The second problem was the need to increase the size of the American force. The substantial losses that occurred during the opening days of the war made drastic measures necessary to secure replacements. The response was to initiate Operation Flush Out among units stationed in Japan.

The idea was to meet the demands in Korea by the identification of superfluous personnel from the occupational billets, requiring that all units in Japan reassign some measure of its troop strength to be used as replacements. What should have been no surprise to the Army was that in combat more riflemen get killed than truck drivers, yet the replacement procedure replaced riflemen with truck drivers, cooks, clerks, linguists, and supply personnel, most of whom were not trained to do what they needed to do. In the process, Operation Flush Out provided 229 officers and 2,201 enlisted men who were reassigned to Korea by 6 September 1950. The process was much like that used in northwestern Europe in 1944 when there was a need for immediate replacement. Along with the men coming into Korea came a great deal of concerns and griping. The number of replacements coming into Korea totaled 11,115 officers and men.

Roy E. Appleman, *South to the Naktong, North to the Yalu.* Washington, D.C.: Office of the Chief of Military History, 1961.
Robert Leckie, *Conflict: The History of the Korean War.* New York: Da Capo, 1996, p. 117.

Operation Get Well   1 March 1952

Referred to by those involved as "a bean counter's holiday," Operation Get Well brought the 40th Infantry Division to a forward assembly area in March 1952. The division was to assume responsibility for its table of organization and equipment and to make an inventory to update the records. On line for some time, the 40th had been defending IX Corps at the "Center Right" near Kumhwa since December 1951 and needed (or was believed to need) an accounting and readjustment of facilities and equipment. The division was called off line and placed in reserve assembly in order to conduct extensive maintenance, reissue, cross leveling, and complete accessibility accountability.

Norman O. Nelson, "Battles, Operations, and Outposts Found in the Korean War." Unpublished manuscript in the Nelson Collection, Center for the Study of the Korean War.

Operation Glory   22 July 1954

The military was very concerned about the bodies of United Nations soldiers who had been killed north of the Demilitarized Zone and whose remains were still located in North Korean territory. An essential part of the negotiations in the cease-fire was an agreement concerning the exchange of military war dead on both sides. The Korean Communication Zone Op. Plan 14-54, called Operation Glory, was established to locate and exchange the bodies of those who still lay in enemy territory.

In preparation the U.S. engineers furnished a reception area, and signal communications were established as the Transportation Corps made whatever plans were necessary for the evacuation of all deceased by rail. The quartermaster corps provided and issued all necessary supplies. During the set up three separate meetings were held with the Communists to develop the procedures and the ground rules for working with photographers and news correspondents.

The disinterment of all enemy deceased personnel was completed and the remains were delivered to Glory Railhead near Munsan-ni, Korea, on 30 August 1954. By that time 4,023 bodies were turned over to the United Nations and 13,528 were returned to the Democratic People's Republic of Korea and the People's Republic of China. At 1300 hours, after the bodies had been removed, a ceremony was held with figures representing the United Nations Command, Far East Command, Military Armistice Commission, and representatives from the Republic of Korea. A religious ceremony was conducted by chaplains of the Catholic, Protestant, and Jewish faiths.

The site chosen was north of Freedom Bridge, which crossed the Imjin River some 45 miles north of Seoul. Company B, 84th Engineer Construction Battalion, built two camps, six miles of road, six hospitals, latrines, storage guard areas, a rail head and a reception area in just fifteen days.

The locating and exchange between the UN and the Communist states continued each day, except Sunday, until 21 September 1954. On that date the UN Graves Registration officials were told there were no more bodies. The UN continued its delivery until 11 October. During the next few months, after the official exchange was over, an additional 144 American bodies were turned over, making a total of 4,167. When anthropologists completed their work in February 1956 they had identified all but 416 of the bodies. Those unidentified bodies were buried at the Punchbowl Cemetery in Honolulu, Hawaii.

Both sides agreed that they would continue searching in more remote areas and if they discovered additional bodies, they would be turned over at the end of the month. Since then efforts have continued to locate and, if possible, to bring home the bodies that still remain. North Korea is sometimes willing to cooperate, sometimes not. Efforts were still being made in 2008, more than fifty-eight years since Operation Glory began.

As could have been anticipated, neither side was happy with the outcome, believing that there were more unaccounted for remains. Since the completion of Operation Glory, the U.S. has been aggressively involved in locating additional remains of Korean War veterans and seeing that, when at all possible, they can be brought home. Despite the care with which the battlefields were searched there are still reports of possible remains. In these cases, when any information is discovered, an investigation is conducted.

The normal process of graves registration was interrupted during the early days when a public controversy arose over the fact that at his death in a car accident, Lieutenant General Walton Walker was flown home to be buried in Arlington National Cemetery. More than one loved one of a deceased wrote to ask the Army why a soldier's rank was used to determine who came home for burial.

"Operation Glory." *Historical Summary*. Graves Registration Division, Army Quartermaster Museum, Fort Lee, Virginia.
"Operation Glory," *Korean War POW/MIA Network*. http://koreanwarpowmia.net/remains/operation_glory.htm
Bradley Lynn Coleman, "Recovering the Korean War Dead, 1950–1958: Graves Registration, Forensic Anthropology, and Wartime Memorialization." *The Journal of Military History*, Vol. 72, No. 1 (January 2008), p. 194.

Operation Haircut 1951

For the Canadian troops heading to the Far East on notoriously overcrowded ships of the U.S. Military Sea Transport, concern grew over the unsanitary conditions of the men, sweltering and seasick below deck. In one case things got so bad it led to the formation of special fatigue parties aboard the USS *Private Joe P. Martinez* to swab the restrooms and enforce high standards of cleanliness. During the voyage, members of the 2nd Battalion, Princess Patricia Canadian Light Infantry, went to the extreme measure of launching **Operation Haircut**. Armed with clippers, the "cue ball club" moved through the troop compartments to shave the heads of members of the battalion. Those who tried to object found they were unceremoniously pinned and their heads shaved.

Brent Byron Watson, *Far Eastern Tour, The Canadian Infantry in Korea, 1950–1953*. Montreal: McGill-Queen's University Press, 2002, p. 52.

Operation Haylift I
22 September 1952

Earlier tests in 1952 had shown that the helicopter could be used to resupply a battalion manning the main line of resistance. The next step, and a much larger one, was to see if it were possible to provided the same level of logistical support for an entire combat regiment. Operation Haylift I was in action between 22 and 26 September 1952 and one of the last of five operations conducted to test the capabilities of the HMR 161. In this case they were to resupply the 7th Marine Regiment under Colonel Moore, who was confronted by an estimated 4,200 men of a Chinese Communist infantry regiment. The helicopter would make the effort to land all Class I, II, III and V supplies that could be accommodated. The effect was to show that for five days at least, a helicopter squadron, using no more than 40 percent of its ships, could sustain a Marine regiment. From this it was determined that the operations could be improve if there was a center where representatives of each participating unit could plan jointly and provide a more flexible landing system.

This exercise set a new record for the movement of all the supplies necessary to keep a Marine regiment at the front for five days. The estimate was that 77,000 pounds had to be lifted to the 7th Marines each day from 22 to 26 September and carried a distance of about twenty miles. The diversity of the supplies required both cargo nets and wire baskets and included everything from ammunition to 55 gallon drums of fuel. The Air Delivery Platoon supervised the loading of the HMR-161 helicopters.

As it turned out, only 40 percent of the capacity of the squadron was required to complete the assignment. Moving less than a maximum payload of 1,000 pounds, altogether 3251,000 pounds were lifted by the ten aircraft employed. This included "seven VIP's at 1,260 pounds." The squadron report concluded: "No unusual problems were encountered and the operation progressed smoothly and throughout" (Montross).

Lynn Montross, *Cavalry of the Sky: The Story of U.S. Marine Combat Helicopter*. New York: Harper and Brothers, 1954, p. 197.

Operation Haylift II
23 February 1953

Having proven that helicopters could supply a Marine Regiment for a five day period (**Operation Haylift I**) Operation Haylift II was designed to see if the same system could be used to supply two frontline regiments for five days. This was a much larger operation than the first attempt, and the 1st Service Battalion and 1st Ordnance Battalion were to move their supplies as well. Opposing the 1st Marine Division were seventy-two infantry battalions, supported by sixteen artillery battalions and one armored regiment. The helicopter pilots were instructed to fly in defilade to the degree possible and to maintain radio discipline. An estimated 130 tons a day would need to be lifted, a figure that was exceeded by 30 tons the first day. Beginning at 0655 on the 25th the crews moved 260 loads in nets or wire baskets slung underneath.

The distance they needed to move was from 7.81 to 8.06 miles and they were able to transport 200 tons in a single day, establishing a record. This was accomplished in 392 lifts made over a 138.4 hour period of flying time. The maximum time for unloading a helicopter was 54 seconds, with some unloading in as little as 28 seconds. Operation Haylift II delivered five times as much as Operation Haylift I. During the five day period — cut short somewhat by weather — a total of 1,612,406 pounds of supplies had been delivered to two regiments. An estimated 95 percent of the squadron's capabilities were devoted to the supply of these two regiments. The helicopters were also able to bring out the bodies of five Marines killed in action. No crew members were hurt or planes damaged.

Lynn Montross, *Cavalry of the Sky: The Story of U.S. Marine Combat Helicopter.* New York: Harper and Brothers, 1954, p. 197.

Operation Helicopter

21 December 1951

This was a part of the overall testing to evaluate the use of helicopters. In the case of Operation Helicopter it was to evacuate patients directly from the front line to a hospital ship. Beginning on 21 December and lasting until 24 January 1952, Operation Helicopter ferried wounded from just behind the battlefield to the USS *Consolation* (AH 19), a hospital ship located in the port of Sokcho, on the Sea of Japan, just above the 38th parallel. At the time the USS *Consolation*, which had arrived in Korea in the summer of 1950, was the only American hospital ship that was equipped with a mounted helicopter platform. The test proved very successful. Richard Wagner, who served as a ward corpsman on the USS *Consolation*, remembered that from 16 December 1951 to 24 January 1952, 23 landings of Army, Marine and Air Force helicopters brought

more than 400 patients. The *Consolation* received three battle stars for its service in Korea and would later serve as the ship for Project Hope.

Paul M. Edwards, *Small United States and United Nations Warships in the Korean War.* Jefferson, NC: McFarland, 2008.

Operation High Tide   June 1952

Even today there remains some question about just when the first of the Operation High Tide flights were authorized and conducted, as well as who was responsible. The argument, however, does not disavow the significance of the operation. It appears that in early 1952 the 116th Fighter Bomber Wing (FBW) was selected to work on this project. It would, if it worked as planned, completely alter the manner in which air combat was conducted. Using a SAC Superfortress that had been modified into a tanker (KB-29), the pilots from the 116th FBW had been trained in this new routine, and by April were proficient enough to try it in action. The test was a mission against a variety of targets in the area of Sariwon, North Korea. Each of the attacking F-84s held two 500 pound bombs. The mission called for each pilot to refuel over Taegu before he turned north for the bombing run. The experiment was so successful that three additional strikes of the same design were completed before 4 July 1952, the date Operation High Tide ended. Gordon Crossley, a member of the 116th FBW, said that this generally reported date is wrong, and that the first flight of F-84s on project Operation High Tide left on October 26, 1952, and were refueled on that same day over Taegu. The answer remains unclear. The 158th Fighter Bomber Squadron, Georgia National Guard, it is also claimed, was involved in the operation.

Paul Wolfgeher, "The Battle Hills, Outposts, Operations and Battle Lines of the Korean War." Unpublished manuscript in the Wolfgeher Collection at the Center for the Study of the Korean War.

Operation Homecoming July 1952

Many of those held in prisoner of war camps in the early days of the Korean War were not really military prisoners but rather civilians of the Republic of Korea who had been arrested for some inexact reason. From July to August of 1952 an effort was made to release as many of these men and women as possible, and eventually more than 27,000 were identified for release. The plan had been originally set for 1 November 1951, and when the talks between the United Nations and the Communist Forces bogged down, President Harry Truman approved the release of the first group. It was called Operation Homecoming. There was considerable protest by the representatives of the People's Republic of China. Another group of about 11,000 were screened and

then released in October and November of 1952.

"Civilian Internee Issue," in James Matray, *Historical Dictionary of the Korean War.* Westport, CT: Greenwood Press, 1991, pp. 1122–113.

Operation Hudson Harbor
October 1951

Several times during the Korean War consideration was given to the use of nuclear weapons, and eventually some preparation was made for their use if it was determined to be necessary. While the initial discussion centered around President Harry Truman's early mention of their use, and pressure by both General Douglas MacArthur and General Matthew Ridgway for consideration, there did not appear to be a great deal of support for their use. Historian Bruce Cumins wrote that Truman's allusion

President-elect Dwight D. Eisenhower makes a promised visit to Korea, December 1952 (Center for the Study of the Korean War).

to the use of nuclear weapons was not a slip of the tongue, but rather a projection of his thinking, for on the same day (30 November 1951) as the president mentioned the use of nuclear weapons, instructions were sent to Air Force generals for the Strategic Air Command to "argument its capabilities." However, as the war progressed and efforts at a negotiated settlement seemed possible, the deployment of atomic weapons was determined to be unprofitable. However, this did not prevent preparation.

In Operation Hudson Harbor, several B-29s conducted individual simulated bomb runs flying from Okinawa to various targets in North Korea. The operation, which was coordinated from Yokota Air Base in Japan, ran a series of test flights during which several "dummy" nuclear bombs, or heavy convention bombs, were dropped. The operation was designed to test what would be involved in making an atomic strike, including the weapon assembly, as well as ground control of bomb aiming. The result of the exercise was to suggest that nuclear bombs would not be as effective as anticipated for many reasons, not the least of which was just how few concentrations of troops or military targets would be worth the cost of nuclear weapons.

After the election of President Dwight D. Eisenhower, the idea was reconsidered. He considered that Truman's evaluation had been a practical one but was aware that something needed to be done to bring about an end to the war. He finally agreed to a plan that he hoped would bring an end to the conflict. He authorized the movement of atomic delivery aircraft to the Far East and instructed the Joint Chiefs of Staff to plan for more intensive action. He then sent Secretary of State John Foster Dulles to India to send word to the Communists that the United States was prepared to move the war to a higher level of involvement unless something was done. It is important to note that the use of nuclear weapons was considered a viable plan only if the final outcome was in serous question.

J. F. Schnabel and R. J. Watson, *History of the Joint Chiefs of Staff: The Korean War.* Washington, D.C.: Joint Chiefs of Staff, 1979.

David J. Wright, "Operation Hudson Harbor." Entry in James I. Matray, *Historical Dictionary of the Korean War.* Westport, CT: Greenwood Press, pp. 350–351.

Operation Immediate   25 June 1950

It was questionable if this was an operation or an "operational immediate," but it refers to the naval response initiated when North Korea crossed the 38th parallel. On the other side of the world, Admiral Forrest P. Sherman, chief of naval operations, received a phone call informing him that the North Koreans had invaded. Soon every admiral in the Navy received a message from the CNO informing them of the outbreak of war. Marked Operation Immediate, it announced, "Due to the Korean incident, place 30 percent of all naval aircraft on one-hour notice and remainder of all aircraft on four-hour notice. Notify CNO soonest of available strength." As a part of this same move, Admiral Arthur W. Radford, commander Pacific, ordered. "Be prepared to move the Seventh Fleet north on short when and if directed" (Karig et al.).

Walter Karig, Malcolm W. Cagle, and Frank A. Manson, *Battle Report: The War in Korea.* New York: Rinehart, 1952, p. 17.

Operation Kiddie Car
December 1950

As the Chinese Communist Forces continued to advance against Eighth Army and began to approach Seoul, much of what was saved was because of the efforts of Combat Cargo Command, which took out men and equipment at an amazing rate. One group that faced considerable danger as the Communists approached was the orphans of the area. Air Force Chaplains Colonel Wallace I. Wolverton and Lt. Colonel Russel L. Blaisdell, and

S/Sergeant Merle Y. Strang his assistant, had been rounding up the children for some time and taking care of them. Originally arrangements had been made so that the approximately 990 children and 80 staff members could board an ROKN LST and be taken to Pusan, and the chaplains were busy arranging trucks to take the children and staff to Inchon, where they were to board. Once they arrived, however, they waited for four days but the planned ship did not show up.

Chaplain Blaisdell then made arrangements with Colonel T. C. Rogers, assistant director of operations for General Howard M. Turner's 5th Air Force, for twelve (some accounts say sixteen) C-54s of the 61st Troop Carrier Group (Heavy) to fly the children to the relative safety of Cheju-do, an island off the southern coast of Korea. Again commandeering trucks, the concerned officers moved the children, staff, and 15 tons of food and belongings to Kimpo Airfield on the morning of 20 December. The airlift was completed satisfactorily. Many reports suggest that the officer responsible for the airlift was the "flying pastor" Colonel Dean E. Hess, but there is little evidence that he was involved. See also **Operations Christmas Kidlift, Kiddie Car Lift, Little Orphan Annie, Santa Claus.**

Allan R. Millett, *Their War for Korea: American, Asian, and European Combatants and Civilians 1945–1953.* Washington, D.C.: Brassey's, 2002, p. 185.

Operation Kiddie Car Lift

December 1950

This is the name usually used in Air Force histories for the evacuation of orphans from the Seoul area in advance of the quickly moving Chinese Communist troops. The children and their supporting staff were flown out of Kimpo to Cheju-do for their safety. See **Operations Christmas Kidlift, Kiddie Car, Little Orphan Annie,** and **Santa Claus.**

Allan R. Millett, *Their War for Korea: American, Asian, and European Combatants and Civilians 1945–1953.* Washington, D.C.: Brassey's, 2002, p. 185.

Operation Leapfrog

18–19 April 1952

At this point in the Korean War the Marine Corps was involved in working out the best means to use the helicopter in transportation and combat situations. Operation Leapfrog was a part of the tests conducted by the Marines on the feasibility of using the helicopter in combat situations. It had a secondary mission, as well, and that of coping with a language barrier in the execution. Operation Leapfrog consisted of transporting the 5th Battalion, Korean Marine Corps, across the Han River to the peninsula and then to lift out the 3rd Battalion, Korean Marine Corps, on the following day. In this case the trip was a six mile round trip, the shortest troop haul yet made, and it took the 12 HRS-1—a single-engine Sikorsky—only three hours and 26 minutes to accomplish the test flight, despite some limitations imposed by the language problem. A total of 1,702 Korean Marines were involved. The area in which the test was conducted was open and out of the way of Chinese artillery, so the pilots were able to use landing sites that were close together. Interpreters managed to keep language problems at a minimum. On 22 April **Operation Circus** tested movement across the Imjin.

Lynn Montross, *Cavalry of the Sky: The Story of U.S. Marine Combat Helicopters.* New York: Harper and Brothers, 1955, p. 184.
Pat Meid and James M. Yingling, *U.S. Marine Operations in Korea, Volume V: Operations in West Korea.* Washington, D.C.: Historical Division, Headquarters, U.S. Marine Corps, 1972, p. 41.

Operation Little Orphan Annie

20 December 1950

This operation refers to a situation in which the U.S. Air Force flew thousands of children, waifs and strays, away from the advance of Communist troops in December 1950. The children, scheduled to be taken away by vessels of the South Korean Navy, were left stranded at Inchon when the boats did not arrive. With the help of Army and Air Force chaplains, arrangements were made for 12 (some sources say 16) C-54 Skymasters to fly the children to safety on the island of Cheju-do. The event, made popular in Dean Hess's book *Battle Hymn* (1956) and the movie by the same name (1957), caused some disagreements as to what actually happened and who was involved. Later inquiry showed that Lt. Colonel (Chaplain) Russell Blaisdell and Staff Sergeant Merle Y. Strang were also critically involved, with Hess responsible for preparations to receive the children. Colonel Blaisdell was later given some of the recognition due, but there was little acknowledgment of Sergeant Strang's contribution. This event is recorded from a variety of sources, many of which disagree on such questions as how many were involved, who was responsible, and why the situation arose. The event was also remem-

bered as **Operations Christmas Kidlift, Kiddie Car, Kiddie Car Lift, Little Orphan Annie**, and **Santa Claus**.

George Drake, "Hess: Fraudulent Hero." *McCormic Speaking*, Vol. 6, December 1952, No. 3, Korean War Children's Memorial. Dean Hess, *Battle Hymn*. New York: McGraw Hill, 1956.

Operation Little Switch
20 April 1953

As the delegates at the armistice discussions began to reach agreement on some points, General Mark Clark, on 20 February, called for an exchange of sick and wounded prisoners from both sides. It was a suggestion originally made by the International Red Cross. General Clark made an indirect appeal to Premier Kim Il Sung and Chinese General Peng Dehuai and, much to the surprise of the UN

General Mark Clark at UN Base Camp, Munsan-Ni, April 1953 (Joseph Adams Collection: Center for the Study of the Korean War).

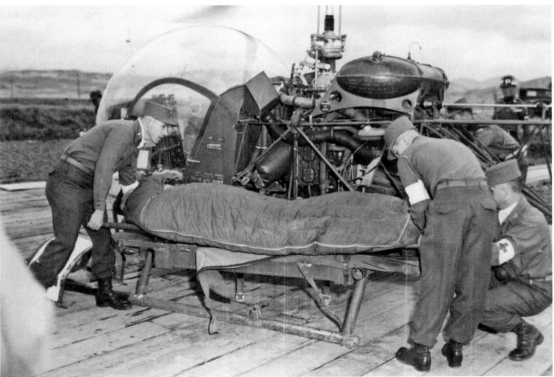

Top: The Chinese Communist Exchange Site for Operation Little Switch, May 1953. *Bottom:* Operation Little Switch, evacuation of wounded prisoners by helicopter (Joseph Adams Collection: Center for the Study of the Korean War).

delegates, it was agreed to at the truce talks at Panmunjom on 11 April 1953. Identified as Operation Little Switch, the exchange began on 20 April. The United Nations exchanged 6,670 Communist prisoners (5,194 North Korean, 1,030 Chinese, and 446 civilians) of which 357 were litter cases. In exchange the UN received 684 prisoners (149 Americans, 471 Korean, 32 British, 15 Turks, 6 Colombian, 5 Australian, 2 Canadian and one each from the Philippines, Greece, the Netherlands and South Africa. The UN agreed to give the term "sick" and "wounded" broad interpretations.

The acceptance was reached with almost astonishing speed, considering the nature of previous attempts to gain agreement. For the purpose of this exchange the Communists had agreed to the return of prisoners without demanding the United Nations abandon its stand on voluntary repatriation. This exchange must be seen as a key breakthrough in the deadlocks that had separated the two sides and suggested a willingness on the part of the Communists to engage in more serious negotiation. Under elaborate security the Communist Chinese, North Koreans, South Koreans, and United Nations exchanged prisoners between 20 April and 3 May 1953.

Exchanged prisoners were immediately transported to processing areas in the Republic of Korea, where they were given a chance to rest and undergo initial medical treatment, and then were flown on the United States. This event, like most associated with the war, was surrounded in disagreement and controversy. Sensational reports appeared on both sides alleging mistreatment, and the UN claimed there were many sick and wounded prisoners still being held by the Communists.

The tension of the exchange was heightened by the Communist launching of an almost suicidal series of attacks along the UN main line of resistance. And yet, while it was not known at the time, Operation Little Switch marked the beginning of the end, for the final agree-

ment of the cease fire came shortly afterwards. At this point, and for their own reasons, most certainly related to the increasing costs of the war, both sides had decided it was time to stop the fighting. Six days after the beginning of the prisoner exchange full armistice talks began again. This time there seemed to be a sense of urgency, though the Communists had by no means given up the fight.

A rather extensive survey was taken of the men returned from Communist captivity and it was generally agreed that they had been exposed to diverse treatment, ranging from acceptable to very bad. The treatment received at the hands of the Chinese was consistently better than that received from the North Koreans. More important, however, was the growing American awareness that some of the men had been subject to "brainwashing" during their imprisonment. Because of this, the military was asked to separate those who were suspected of being pro–Communist and send them back to the United States in isolation. General Mark Clark refused, and the men, most very sick or badly wounded, were sent home as quickly as possible.

Walter Hermes, *Truce Tent and Fighting Front, United States Army in the Korean War*. Washington, D.C.: United States Army Center of Military History, 1966.

United Nations, *Report of the Neutral Nations Repatriation Commission Covering the Period Ending 9 September 1954*. New York, 1954.

Operation Long-Johns
December 1950

Chaplain Lt. Colonel Russell Blaisdell, who was also involved in the earlier **Operation Little Orphan Annie**, supervised Operation Long-Johns, a plan to provide much needed underwear for Korean orphans. Everywhere he was discovering children unable to take care of themselves and facing the cold weather without proper clothing. In conjunction with the American Red Cross, the Korean Red Cross, the Roman Catholic Mission and Protestant Missions, 5th Air Force became a participant when it ordered $1,000 in children's underwear purchased in Japan, as arranged for by two of the wives, Mrs. Raymond W. Carlson and Mrs. Harry G. Libbey. Within a week of the order Colonel Blaisdell returned with 829 suits of long underwear which were distributed to the needy children through the Myung Chin Su orphanage in Seoul. Money to pay for the purchase came from 5th Air Force bases in Korea and Japan, as "the airmen in Korea remain the most generous group of contributors" (Stewart). The project continued through the course of the war and funds, primarily from the Air Force, were used to maintain the much needed supplies.

Jean Stewart, "War Orphans: Fighters Pause to Aid the Helpless." *Pacific Stars & Stripes*, December 9, 1950.

Operation Marlex I   5 April 1952

The stated purpose of this operation was "to gain experience for HMR-161 personnel and I Company (3rd Battalion, 5th Marines) personnel in vertical envelopment combined with an amphibious operation" (Montross). The original plan for Operation Marlex had been to take off from a carrier, but since none were available, the island of Sung Bong-do, 40 miles to the southwest of Inchon, was selected as the loading area. The destination of the operation was Tokchok-to, a small island about five miles long. During the operation seven helicopters moved 236 men and their equipment during 59 flights the first day, to be repeated on the second day. Several problems were discovered. First of all communications was not effective. Also, the distance traveled in the exercise meant that small number of planes in the area required too many air-hours (43.6) and suggested the need for more aircraft to be involved.

The exercise was attempted again on 24 June with 235 men of George Company, 5th Marines, flown to Tokchok-to, but this time

the flying distance was cut to just over two miles. This time communications was announced as "excellent" and the one day operation required 56 flights.

Lynn Montross, *Cavalry of the Sky: The Story of U.S. Marine Combat Helicopters*. New York: Harper and Brothers, 1954, p. 186.

Operation Mascot

For several months U.S. troops had picked up orphan boys that had lost their parents during the war. They were turned over to orphanages when possible, but they were not always available. In the main these homeless children were well taken care of by the soldiers who supplied whatever food and clothing they needed. The children were called the "mascots." The 1st Cavalry Division commander grew concerned about the boys and what would happen when the troops moved on. He asked Chaplain Harold O. Prudell to take charge. Prudell organized Operation Mascot, which gave 43 boys medical examinations, fed and clothed them, and then sent them off to established orphanages. To be sure they were taken care of, the members of the 1st Cavalry contributed more than 1,600 dollars to their continued upkeep. During Operation Mascot two of the young boys decided they liked it better with the division and escaped and hiked over a hundred miles back to join their former friends. They had to be returned.

Rodger Venzke, *Confidence in Battle, Inspiration in Peace: U.S. Army Chaplaincy 1945–1975*. Washington, D.C.: Office of Chief of Chaplains, 1977, Chapter Three.

Operation MiG   17 April 1952

The United States Air Force ran into a powerful adversary when it came in contact with the Soviet-built MiG. Because of its advanced state every effort was made by the U.S. to get their hands on one. Money was offered in case a North Korean or Chinese pilot was willing to sell (See **Operation Moolah**). On 9 July 1951 a pilot from the People's Republic of China felt it necessary to eject from his MiG while over the coast, and his pilot-less plane crashed on to a small sandbar. Communist pilots were forbidden from flying over the water in South Korean territory for this very reason. Operation MiG was set up to recover the wreck. The Communists went to considerable effort to bomb the location and destroy what was left, but the salvage operation using an YH-19 helicopter managed to recover many of the pieces; they were sent back to the United States for study.

Callum A. MacDonald, "Operation MiG," in James I. Matray, *Historical Dictionary of the Korean War.* Westport, CT: Greenwood Press, 1991, pp. 353–54.

Operation Moolah   April 1953

This was certainly one or the more unique of the Psy-War efforts and operations during the Korean War. It was a program of open and unashamed broadcasts of a program to publicly bribe a Communist fighter pilot to bring in his MiG-15 to a United Nations airfield. While the broadcasts and leaflets were in Korean, Chinese and Russian, they were primarily directed toward Russian pilots believed to be flying for the Communists. The combat success of the Russian MiG 15 led the American Joint Chiefs of Staff to offer a 100,000 dollar cash bonus and defector status to any Communist pilot that would successfully land a fully operational MiG 15 at an air base held by the United Nations. The Soviet fighter was a high-altitude interceptor that could reach speeds of Mach-1, was well-armed, and had the ability to stay in the air for over an hour. Without a doubt it out-performed any Western fighter, even American's best, the swept-wing F-86 Sabre jet. *The Saturday Evening Post* suggested that the idea for purchasing an enemy plane had come from the Russian Research Center at Harvard University, but they would later deny it. Alan K. Abner, then a

captain in the Psychological Warfare Branch, suggested that their "think tank" had come up with the idea, but there is little evidence to support this. General Mark Clark remembered that the idea had come from a newspaper correspondent named Edward Hymoff, the bureau chief of the International News Service, who it was believed personally launched the campaign.

Whatever the source of the idea, Operation Moolah was approved in Washington and the offer made. News of the offer was released through the 1st Radio Broadcasting Leaflet Group in Russian (as they were believed to be flying MiG for the Chinese), Chinese and Korean, and via VUNC network, the voice of United Nations Command. Half a million leaflets were dropped over Sinuiju and Uiji, MiG airfields. In anticipation the Air Force provided a quarter of a million dollars to conclude the operation. There had been a MiG downed earlier and attempts were made to recover it (see **Operation MiG**) but the wreckage did not prove fruitful.

No MiG 15 pilot responded to the offer during the war. Much too late to influence the war in Korea, a North Korean pilot, Lieutenant No Kum-Sok, landed a MiG 15BIS at Kimpo field on 21 September 1953. The young North Korean pilot surrendered himself to the astonished airman at the base. He reported that he had been raised and educated in a Catholic Mission school and had always dreamed of going to the United States. During all the questioning that followed, Lt. No maintained the position that he knew nothing of the offer and was simply defecting because of his disillusionment with the Communist cause. For most Americans the offer had long since been forgotten. President Dwight Eisenhower, when he heard of it, said he believed the offer was unethical. He was not happy with the execution of the Psy War in general and believed the offer had been phased out with the Armistice.

Lieutenant No changed his name to Kenneth

Rowe and became and American citizen. He later taught aeronautical engineering at several American universities. The exercise was costly and took several lives once the Communists became aware of his actions, including the death of Lt. Kon Soo Sung, who knew of Lieutenant No's plans and had not turned him in.

Note: In April of 1951, the United Nations conducted a mission into enemy territory to salvage some parts from a downed MiG-15. The wreckage was more than a hundred miles inland and too far to retrieve, but David Nichols and his small crew of specialists managed to photograph and record considerable technical data.

Michael E. Haas, *In the Devil's Shadow: UN Special Operations During the Korean War*. Annapolis, MD: Naval Institute Press, 2000, p. 77.
No Kum-Sok, *A MiG-15 to Freedom: Memoir of a Wartime North Korean Defector Who First Delivered the Secret Fighter to the Americans in 1953*. Jefferson, NC: McFarland, 1996.

Operation Mousetrap 24 May 1951

The 1st Marine Regiment had reached a line five and a half miles north of Sango-ri. On the night of 22 April 1951 the Chinese launched a major offensive and with two days of intense fighting they began to overrun the UN position. The advancing Communist forces endangered the Marine flank, placing them out on a limb, and required them to pull back in order to avoid being overrun. Operation Mousetrap consisted of series of helicopter transports designed to test both the ability of the machines, and the troops mounted in them, to carry out anti-guerrilla attacks on short notice and in very rough country. Undertaken by HMR-161, with only a few hours' notice, they were to lift two companies at 1000 that morning. Acting quickly, the unit moved about 500 men of the 2nd Battalion, 5th Marines, without a hitch. The report of the activity concluded that "a relatively large num-

ber of troops can be moved by helicopter on very short notice ... the entire operation was completed with only minor difficulties" (Montross).

As the 2nd ROK Regiment collapsed, the UN fell back about 20 miles and quickly reorganized. Once a line was established Marine patrols went out daily in an effort to keep contact with the Chinese advance. The wet rainy weather made these efforts nightmares, and the normal supplies of food, ammo, and water became very difficult to obtain. Nevertheless the Marines held.

About 24 May elements of the 7th Marines were ordered to advance well to the front of other units. This action caused the Chinese to attempt another massive strike in an effort to break through the lines. In this case Operation Mousetrap, and Dog Company, were acting as the bait. The hope was to lure the Chinese into moving forward into a space set up between two Marine units that were waiting for them. Operation Mousetrap turned out to be very successful, with about 450 to 500 enemy troops killed, with only 28 casualties for Dog Company. As the Marines moved through the area bulldozers were digging a massive grave to bury the enemy dead.

Lynn Montross, *Cavalry of the Sky: The Story of U.S. Marine Combat Helicopters*. New York: Harper and Brothers, 1954, p. 178.

Operation Muletrain 1952

One of the most ambitious of the helicopter supply missions, Operation Muletrain attempted to supply a battalion on the main line of resistance for a week using only four helicopters. The objective was Hill 884 and the task was given to Colonel Keith B. McCutcheson's HMR 161. They were to fly in tentage, stoves, rations, and ammunition to the men of the 1st Battalion of the 1st Marine Regiment under the command of Lieutenant Colonel John E. Gorman. This was the first test of the flying crane approach — an under slung net controlled manually from the cockpit of the helicopter — which worked better than pallets for much of the cargo.

An average of four helicopters each day were employed in Operation Muletrain. In this operation the helicopters replaced 580 Korean day laborers who had been taking supplies from the battalion supply area over mountain trails to the line. The main problem turned out to be that the cargo was brought in faster than the unloading teams could keep up. In the operation 159,730 pounds were lifted in 91.7 hours of flight time. Each trip was an average of 9.6 miles. The height of the landing area was 2,300 feet, so it was necessary to reduce the payload to about 850 pounds. Using about third of its aircraft, the HMS 161 kept well ahead of the schedule.

Lynn Montross, Hubard D. Kuokka, and Norman W. Hicks, *U.S. Marine Operations in Korea*. Volume IV. Washington, D.C.: Historical Branch G-3, Headquarters U.S. Marine Corps, 1962, p. 240.
Montross, Lynn, *Cavalry of the Sky: The Story of the U.S. Marine Combat Helicopters*. New York: Harper and Brothers, 1954, p. 177.

Operation Native Son Dog

6 March 1952

This operation consisted of the movement of a complete early warning detachment and all of its equipment from its position on the Naktong River Estuary in Korea to Tsushima, Japan, the island archipelago in the Korean Straits, often called the "gateway to Japan." Operation Native Son Dog moved Marine Ground Control Intercept Squadron 3, whose job was "to detect, identify, control the intercept of hostile aircraft, as well as to provide aid to friendly aircraft." This command consisted of two officers and 18 enlisted men, called Doodlebug Dog (its call sign), and its vast amount of electronic facilities.

Paul M. Edwards, *Korean War Almanac*. New York: Facts on File, 2006, p. 282.

Operation Nebraska   13 October 1952

Planned as a "tactical move by helicopter," Operation Nebraska was to move a unit from a combat position on one of the phase lines to another. HMR-161 was given the assignment of transporting the 2nd Battalion, 1st Marines, as well as a platoon of the 4.2 inch mortar company. Ten helicopters were used in the operation to form a shuttle service with the loading and landing zones located in defilade for concealment. In the operations, 820 troops were moved in 169 flights in just over two and a half hours.

Lynn Montross, *Cavalry of the Sky: The Story of U.S. Marine Combat Helicopters*. New York: Harper and Brothers, 1954, p. 195.

Operation Paper   Summer 1951

The Civil Air Transport Company (CAT) was the private airline of the Central Intelligence Agency. Originally created during America's clandestine operations in China, and operating briefly as a scheduled airline, it was purchased by the CIA in 1950. During the Korean War the CAT worked with the United Nations under **Operation Booklift**, a working agreement between the CIA and the military. This operation, which continued throughout the Korean War, was designed to transport men and materials throughout the Far East. Their services, however, went far beyond what was suggested in the beginning. In Operation Paper, for example, the CAT supported Li Mi's Kuomintang (KMT) forces in the Shan provinces of northeast Burma. The attacks were a part of two invasion attempts in southwest China to divert Chinese Forces from Korea. In the summer of 1951, shortly before General Li Mi attacked, "hordes of big green C-47s" (Best) were seen delivering supplies. When the efforts turned out to be unsuccessful, and their actions had become an embarrassment to the governments of Burma and Thailand, the CAT was pulled out. It was later used to repatriate KMT forces and their families to Taiwan after the fall of that government. The U.S. never acknowledged any involvement.

Martin Best, "The CIA's Airline: Logistic Air Support." http://www.vitenam.ttu.edu/airamerica/best/.

Michael E. Haas, *In the Devil's Shadow: U.N. Special Operations During the Korean War.* Annapolis, MD: Naval Institute Press, 2000.

Operation Pelican 27 September 1951

As in any military situation, the ability to move men and supplies quickly was of major significance during the Korean War. In September 1951 it was determined to test the capability of a new adaptation of the Douglas C-124 Globemaster. The C-124-A was a four-engine, long range, heavy transport plane with a crew of five or six that could carry up to 60,000 pounds. When configured with its two decks it was capable of carrying 200 armed troops. Later referred to as "Old Shaky," the C-124-A flew its first test in Operation Pelican on 27 September 1951, taking a payload of 30,000 pounds of aircraft parts from Japan to Korea. In a little over a month, the cargo plane flew twenty-six million pounds between Japan and Korea, carrying an average load of 34,000 pounds. This amount was double that of the C-54. In one mission, the C-124-A lifted a record 167 patients from Kimpo Airfield to hospitals in Japan. Once the test was concluded, on 31 October 1951, the test plane returned to the United States. Soon afterward the C-124-A entered service in Korea.

The large plane was not without its difficulties, however, for it tended to have trouble with the fuel lines, and as heavy as it was, there were only four airfields in Korea large enough to receive it. Even then, to land the plane safely, the cargo load was limited to 36,000 pounds. A major crash occurred 18 June 1953 near Tachikawa due to an engine fire, during which 122 lives were lost.

Paul M. Edwards, *Korean War Almanac.* New York: Facts on File, 2006, p. 243.

Operation Pimlico 22 November 1952

Company D of the 1st Royal Fusiliers was assigned to take one of the hills in the area known as "The Apostles," which rose nearly 400 feet above the valley in an area called Kigong-ni. The mission assignment was to kill as many Chinese troops as possible and destroy the fortifications on the hill. In preparation for the attack the company was carefully rehearsed. Companies A and C were in flak positions, and the divisional artillery, including tanks and mortars, were in place.

Then, at the last minute the operation was cancelled. Intelligence had reported the Chinese were aware of the plan and were on alert. Two days later it was on again and the unit moved out and managed to reach its objective without undue opposition by 2000 hours, but then came under pre-positioned mortar and machine-gun fire. Moving across the ridge, the men ran into an ambush of more than fifty Chinese firing burp guns. The Chinese moved through them and on to the ridge. Men began to slip back into the safety of the Fusiliers' minefield. Second Lieutenant R.F. Hoare and all his NCOs were killed or fatally wounded. The Chinese finally took the hill. Of the 21 men making up the attack force, only seven wounded men remained as the Chinese took over. Four men finally made it back. Operation Pimlico cost 22 killed or missing and 19 wounded.

Papers later found on the enemy dead suggested Pimlico had blundered into the launching of a full scale Chinese attack on the battalion bunkers.

Brian Catchpole, *The Korean War.* New York: Carroll and Graf, 2000, pp. 176–179.

Operation Pink 5 December 1950

Following the disastrous retreat from the Chosin Reservoir on the east and the Yalu on the west, the surviving troops had been reduced to a bare minimum of supplies and equipment and were often limited to just what they were able to carry. Both individuals and groups had lost a good deal of materials through enemy action, abandonment, and voluntary destruction. This loss included bedding, tentage, ordnance, signal and communications equipment, engineering gear, and weapons as well as numerous vehicles of every description. In addition to Eighth Army and X Corps losses, it was necessary to replace the equipment for the Turkish Brigade.

General Thomas B. Larkin, G-4, ordered Operation Pink, the immediate preparation, loading, and priority shipment of a division's list of equipment to the Far East Command to replace items lost during the retreats. General Douglas MacArthur felt this was not enough and raised his request to ask for two divisions' worth, but this was denied because the pending augmentation of the Army required equipment, and additional supplies could not be provided. Most likely this amount of material was simply not available. However, the effort to procure the needed replacements required in Operation Pink took place with great urgency. Four ships from San Francisco, California, and four from Seattle, Washington, began loading on 5 December, finished four days later and were ready to move out. Among the other materials delivered were 140 medium tanks. The necessary supplies were scrounged from everywhere, some from the Mutual Defense Assistance stocks, and others from troops stationed in the area. Operation Pink was a success.

James F. Schnabel, *United States Army in the Korean War, Policy and Direction: The First Year.* Washington, D.C.: Office of the Chief of Military History, United States Army, 1973, p. 297.

Operation Plan 116-50
13 November 1950

The onslaught of the Chinese intervention into the Korean War in late October and early November 1950 put the United Nations on the defense. For Admiral C. Turner Joy it was necessary to be sure that the details of Operation Plan 116-50, which authorized the plans for an emergency evacuation of all UN forces from Korea to Japan, were in order. The procedures were issued on 13 November 1950 and stressed that any such action should be based upon the principle of an "assault in reverse," and provided what information was needed for both Korean and Japanese ports set up for evacuation. Also considered was the troop capacity that could be moved if both commercial and combat shipping was called into play. Command of the event, if necessary, would be CTF 90, supported by the other naval forces that would provide the protective cover required. At 1534 on 28 November 1950 Admiral James H. Doyle was alerted for a possible emergency. The emergency was the belief (at that time) that the North Koreans might well push the UN out of Korea, and emergency plans were in operation for a last minute evacuation if necessary. It was never implemented.

James A. Field, Jr., *History of United States Naval Operations: Korea.* Washington, D.C.: Government Printing Office, 1962, p. 265.

Operation Plan Big Star Power
May 1953

While there seemed to be some progress at the negotiation table in May of 1953, and there was hope that the war might be coming to an end, the UN Command was not unaware of the danger the Communists still represented. There continued to be some lingering concern that the Chinese Communists would unleash a last minute attack on the UN lines, perhaps expecting to catch the UN unaware. In anticipation, Operation Plan Big Star Power was formulated to provide for the cautious withdrawal under fire from Line Minnesota to Line Kansas, where the UN had set up a secondary line of defense. The anticipated attack did not come against UN lines and the operation was never executed.

Operation Rabbit Hunt
22 October 1951

As the war in Korea began to settle down and was becoming a war fought between smaller units, with only few large scale troop involvements, the 1st Marine Division, in Operation Rabbit Hunt, used helicopters to conduct a series of systematic patrols of the vast areas behind the main line of resistance. They were looking for some of the guerrilla outfits that continually gathered behind the lines to cause as much trouble as possible. If nothing else, the presence of these Communist supporters required the UN to keep troops in the area in order to provide protection.

The Marines, however, were also seeking other ways to conduct the tedious and dangerous patrols in a better manner, believing the helicopter was the answer. In this case the value of the exercise was extended because Commandant General Clifton Cates, Major General Gerald Thomas, and Brigadier General Clayton Jerome were aboard some of the helicopters during the patrols and were impressed by how smoothly the operation was conducted.

Lynn Montross, *Cavalry of the Sky: The Story of U.S. Marine Combat Helicopters.* New York: Harper and Brothers, 1954, p. 172.

Operation Rainbow   5 April 1953

This was the name given to the building of the facilities necessary to conduct the prisoner of war exchange. In a little over a day (about 31 working hours) more than 100 Marine

Setting up signs at Freedom Village for Operation Rainbow, 1953 (Center for the Study of the Korean War).

construction personnel, most from Company A, Shore Party Battalion, under Major Charles E. Gocke, and Company D platoon of the 1st Engineer Battalion had constructed Freedom Village, the POW recovery station. Everything that would be needed was provided. Furniture, equipment, supplies, and tents were transported from supply units. When they were done, the area consisted of three sections: the command and receiving unit, processing, and press facilities. They also constructed facilities for the United Nations troops that would be conducting the exchange. In support, the 45th Mobile Army Surgical Hospital unit was set up, a three mile gravel road was built, more than two miles of electrical wiring was installed, and more than 100 signs in Korean and English were erected, including six massive welcome home signs. Adequate parking was provided for ambulances and a helicopter landing strip. Storage areas for food and supplies, five 50 foot flagpoles, boot paths, and the necessary sanitation facilities were constructed.

Pat Meid and James M. Yingling, *U.S. Marine Operations in Korea, Volume V: Operations in West Korea.* Washington, D.C.: Historical Division, Headquarters, U.S. Marine Corps, 1972, p. 316.

Operation Rebuild   August 1950

The damage and destruction of U.S. vehicles and the lack of essential replacement supplies and ammunition set in motion a Far East Command program called Operation Rebuild. Not to be confused with **Operation Rollup**, this was a program to repair vehicles and to make provisions for ordnance. The operation quickly assumed the proportion of a major production and repair facility as more and more damaged equipment was refurbished. By the end of 1950 Operation Rebuild had expanded to the point it employed 19,908 men and women in eight different shops across Japan. Reports are that in August 1950 alone, more than 950 2½ ton trucks were repaired.

During the first three months of the war a major portion of the ammunition available to the United Nations and South Korean troops had been supplied or rebuilt from Operation Rebuild stocks in Japan.

Roy E. Appleman, *South to the Naktong, North to the Yalu.* Washington, D.C.: Office of the Chief of Military History, Department of the Army, 1961, pp. 379–380.

Operation Relax   30 December 1950

Essential to the morale of the troops that served in Korea was a rest period known as R & R (rest and recuperation.) On 30 December 1950 Eighth Army initiated Operation Relax by which each day some 200 battle-fatigued men were given five-day passes to Japan. The Far East Air Force initiated similar plans for its personnel on 19 January 1951. The program was standardized on 18 September 1951 when it ordered that groups of 46 men, with an officer or NCO in charge, would be airlifted to some spot for relief from the war. At first the responsibility for the transportation was given to the Military Air Transport Service, but on 1 May 1952 the 315th Air Division assumed responsibility for operating the scheduled flights. During 1952 the R & R traffic was an essential portion of all the persons airlifted, and by the end of January 1953, the 315th Air Division had lifted 800,000 R & R passengers.

Robert Futrell, *The United States Air Force in Korea.* Washington, D.C.: Air Force History and Museums Program, 2000, p. 558.

Operation Removal   May 1952

When the Communist prisoners at Koje-do revolted and managed to capture the camp commander, Brigadier General Francis T. Dodd, it created a military standoff and a public relations nightmare. This problem grew even graver when Dodd's second in command,

Brigadier General Charles F. Colson, in an effort to preserve Dodd's life, agreed to many of the Communists' demands. Lieutenant General Mark Clark, who had recently been named Eighth Army commander, was a hardline anticommunist, and in response to the problems at Koje he sent in Brigadier General Haydon L. Boatner, a combat officer who was fluent in Chinese. Boatner was a no-nonsense combat leader, and as he was taking over he was faced with the evidence that the Communist prisoners were about to stage a major breakout from the compound. He was determined that this would not happen and he acted quickly. As one of his first actions, at the end of May 1952, he initiated Operation Removal during which he had all the Korean refugees removed who were living in proximity to the camp. He believed, and he was right, that they were being used by the prisoners to communicate with the Chinese high command. This clearing of the peripheral area was a first significant step in taking control of the prisoners.

"Boatner, Haydon L.," in James Matray, *Historical Dictionary of the Korean War*. Westport, CT: Greenwood Press, 1991, pp. 55–56.

Operation Ripple I 19 August 1952

Operation Ripple I took off from the HMR-161 base at 1800 hours on 19 August 1952, and its assignment was completed when it departed from Firing Zone 2. During the Korean War helicopters demonstrated their great value in search and rescue, covert operations, minesweeping, medical evacuation, and supply. But they were also adapted to quick transportation when needed. Operation Ripple I tested the ability of the helicopter to move units, in this case rocket launchers and their personnel and equipment, from one firing position to the other. In this exercise, dubbed "hit n'git," they would drop the crew in a suitable firing position, let them fire off a

few rockets, then pick up the still hot tubes and move them somewhere else before they could be located by the enemy artillery. The rocket launcher was under the helicopter in a sling while it was in flight. There was some delay due to a sling-hoist mechanical problem at Firing Zone 1, and the fact that several of the rocket launcher crews used too much time entering and leaving the helicopter. Nevertheless, in Operation Ripple I, HMS-161 transported a 4.5 inch rocket battery from point to point in order for the smoke from the rockets not to give them away, and thus put them in danger from enemy artillery. HMS 161 later perfected the techniques of ship borne assault and launching from the USS *Sicily*.

Lynn Montross, *Cavalry of the Sky: The Story of the U.S. Marine Combat Helicopters.* New York: Harper and Brothers, 1954, p. 197.

Gary W. Parker, *A History of Marine Medium Helicopter Squadron-161.* Washington, D.C.: History and Museum Division Headquarters, United States Marine Corps, 1978, pp. 11–13.

Operation Ripple V February 1953

Ripple V was a mission designed to move a rocket launching team from one fire zone to a second position. Like the earlier Ripple exercises, the purpose was to "evaluate under combat conditions the feasibility of logistically supporting both MLR regiment, and to determine the planning factors involved" (Montross). The operations accomplished both of these purposes.

Note: Two other Ripple missions that place in August and September of 1952, but information on these particular operations is not available.

Lynn Montross, *Cavalry of the Sky: The Story of U.S. Marine Combat Helicopters.* New York: Harper and Brothers, 1954, pp. 193–7.

Operation Rollup 1947

At the end of World War II the American people discarded arms and equipment as if they would never be used it again. An incredible amount of equipment was destroyed, or abandoned, or sold in the emerging Army and Navy surplus stores. Units, when deactivated, had turned in huge amounts of equipment, but most of it was unserviceable. When it came time to fight the Korean War there was little to fight it with. Far East Command had received no new vehicles since the end of World War II, and an estimated 80 percent of the Army's 60-day reserves were, on 25 June 1950, unserviceable. Eighth Army was authorized 226 recoilless rifles but had only 21. Of the 18,000 quarter-ton trucks available, more than 19,000 were unserviceable and only 4,441 of the 13,789 two-and-a-half ton trucks were in running condition.

So, while Operation Rollup is outside our time period, it is nevertheless highly significant to it. The operation was initiated by Far East Command and its mission was to locate vehicles and equipment that were left to rust on past Pacific battlefields. The assignment was to locate the equipment, catalogue it, and see that it was retrieved and refurbished. It was sent to the Tokyo Ordnance Depot facilities, where workers were able to repair much of what had been found. Critical shortages of qualified U.S. personnel meant that the Army relied on hundreds of Japanese laborers.

When the war broke out on the Korean peninsula there were not enough provisions in theater, or available to be sent there, nor were there enough transports to move the materials had they been available. So, as it turned out, much of what General Walton Walker had to fight with during the early months was made available through the efforts of Operation Rollup. Ninety percent of all armaments and seventy-five percent of all automotives issued at the start of the war were from the project.

During the operation more than 200,000 measured tons of ordnance and thousands of vehicles were brought back. By June 1950 more than 46,000 vehicles had been reworked, and during July and August 1950 an additional 4,000 vehicles were made available for the troops in Korea. While not all repaired equipment was successful — some vehicles were so rusted under their new paint jobs that they actually broke when driven over rough territory — they made a significant difference.

Stanley Sandler, *The Korean War: No Victor, No Vanquished.* London: University College London, 1999, p. 63.
James F. Schnabel, *Policy and Direction: The First Year.* Washington, D.C.: Office of the Chief of Military History, 1972, pp. 58–59.

Operation Rotate   24 February 1951

In an unusual and highly significant move, helicopters from Marine Helicopter Squadron 161 were able to rotate Marine battalions stationed in an out-of-the-way location. In Operation Rotate the 1st battalion of Lt. Colonel Harold C. Howard's 7th Marine Regiment was lifted out and was relieved by the 2nd Battalion of the same regiment. Using nine aircraft of HMR 161, the units and all of their supplies and equipment were delivered to the top of Hill 884. The hill, later dubbed "Mount Helicopter" was a steep, roadless area that, even when traveled by foot was precarious. Nevertheless, the operation was completed with so little difficulty that it could not add much to what had been learned from previous exercises, other than to reinforce belief in the success of potential operations.

Lynn Montross, Hubard Kuokka, and Norman Hicks, *U.S. Marine Operations in Korea 1950–1952. Volume IV, The East Central Front.* Washington, D.C.: Headquarters U.S. Marine Corps, 1962, p. 241.

Operation Santa Claus
December 1950

Yet another name by which to identify the airlift of orphans from Kimpo Air Field at Seoul during the Chinese Communist Forces' advance on the area. The children were flown out of the area by planes of the 5th Air Force. Also called **Operations Christmas Kidlift, Kiddie Car, Kiddie Car Lift,** and **Little Orphan Annie.**

Allan R. Millett, *Their War for Korea: American, Asian, and European Combatants and Civilians 1945–1953.* Washington, D.C.: Brassey's, 2002, p. 185.

Operation Santa Claus
20 December 1952

This operation involved a specially set up holiday flight called **Operation Sleigh Ride,** in which a C-124 Globemaster military transport, called the "Christmas Special," was fully loaded with fuel and service men from all over to bring them home for Christmas. The selection process was done by numbers. The intent was to provide them special transport to spend Christmas at home. However, in December 1952 the plane carrying the soldiers crashed. Eighty-two passengers and five crewmen were killed. The accident took place at Larson Air Field not far from Moses Lake, Washington. The plane, brimming with servicemen heading home for the holiday, took off from the runway, climbed to about 100 feet, started to bank left, and then without any warning, fell to the earth. The victims were rushed to the Air Force Base hospital, but only a few survived. The cause of the crash was ruled as pilot error, for some member of the crew had failed to unlock the rudder and elevation locking pin. Several investigators, however, point to the C-124s poor safety record for an excuse.

"Airplane Crashes: Globemaster Crash, December 1952." http://www.koreanwar-educator.org/topics/ airplane_crashes/#globemasterMosesLake.

Operation Saturate   3 March 1952

Having completed **Operation Strangle** and not yet ready to give up on the idea that saturation bombing could be instrumental in keeping the Communists at the negotiation table, Colonel Jean H. Daugherty, the 5th Air Force director of Intelligence, suggested in late February 1952 that around the clock bombing be implemented; they called it Operation Saturate. As suggested by the name, this was a change in the policy of implementation: no longer designed to continue the wide and indiscriminate bombing of Operation Strangle, this operation instead focused on major sectors and targets with the intention of completely destroying them. The focus was to be on the four main railway lines: Kunu-ri to Huichon, Sunchon to Samdong-ni, Sinanju to Namsiong, and Pyongyang to Namchonjom. The hope was to cause so much destruction that the damage could not be repaired, or if it was, it would require the employment of scarce heavy equipment that would need to be brought in. Targets were especially selected and flights controlled by the 5th Air Force Joint Operations Center. It also tried to select targets that were as free of anti-aircraft protection as possible.

The fighter-bombers involved employed mass formations and planned to deliver an average of 300 sorties and 600 bombs on each railway segment each day. During the day the fighter-bombers would sortie and then at night the B-26s would bomb with 500 pounders under flares. By the end of April the Communists had stationed anti-aircraft fire along the target areas, and before long there were no flak-free areas remaining.

In late May the attackers went after a particular strip of railway and delivered bombs for two days, only to find it back in operation in a week. The exercise was not without cost, for chiefly through strikes the 5th Air Force had lost 243 fighter-bombers and damaged 290 others. By mid–May, Operation Saturate was running down and finally phased out.

Once again concern was raised about the validity of such an operation. While there was no doubt that the planes were hitting their targets, in one specific case the rails were back in working condition in two days. Nevertheless,

5th Air Force continued Operation Saturate during April and May, but it was not long before planners were seeking more profitable operations.

Walter G. Hermes, *Truce Tent and Fighting Front*. Washington, D.C.: Office of the Chief of Military History, 1966, p. 170.

Robert F. Futrell, *The United States Air Force in Korea*. Washington, D.C.: Air Force History and Museum Program, 2000, p. 453.

Operation Shakedown May 1953

During the last few weeks prior to the signing of an armistice, some consideration was being given to Operation Shakedown, a contingency plan to make a drive to the Yalu using nuclear weapons and calling on the support of Nationalist Chinese troops. The National Security Council had once again considered nuclear weapons as a means of breaking the deadlock in Korea. By this time there was no lack of weapons, or bombers to deliver them, and it was believed that the Soviet Union was not yet in the position to challenge the United States in the nuclear conflict. This consideration was not addressed in the National Security Document 147, however, so the rationale for their view is not known. President Dwight D. Eisenhower, it is reported, was ready to execute Operation Shakedown but perhaps more significantly allow knowledge of its existence to be leaked out through trusted intermediaries. It will never be known, until the Chinese and North Koreans open their archives, what effect this had on conditions, but the assumption is that Chinese Communists reconsidered the outcome of a nuclear war and decided to settle the conflict with the concessions that had been made at the table so far. Soon after that, the war ended.

Laurence Oglethorpe, *Memoirs*, Center for the Study of the Korean War.

Operation Silent Redline I

13 September 1952

This operation was set up to accomplish the relief of a unit on the main line of resistance and return it to reserve as quickly as possible. Operation Silent Redline I was initiated in September 1952. In this case it was the 1st Battalion of the 1st Regiment, Korean Marine Corps, that was to be taken across the Han River to relieve the 5th Battalion that needed rest and reorganization. Intelligence sources identified the enemy as having elements of two regiments of a Chinese Communist Force Army with six battalions in line. Operation Silent Redline I was completed without enemy opposition between 0900 and 1531. Ten helicopters were involved and made 277 flights carrying six men each. In 61 hours of aircraft time, 1,618 troopers were transported.

Lynn Montross, *Cavalry of the Sky: The Story of U.S. Marine Combat Helicopters*. New York: Harper and Brothers, 1954, pp. 194–195.

Operation Silent Redline V

February 1953

Like **Operation Ripple** I and V the purpose of this operation was both to move troops and equipment, but also to "evaluate under combat conditions the feasibility of logistically supporting both MLR regiment, and to determine the planning factors involved" (Montross).

Lynn Montross, *Cavalry of the Sky: The Story of U.S. Marine Combat Helicopters*. New York: Harper and Brothers, 1954, p. 197.

Operation Skunkhunt

15 December 1951

During the period between 6 December 1951 and 13 February 1952, the guerrilla raids in the area maintained by the Commonwealth Division had increased dramatically. There had been at least five separate raids and several of them were directed against the area held by the 28th Brigade. A Canadian ambulance had been ambushed just three miles from the New Zealand position. Booby-traps has been located in the division area and several men hurt. Two prisoners admitted that they were part of a unit that was setting up infiltration routes, planning ambushes, setting booby-traps, and placing agents in the area. One unit reported, "We are having to get more and more alert on piquet's at night" (McGibbon), and travel in and out of the divisional area was more dangerous.

In December 1951 a detachment of New Zealand gunners joined up in Operation Skunkhunt, a sweep of the entire division area to clean it out. In the process more than 600 civilians were screened and 200 found questionable enough to evacuate them to the rear. Twelve were held for interrogation. During the exercise, while few guerrillas were found, four troopers from the division were wounded by booby-traps.

Greater control was imposed on members of the Korean Service Corps and a new set of checkpoints was introduced. Operation Skunkhunt did not do the job, however, and as the problems increased a new divisional sweep was planned. **Operation Polecat** was set in motion on 18 February.

Ian McGibbon, *New Zealand and the Korean War: Combat Operations.* Melbourne: Oxford University Press, 1996, page. 243.

Operation Skyhook   22–24 May 1953

While the Marines had been experimenting with the helicopter during much of the Korean War, it was not until late that the U.S. Army's 6th and 13th Transportation Company (Helicopters) arrived in Korea at the request of General Matthew Ridgway. The general had been impressed with the successful operations illustrated by the Marines and had encouraged the Army to speed up deployment. Nevertheless, it was not until January 1953 that the U.S. Army's first helicopter transportation units became active. Flying the H-19 Chickasaw helicopter in Operation Skyhook, the 6th and

13th Transportation Companies (soon unified as the 1st Transportation Army Aviation Battalion, Provisional) cooperated to fly 34,000 pounds of supplies to the aid of three front line regiments of the 25th Infantry Division that had been cut off in May 1953. On the basis of this success, Lieutenant General Maxwell Taylor said, "The cargo helicopter, employed en masse, can extend the tactical mobility of the Army far beyond its normal capability" (Kreisher) and urged greater adoption into the service.

Otto Kreisher, "The Rise of the Helicopter During the Korean War." *Aviation History*, January 2007.

Operation Skyway   June 1953

During the final days of the fighting, while everyone waited to see if President Syngman Rhee's attitude would prevent the armistice, United Nations units were still on high alert, but the pressure was easing off somewhat. The gunners of the New Zealand 64th Field Artillery Battalion replaced the 16th Field Regiment so that the latter could get some rest. At one point in this replacement, for three days late in June, elements of the New Zealand 64th Field Artillery Battalion took part in Operation Skyway. The operation involved the use of helicopters to move supplies to units of the Commonwealth Division that were located north of the Imjin River. The operations, generally experimental, were proclaimed a success.

Ian McGibbon, *New Zealand and the Korean War: Combat Operations.* Melbourne: Oxford University Press, 1996, p. 340.

Operation Sleigh Ride   December 1950

This was a plan to select a few U.S. servicemen by lottery and provide them an air flight home for Christmas. For the tragedy of the flight of 1952 see **Operation Santa Claus** (20 December 1952).

"Airplane Crashes: Globemaster Crash, December 1952." www.koreanwar-educator.org/topics/air plane_crashes/#globemasterMosesLake.

Operation Smack   25 January 1953

This was an exercise with considerable potential that ended up costing the Army and Air Force a significant bit of embarrassment and criticism. It was planned as an attack against Spud Hill, an enemy held position on the east side of T-Bone Hill on the east-central front. It was designed to illustrate the possibility of launching a combined artillery, armor, air, and infantry attack. In this case the goal of the operation was to take prisoners. The 7th Infantry Division was assigned to the operation and Major General Wayne C. Smith, the division commander, proposed a daylight raid supported by tactical air and tanks.

Operation Smack was in trouble right from the beginning. It had been booked as an exhibition with several high ranking officers on hand to witness the effort, and the word "scenario" was used in describing the plan. The attack, when it came, consisted of one platoon from Colonel William B. Kern's 31st Infantry Regiment. But it was late getting underway due to a radio malfunction. Air support came from the 58th Fighter Bomber Wing that was to provide ground support. As the advancing troops reached a point about a third of the way up the hill, they came under murderous enemy fire. It quickly became apparent that the enemy was too strong and well fortified and Colonel Kern called off the attack.

Much to the discomfort of all involved, a reporter who was not there but heard about it linked the operation to the gladiators in the Coliseum and suggested American soldiers had been killed for the entertainment of visiting brass. The uproar was enough that eventually General J. Lawton Collins, Army chief of staff, was called before a Congressional Committee to explain what had happened. He did so adequately enough to avoid censure.

Later General Mark Clark would write: "The object of Operation Smack was to capture prisoners. In that, it failed. No prisoners were taken. The results of the fight were thirteen enemy dead, twenty-five enemy estimated killed in action and three enemy known wounded. Our losses were three killed in action and sixty-one wounded" (Clark). The official military view of the incident was that while this particular operation was not an immediate success it proved the value of the basic principles set forth.

Mark W. Clark, *From the Danube to the Yalu*. New York: Harpers, 1954, pp. 335–336.

Operation Snap   December 1950–January 1951

Suddenly in December 1950 the logistical situation in the Korean War changed. Up to this time the problem had been to keep up with the quickly advancing units that were outrunning their supplies and services. Then quickly, with the massive Chinese intervention and the immediate call for retreat, the quartermaster unit found itself in the position of having to withdraw supplies and redistribute them faster than the Chinese were advancing. A significant amount of supplies simply could not be moved in time and had to be destroyed. Some, unfortunately, fell into the hands of the enemy. Most, however, were moved out and new depots established farther to the south. In addition, about 160,000 tons, under Operation Snap, were moved out of Korea and sent back for storage and later dispersal in Japan. This operation continued from 15 December until mid–January 1951.

James A. Huston, *Guns and Butter, Powder and Rice: U.S. Army Logistics in the Korean War*. Selingrove: Susquehanna University Press, 1989, pp. 153–15.

Operation Snowball   1–3 October 1951

Napalm was one of the more effective weapons of the Korean War. Napalm (a trademark) is a combination of power and gasoline that is sticky, stringy, and adheres to objects while it is burning. In addition, the explosion of the rapidly burning fire creates a large amount of carbon monoxide that makes it hard for persons in the area to breathe. During the early days in Korea it was delivered in 100 gallon plastic jugs that cost about 40 dollars each. During the war an average of 250,000 pounds of Napalm was dropped each day in support of United Nations troops, and against specially designated targets. Delivery was made by just about every means available but primarily by plane. Operation Snowball was an experiment to see if it was possible to successfully drop this deadly mixture from one of the C-119s of the 315th Air Division (Troop Carrier). During this operation the C-119s dropped 55 gallon tanks filled with Napalm onto positions behind enemy lines in North Korea. While the operation was successful, it was not necessarily efficient, and few such missions were flown thereafter.

Many Americans know the term from the remarkable scene in the movie *Apocalypse Now* (1979): "I love the smell of Napalm in the morning."

Paul M. Edwards, *Korean War Almanac*. New York: Facts on File, 2006, p. 244.

Operation Spreadout   19 April 1952

In early April 1952 the Communists asked for an estimate of the number of POWs held by the United Nations who would want repatriation. In order to reach this number, both sides agreed to a screening to determine which soldiers wanted to return to their homeland and which did not. The Communists were pushing for a figure and the one given, taken hastily, showed that an unrealistic 116,000 did not want to be repatriated. But during later screening it was determined that only about 70,000 of the Chinese POWs wanted to be repatriated. A significant number of the Chi-

nese POW indicated they did not want to be repatriated and asked to be sent to Taiwan.

This screening necessitated that those refusing repatriation be moved to camps away from those other prisoners who wished to be repatriated. This process was conducted under the identity of Operation Spreadout, and it took place from 19 April to 1 May 1952. In this process more than 80,000 non-repatriate prisoners and civilian internees from Koje-do Camp 1 were moved to new camps set up on the Korean mainland. Anti-Chinese Communist prisoners were sent to Cheju-do. The Communists, upset with the numbers released, claimed the screening had been done unfairly, and it was the death blow to any hope of an immediate cease-fire.

Callum A. MacDonald, *Korea: The War Before Vietnam*. New York: Free Press, 1986.

Operation Spyglass   August 1953

As soon as the cease-fire agreement was signed, most military units went into new operational modes, including an increase in training exercises. Shortly after the fighting stopped the pilots of Marine Air Group 33 were involved in Operation Spyglass, which began in August of 1953. This Far East Air Force exercise stressed interception flying and working with Ground Control Intercept Squadrons. Acting as the aggressors, the Pohang-based airmen would make simulated attacks on various South Korean targets that were defended by Air Force and land-based Marine units. The operation was followed, in September, by **Operation Back Door**.

Pat Meid and James M. Yingling, *U.S. Marine Operations in Korea, Volume V: Operations in West Korea*. Washington, D.C.: Historical Division, Headquarters, U.S. Marine Corps, 1972, p. 473.

Operation Strike

The whole plan for strategic bombing of North Korea was called Operation Strike, and the bombing phrases (see Appendix Four) reflect the general operational policy rather than any specific event. In intent the operation was set up with two purposes: the destruction of key supply areas and as a warning to show that the United Nations forces were maintaining complete control of the air. It was important for the Communists to know that the United Nations air forces were able to strike at any time they wanted. In many cases civilians were warned that they were about to be bombed because military targets were located in the area. Radio Seoul also broadcast additional warnings. Then, after the bombing raids were completed, the planes dropped leaflets to remind the citizens that they had been warned, and further warning them their town or area would be bombed again.

The warning sent out by Radio Seoul was this: "People of North Korea. Attention. This may save your life. Today the United Nations Air Force bombed fifty villages, towns and cities that were military targets. These were military targets along highways and railways. You may be next. Save your lives. Flee to the hills. The United Nations Command wants to protect Korean civilians. You must obey these instructions to leave. Leave the doomed area at once. Remember. You may be the next to die!" (Friedman). These announcements were not, of course, simply humanitarian. It was believed that such warnings would lead to a mass exodus from the area identified, and thus complicate the Communist response.

The evaluation of Operation Strike during the Korean War is still being made, and is a point of disagreement between those who felt the near saturation bombing was unnecessary and those who believed that the war could not have been successfully waged without it.

Herb Friedman, "The Strategic Bombers and American Psyop." *Fallen Leaf: The Journal of the Psychological Society*, October 2000.

Operation Summit   21 September 1951

This was the first helicopter-borne landing of combat Marines to take place. H-hour was set for 1000 hours on 21 September 1951. The early plan called for a landing of a reconnaissance company's rifle squad to secure the area, and the location of a landing point team from the 1st Shore Party Battalion under Lieutenant Colonel Harry W. Edwards to clear the sites. They were to disembark from the hovering helicopters via a 30 foot rope. Heavy winds at the drop zone made this a very difficult operation. It was carried out by aircraft landing at 30 second intervals, each carrying five fully equipped men.

The disembarkation took 20 seconds per man. Despite dense fog, HMR-161 managed to lift 224 fully equipped Marines to Hill 884. Hill 884, on the extreme right flank, was so remote that it could not be approached by road and, it was determined, it would take nine hours for Korean Service personnel to reach the site. In addition, the HMRs transported 17,772 pounds of cargo in support of the operation. The entire venture required 65 flights, 31.2 flight hours, and took about four hours. The operation concluded with the laying of two telephone lines between the command post and the Marines on Hill 884.

It was not, according to air historian Lynn Montross, an unqualified success. Flare pots illuminating the area were blow away by the wash of the rotors and the glare often blinded pilots. The operation was, however, highly significant in the progression of helicopter use. The concluding report read, in part: "Helicopter functions will be progressively enlarged as time passes, and that the aircraft type must be recognized as a requisite component of a balanced military force" (Montross et al.). Lieutenant General Lemuel C. Shepherd, Jr., stated that it was "a bright new chapter in the employment of helicopters by Marines" (Montross).

Lynn Montross, Hubard D. Kuokka, and Norman W. Hicks, *U.S. Marine Operations in Korea 1950–1953*. Volume IV. Washington, D.C.: Historical Branch G-3, Headquarters, U.S. Marine Corps, 1962, p. 208.

Lynn Montross, *Cavalry of the Sky: The Story of U.S. Marine Combat Helicopter*. New York: Harper and Brothers, 1954, p. 164.

Operation Switch 11 November 1951

The Marines were way ahead of both the Army and the Air Force in the operational use of helicopters. Operation Switch was an exercise in which Marine Helicopter Transport Squadron (HMR) 161 effected the relief of a frontline battalion, a project that involved the movement of nearly 2,000 troops. Beginning at 0635 when the first of twelve helicopters took off from X-83, the group made 262 trips in an overall time of 10 hours (95.6 hours of flight time). The advantage of such a tactical operation was quickly apparent. Refueling and flight operations continued smoothly. So impressed were the Eighth Army observers who witnessed the transporting of men and combat equipment in such a short amount of time that in November 1951 General Matthew B. Ridgway asked the Army to provide four helicopter transport battalions, each to be equipped with 280 machines.

Lynn Montross, Hubard D. Kuokka, and Norman W. Hicks, *U.S. Marine Operations in Korea*. Volume IV. Washington, D.C.: Historical Branch G-3, Headquarters U.S. Marine Corps, 1962, p. 219.

Operation Terry Blue March 1953

The success of Marine helicopter exercises during the first two years of the Korean War led General Matthew Ridgway to ask for helicopters for the Army. It was not until January of 1953, however, that the U.S. Army's first helicopter transportation units became active. Flying the H-19 Chickasaw helicopter, the 1st Transportation Army Aviation Battalion (Provisional) had twelve ships and was stationed in and around Uijongbu. In Operation Terry Blue, the 6th and 13th Transportation Companies (prior to their unification) joined to fly 34,000 pounds of supplies to the aid of the 3rd Infantry Division that had been cut off, in March 1953, by rising flood waters.

"Helicopters in Korea," *U.S. Transportation Museum*. http://www.transchool.Eustis.army.mil/museum.

Operation Thanksgiving December 1952

One of the major questions of facing General Matthew Ridgway was the number of civilians being held as prisoners of war who were, in reality, simply civilians caught in one of the many roundups. The decision was that each case should be considered and if they qualified, they were to be reclassified from prisoners to civilian internees. Under **Operation Scatter** in June of 1952, Eighth Army released about 27,000 civilian internees who had been improperly identified as POWs. These were men and women who indicated that they did not want to be repatriated. In July, **Operation Homecoming** released 18,746 more civilians who also indicated that they did not wish to be repatriated. In later investigations another 16,000 or so were reclassified as civilian internees. The United Nations Command recommended that these civilians be released as well, believing that such an action might impress the Communist negotiators at Panmunjom. With Washington's approval, the plan, Operation Thanksgiving, authorized their release and this was accomplished by 4 December 1952. Contrary to expectations, the Communists protested the release of persons they considered POWs. There is some evidence as well that the action caused the North Koreans to retain many South Korean civilian POWs.

Laurence Oglethorpe, *Memoirs*, Center for the Study of the Korean War.

Operation Timber   May 1952

Setting up the bunkers and fortifications for their defensive positions along the newly established line was made more difficult for the 1st Marine Division, as the supply procedure was particularly hard for the Marines who were not accustomed to the Army system. But in this case it was more than that; the necessary materials were not available anywhere. The plight led to Operation Timber, an exercise undertaken to provide the raw lumber needed to complete bunker construction along the Jamestown, Wyoming, and Kansas Lines. The 1st Marines had estimated that three million linear feet of timber would be needed to complete the necessary defense establishment. Unable to acquisition such amounts, the Corps identified a tract of deeply wooded ground about 50 miles east of the 45th Infantry Division sector. On 12 May an engineering platoon under 2nd Lieutenant Robert E. Gal-

lagher, a truck platoon, and about 500 Korean Service Corps personnel were sent to the area and began the cutting and hauling of timbers. By the time the operation had ended in July more than 34,294 sections of timber had been cut. Despite this effort, it was still not enough timber and finally, in July, Eighth Army was able to make up the difference. The Marines were able to complete most of the fortifications planned.

Pat Meid and James M. Yingling, *U.S. Marine Operations in Korea, Volume V: Operations in West Korea.* Washington, D.C.: Historical Division, Headquarters, U.S. Marine Corps, 1972, p. 100.

Operation Trojan   November 1952

This was one of the many operations set up to try and confuse the Communists and hide the UN intentions. Commonwealth troops were given American style helmets in order to

Operation Timber, collecting logs for construction of dugouts (Center for the Study of the Korean War).

make the Chinese Communist spotters believe that the U.S. troops had moved away from their customary spot on Hill 355. The other side of the deception was that UN troops were ordered to wear their shirt sleeves down and buttoned, as was the Commonwealth practice. Canadian radio operators used American procedures and when possible Commonwealth troops were provided with American weapons. The idea was to tempt the Chinese into probing what was hoped would be seen as the new troops on the line and give the UN the chance to take more prisoners. The deception seemed to be working until the Canadians began firing their Vickers medium machine guns, a sound well known to the Chinese. The following day Chinese loudspeakers welcomed the Canadians to the line.

Ted Barris, *Deadlock in Korea: Canadians at War, 1950–1953*. Toronto: Macmillan Canada, 1999, pp. 197–198.

Operation Turnaround

7 December 1950

The 65th Regimental Combat Team had been moving north when it received orders to turn around and move to the Hamhung-Hungnam area. Operation Turnaround presented the 65th RCT with a five phase mission without providing the unit with much detailed instruction as to how to accomplish it. They were to set up a defensive position along the Charlie Line, the boundary with the 7th Infantry Division on the right, and Line George on the left. There they were to anticipate opposing a large enemy force that was arriving from the north, which would mean defending the village of Majon-dong, and clearing the main supply route from there to Sudong, north of Koto-ri, of all enemy forces. Last, but not least, the 65th RCT was to protect the withdrawal of the 1st Marine Division that was moving out of Hagaru-ri, where it had been surrounded by Chinese Communist forces. In support, the 65th had the 3rd Battalion of both the 15th RCT and the 7th RCT and the arrangement was to set up a mobile defense, that is, fire and fall back when necessary.

The plan was straightforward. As the Marines, came moving down the road, the troops along Charlie Line would hold the Chinese long enough for the Marines to load aboard the ships at Hungnam Harbor. The perimeter defense then would fall back in a series of lines, from Charlie, to Tare-King, to Mike-King, Peter-Queen, Able and finally to Line Fox. As the enemy was being delayed the 7th Infantry Division would load with the 3rd Division being the last unit to leave. The 65th RCT was drawn into a tighter and tighter perimeter providing defense around the harbor itself. By late on the afternoon of 24 December, most of the other troops had been loaded and headed out, and the Puerto Rico 65th was ordered to start loading on the Liberty Ship *Freeman*. Colonel W.W. Harris, commander of the 65th, remembered it: "My small command loaded on the last LCT with elements of the 2nd Battalion at 1430 hours on 24 December 1950. So far as I know, we were the last to leave the area" (Harris).

W.W. Harris, *Puerto Rico's Fighting 65th U.S. Infantry: From San Juan to Chorwan*. California: Presidio Press, 2001, pp. 125–131.

Operation Wedge   15 October 1951

Republic of Korea (ROK) forces had been completely surrounded and called on helicopter support from the 1st Marine Division. Operation Wedge took place on 15 October 1951 when Lieutenant Colonel William P. Mitchell led six Marine helicopters from HMR-161 in response to the request and flew to the defense with 19,000 pounds of ammunition. During the operation the squadron's surgeon, Lieutenant Donald L. Hillian, landed to offer medical aid and eventually the helicopter team evacuated twenty-four wounded men. Captain James T. Cotton and Captain Albert A.

Black each made four flights into the area as needed. The rescue effort was acknowledged by Major General Claude F. Ferenbaugh, commanding IX Corps, when he reported that in this case the exercise proved the reliability of the helicopter transports to respond in emergency situations without a lot of pre-planning.

Lynn Montross, *Cavalry of the Sky: The Story of U.S. Marine Combat Helicopter.* New York: Harper and Brothers, 1954, p. 171.

Operation Wellsend   4 March 1951

The 68th Chemical Smoke Generating Company arrived in Korea in October of 1950. In March it began its normal mission of generating smoke. On 4 March 1951 the men set up smoke generators as a part of the feint in Operation Wellsend. A short test prior to the operation showed that the wind was blowing in the wrong direction. In fact, this was the case in most of the missions they were given, and as a result they were not often used. The exercise was eventually cancelled.

John G. Westover, *Combat Support in Korea.* Washington, D.C.: Center of Military History, United States Army, 1987, pp. 80–81.

Operation Windmill I

13 September 1951

Elements of the North Korean People's Army, 6th Division, were dug in at concealed bunkers and were holding up the advance of the 23rd Regiment of the 2nd Infantry Division. The UN troops began receiving heavy fire and in the return of fire were running out of ammunition and supplies. At 1600 hours, Operation Windmill I was executed. In other circumstances it would have been necessary to call for a parachute drop but the situation was perfect for illustrating the Marine helicopter capabilities. The operation consisted of moving one day's supplies to the 2nd Battalion, 1st Marines, over a distance of seven miles from X-83. First they landed a team under Lieutenant Colonel Harry W. Edwards, which went in to clear off an area, and then the first helicopter from Marine Helicopter Squadron 161 began dropping nets of cargo and then troops. The landing point was about 600 feet from the floor of the valley. The first helicopter arrived at 1610 hours. In two and a half hours, the helicopters were able to deliver 18,848 pounds of highly necessary cargo and to evacuate 74 casualties on the return trip.

Lynn Montross, Hubard D. Kuokka, and Norman W. Hicks, *U.S. Marine Operations in Korea.* Volume IV. Washington, D.C.: Historical Branch G-3, Headquarters U.S. Marine Corps, 1962, p. 189.

Operation Windmill II

19 September 1951

The battle for Heartbreak Ridge continued with an attack on Hill 931. Eighth Army was pushing north of the Punchbowl seeking a better defensive line. The 1st Battalion, 5th Marines, relieved the 1st and 2nd Battalions of the 1st Marines and occupied a defensive line that stretched more than two miles to the east along a ridge that ran almost to the Soyang-gang River. Here Operation Windmill II dropped badly needed supplies to help in the construction of fortifications in an area called the Rock.

Lynn Montross, *Cavalry of the Sky: The Story of U.S. Marine Combat Helicopter.* New York: Harper and Brothers, 1954, pp. 162–63.

V. Covert and Clandestine Operations

As generated by the changing nature of war itself, the war in Korea witnessed an expansion of propaganda, intelligence, and covert and clandestine activities. In 1950 when the Korean War broke out, the United States Special Forces was not operational, and paramilitary activities that took place in Korea were limited by infighting and turf wars between the Army's G-2 and the CIA. Perhaps the first and most active force functioning was the United Nations Partisan Force Korea, which operated on off shore islands and behind enemy lines. This group would be later identified as the 8086th Army Unit, and then later as the Far East Command Liaison Detachment, Korea. The purpose of these units was to direct North Korean partisans in raids, interdiction, reconnaissance, and even rescue attempts. There was, however, considerable tension between CIA tactical support for Eighth Army and its own agenda. The Army and the CIA never really worked well together in these counterintelligence operations.

While some very interesting books have been published in the last few years about the covert and clandestine activities that took place during the war, there is still not a great deal of information available. Understandably, these accounts are more about the organization of units and the planning of missions than they are about the mission themselves. It should not come as a surprise that U.S. government records that authorized American missions of destruction and infiltration into North Korea and China during the Korean War have either been destroyed or are so buried in the system they will probably never reappear. Nevertheless, there is enough evidence of the many efforts being made to identify them, even if there is often very little information about the actual execution of the mission, or more important, the final disposition of those involved.

What cannot be denied, however, are the memoirs and oral histories of the agents, both military and civilian, as well as the partisans and airmen who willingly presented themselves for these high risk missions into enemy territory. The researcher's difficulty is in determining the legitimacy of this "self-reported" information.

The National Security Council, in June of 1948, defined a covert operation as one in which "actions conducted by the United States against foreign states which are so planned and executed that any U.S. Government responsibility for them is not evident to unauthorized persons and that if uncovered the U.S. Government can plausibly disclaim any responsibility for them" (Department of Defense). It then proceeded to authorize the Central Intelligence Agency to conduct such actions, though the language is not particularly clear about just what was being expected or authorized.

The fact is that the intelligence community in 1950, in contrast to what it is today, was in its infancy as the Korean War broke out and, in a large measure, this was the war that marked the turning point in American intelligence activities. Prior to the war in Korea, the budgets of intelligence agencies had been lean. But because of lessons learned during the war Congress would greatly increase funds for its expansion.

While the CIA was new at this time, having only been established by the National Security Act of 1947, the operations which they conducted were not all that new. The U.S. government had been involved in such undertakings since President George Washington drew on his contingent Fund of Foreign Intercourse to ransom Americans held hostage. Behind the scenes planning and behind the lines operations have always been a part of warfare, and the manner in which they were carried out had been greatly sophisticated by the American experience in World War II. In Korea the covert actions became more organized and formalized and, while covert, they were certainly not unknown.

Early clandestine operations in Korea were limited by General Douglas MacArthur's rather basic dislike of such behavior. During World War II he had prohibited unconventional warfare in the Pacific and that order was still in effect when he took command of the United Nations Forces in Korea. He did not like the manner in which the CIA functioned, but more specifically he did not like his lack of control over their activities. In time MacArthur would lose out in this argument, as the Central Intelligence Agency gained credibility and authority, as well as under the pressure of thousands of North Korean refugees demanding to be used.

The degree to which such actions were conducted in Korea is still a matter of considerable discussion as more and more veterans tell their stories, and military analyses evaluate the success or failure of what happened. In most of the available accounts the term "partisan" is used to identify North Koreans who operated behind Communist lines in support of United Nations efforts. The term "guerrilla" is more often used to identify those North Koreans operating behind United Nations lines on behalf of the Communists. The stories of these operations are complex and the intention here is simply to identify those operations for which we have some information.

Department of Defense, *Dictionary of Military and Associated Terms.* Washington, D.C.: GPO, January 2007.

William B. Breuer, *Shadow Warriors: The Covert War in Korea.* New York: Wiley, 1996.

Ed Evanhoe, *Dark Moon: Eighth Army Special Operations in the Korean War.* Annapolis, MD: Naval Institute Press, 1995.

Michael Haas, *In the Devil's Shadow: UN Special Operations During the Korean War.* Annapolis, MD: Naval Institute Press, 2000, p. 111.

Frank Holober, *Raiders of the China Coast: Covert Operations During the Korean War.* Annapolis, MD, Naval Institute Press, 1999.

Operation Alcatraz 12 March 1952

Little is known of this operation other than it was a well-defined reconnaissance landing made at a small enemy-held island in the territory just south of the Suwon Dam lighthouse. The landings of Operation Alcatraz went smoothly and the mission was accomplished with limited casualties.

Charles Givens, *Memoirs*, Center for the Study of the Korean War.

Operation Aviary 26 September 1950

Operation Aviary got underway as a limited mission right after General MacArthur's invasion at Inchon. It would expand to be the operational name for a vast, but limited-success clandestine service. It had the identified mission of meeting the needs for the highly secret process of training Koreans for insertion into North Korea. The missions on which they were sent would soon claim the life of almost every graduate of this school. Because of its airport emphasis, it was termed Operation Aviary.

The first mission came as a result of the success of the landing at Inchon. The Communists seemed to have just faded away following the fall of Seoul, and it was necessary to find out where they were. On the night of 26 September 1950, nine teams carried on two U.S. Air Force C-47s flew from South Taegu in southern Korea to enemy territory. Five of the men were deposited in one drop zone, four in the other. The locations were such that they were in proximity of the main evacuation routes. Within a few days eight of the nine agents reported back on their findings. The first mission was deemed a complete success.

Aviary soon went on to perform many missions, all carried out with courage and determination. But they were not all successful, and some turned out to be very dangerous. One, in particular, displayed the inherent danger faced in all operations. On this jump one of the members, who was in fact a Chinese agent, turned as he parachuted from the plane and lobbed a live grenade into the forward cabin section. The explosion killed or seriously wounded the four remaining team members, as well as their American handler. Captain Lawrence E. Burger remained at the control of the burning plane long enough for the last to parachute.

Michael Haas, *In the Devil's Shadow: U.N. Special Operations During the Korean War.* Annapolis, MD: Naval Institute Press, 2000, pp. 19–22.

Operation Beehive   25 May 1953

This plan, in association with **Operation Camel**, was designed to maintain units in North Korea after the close of the war in order to continue to disrupt government functions. It called for separate groups of 124 partisans to be sent into North Korea just prior to the cease-fire agreement. There they were to remain dormant until after the truce had been signed. Once the fighting had stopped they were to infiltrate North Korean military groups and civilian offices in order to develop a network of agents who, when called upon, could cause disruption in the Communist government. Operation Beehive commenced on 26 May 1953 and continued until February 1954. During that time 102 partisans were sent across the Demilitarized Zone. When reporting to headquarters, they said that had been able to recruit an additional 674 who were willing to serve as members of their underground team.

Ben S. Malcom and Ron Martz, *White Tigers: My Secret War in North Korea.* Washington, D.C.: Brassey's, 1996, p. 188.

Operation Big Boy   2 September 1951

A fifty man Kirkland partisan force, identified as Operation Big Boy, was sent into the Kumgang Mountain area to establish an inland operation. Landed by the USS *Begor*, they headed into the mountains undetected. There were some initial successes but they did not last a long time. Most of those selected for Big Boy were not from the area and were not well prepared to fit into the areas where they were dropped, despite the fact they were supposed to provide for their own supplies. By the end of the month the group had been reduced to fifteen, a result of some casualties and several desertions. Despite asking to be withdrawn, the group was left in place to act as a reception body for intelligence agents coming in. Shortly after, the remainder of the group either defected or was killed. Aircraft continued dropping supplies for some time, but radio contact was soon lost.

Ed Evanhoe, *Dark Moon: Eighth Army Special Operations in the Korean War.* Annapolis, MD: Naval Institute Press, 1995, pp. 80–84, 138–140.

Operation Blossom   Winter 1950

Hans Tofte's Office of Policy Coordination (OPC) began Operation Blossom in the winter of 1950. The OPC was set up to direct covert psychological operations and was activated in 1948 by the National Security Council. They were absorbed by the Central Intelligence Agency in 1951. This operation was designed to develop a general resistance warfare group. It envisioned selected North Korean refugees who would be returned to their homes in North Korea, where they would form resistance groups designed to operate indefinitely in Communist held territory. It was assumed they would receive unlimited support from cooperative civilians in the area. Originally seen as a fairly passive resistance network, they eventually became a more heavily armed and aggressive group. A good number of the Operation Blossom teams were sent into central and northeast Korea during the following year. The Blossom operators had mixed luck; some were lost immediately upon re-entry, while others managed to survive through October of 1951.

By January 1952, the lack of adequate intelligence and limited communications caused the agency to come to the conclusion that most, if not all, of the groups had either been captured or compromised. By September 1952 it was determined that if any groups were still operating, they had undoubtedly been doubled by the Communists. The fate of the team was finally settled when a defecting Communist confirmed that the teams in his area had indeed been doubled. The contacts were terminated and the teams not heard from again.

Michael Haas, *In the Devil's Shadow: U.N. Special Operations During the Korean War.* Annapolis, MD: Naval Institute Press, 2000.

Operation Boxer   7 February 1953

All of the Boxer operations were carried out by the Central Intelligence Agency, Special Operations Group, Joint Assistance Commission, Korea (SOG-JACK). These teams were parachuted in on specially assigned missions and then evacuated when the job was done. Each of the units consisted of twelve men. While most records concerning the Boxer drops are unavailable, Ed Evanhoe suggests that they were an American-led Korean partisan team. During Operation Boxer I (7 February), the entry team was dropped along the east coast above Hungnam and about forty miles south of Vladivostok, Siberia. Their mission was to disrupt rail lines carrying supplies between North Korea and the Soviet Union.

Douglas Dillard, *Operation Aviary: Airborne Special Operations in Korea, 1950–1953.* Victoria, B.C.: Trafford, 2003.

Operation Boxer II   7 February 1953

This operation had as its mission a disruption of the main supply route and rail line that ran close to Tong-ni, a coastal town northeast of Yongdae-ri. Though there is no further disclosure of the operation, it is believed all involved were evacuated successfully.

Douglas Dillard, *Operation Aviary: Airborne Special Operations in Korea, 1950–1953.* Victoria, B.C.: Trafford, 2003.
Ed Evanhoe, *Dark Moon: Eighth Army Special Operations in the Korean War.* Annapolis, MD: Naval Institute Press, 1995, p.159.

Operation Boxer III   9 February 1953

Unlike the others, Operation Boxer III was dropped twenty miles farther northeast and up the coast near Tanchon. Best evidence is that all agents were withdrawn successfully.

Douglas Dillard, *Operation Aviary: Airborne Special Operations in Korea, 1950–1953.* Victoria, B.C.: Trafford, 2003.

Ed Evanhoe, *Dark Moon: Eighth Army Special Operations in the Korean War.* Annapolis, MD: Naval Institute Press, 1995, p. 159.

Operation Boxer IV 11 February 1953

This operation landed the agents on the east coast northeast of Hungnam. The best available evidence is that the raids were successful and that team members were evacuated by U.S. Navy vessels.

Douglas Dillard, *Operation Aviary: Airborne Special Operations in Korea, 1950–1953.* Victoria, B.C.: Trafford, 2003.

Ed Evanhoe, *Dark Moon: Eighth Army Special Operations in the Korean War.* Annapolis, MD: Naval Institute Press, 1995, p.159.

Operation Broken Reed

January 1952

According to author and survivor Lieutenant Arthur L. Boyd (lieutenant colonel, U.S. Army retired), Operation Broken Reed was a secret mission into North Korea on the orders of President Harry Truman. President Truman, it was suggested, felt it was necessary to have first hand information about the intentions of the People's Republic of China. Boyd, who served as a cryptographer, was part of a team that consisted of Army Rangers, Navy Frogmen, Air Force officers, and CIA operatives who disguised themselves as the captured crew of a B-29 bomber. Transported by Chinese Nationalists, wearing the uniforms of the Chinese Communists and posing as guards, the party was able to move across North Korea gathering information about troop strength, weapons, displacement and most of all, trying to assess the intentions of the Chinese Communist Forces and the involvement of the Soviet Union.

Despite the fact that seven of the team were killed, the mission was considered a great success. The group was able to determine that the Chinese involvement was serious, and that there was increasing evidence of a massive Chinese and Soviet buildup, even the possibility of atomic weapons. This information was vital to President Truman as he tried to avoid any expansion of the deadly events in Korea. Eventually picked up by helicopter, Boyd and one other man were taken out. The second man died, leaving Boyd as the only survivor from the mission. Sworn to secrecy, he held his story for half a century, only to release his information in the 2007 publication from Da Capo Press.

As there was only one survivor, and fully aware that the government would not make available any records of such an operation if it had occurred, we are left to judge the story on the basis of evidence provided in Boyd's book, and in his 2008 oral presentation at the Center for the Study of the Korean War annual conference at the Truman Library.

Arthur L. Boyd, *Operation Broken Reed: Truman's Secret North Korean Spy Mission That Averted World War III.* Philadelphia: Da Capo Press, 2007.

Arthur L. Boyd, "Broken Reed." Manuscript of speech delivered to the Center for the Study of the Korean War 8th Annual Conference, Truman Library, 26 February 2007. Copy available at the center.

Operation Camel 27 July 1953

The plan, associated with **Operation Beehive**, was designed to maintain units in North Korea after the close of the war in order to disrupt the functioning of the North Korean government. It called for separate groups of 114 partisans to be sent into North Korea just prior to the cease-fire agreement. There they were to remain dormant until after the signing of the truce agreement. Once the fighting had stopped they were to infiltrate North Korean military groups and civilian offices in order to develop a network of agents who, when called upon, could harass and disrupt. Operation Camel started on 27 July 1953 and ran until it was disbanded in February 1954. During that time

102 partisans were sent across the Demilitarized Zone. They reported success in their mission, but in this case it is very hard to know what that means.

Ed Evanhoe, *Dark Moon: Eighth Army Special Operations in the Korean War.* Annapolis, MD: Naval Institute Press, 1995, p. 166–167.
Ben S. Malcom and Ron Martz, *White Tigers: My Secret War in North Korea.* Washington, D.C.: Brassey's, 1996, p. 188.

Operation Green Dragon
25 January 1953

One of the largest behind-the-lines parachute drops among the partisan groups during the Korean War, Operation Green Dragon was an enterprise of the Combined Command Reconnaissance Activities Korea (CCRAK), and included ninety-seven partisans. They parachuted from five C-47s into the mountainous area of the west of Kokchang, a town 40 miles west of Pyongyang. The landings were a second drop in the zone of **Operation Spitfire.** The mission was to establish semi-permanent bases for future operations, and at first it seemed to have been pulled off successfully. The group was later augmented by an additional fifty-six partisans. Command received a transmission saying that five downed airmen were with the unit and a rescue pick up was considered, but when the rescue effort was attempted, the plane came under fire and the rescue operation was cancelled. For seven months supplies were dropped and sporadic radio communication maintained. But after the last drop, suspicions began to be raised about who was left and what they were doing. Then, communications faltered and finally stopped all together. No Green Dragon partisan agent was ever returned to the United Nations lines.

Ed Evanhoe, *Dark Moon: Eighth Army Special Operations in the Korean War.* Annapolis, MD: Naval Institute Press, 1995, pp. 158–159.

Operation Haul Ass
20–22 February 1954

The night of 20–21 February 1954 was well below zero and a light snow was falling. It was seven months after the signing of the armistice and in an area that definitely belonged to North Korea. Operation Haul Ass was a clandestine mission designed to clear up loose ends. It began as two 50-foot patrol boats moved slowly across the Han River Estuary during the night. Just before 2400 hours they reached a point 200 yards off the coast at Haenam-ni, North Korea. Pulling in as close as they could, they quickly boarded thirty-two survivors who had been members of the failed **Operation Beehive**, a stay-behind mission that had gone astray. At 0043 hours the boats pulled out, bringing an end to Operation Haul Ass, and ending the last operational mission of the United Nations Partisan Infantry Korea (8240th Army Unit).

Charles Givens, *Memoirs,* Center for the Study of the Korean War.

Operation Hurricane   30 March 1953

This was a five member radio team that was dropped on the night of 30–31 March 1953 with the assignment to establish a partisan base in the mountains southeast of Anju. The team was able to make contact shortly after landing. Two days later the Operation Hurricane team reported that they had been spotted and asked that they be evacuated by helicopter. The request was turned down by CCRAK on the belief that any helicopter operating overland in or near Red China would most likely be destroyed. Team Hurricane was last heard from on 5 April 1953.

Ed Evanhoe, *Dark Moon: Eighth Army Special Operations in the Korean War.* Annapolis, MD: Naval Institute Press, 1995, p. 159.

Operation Jesse James
28 December 1952

This was one of the final operations of the

war. It took place in three phases (I, II, III) on 28 December with a team consisting of ten men. The drop was in the mountainous region southeast of Sariwon and near the Pyongyang-Kaeson railroad. The team was built around a radio operator and was sent to augment Donkey units already in the area. The plane carrying Operation Jesse James I developed mechanical troubles and had to return. It was rescheduled and dropped on the following night (29 December 1952). Nothing was heard from the team members after that, but the Donkey team, including the radio operator, came out of North Korea a few weeks prior to the cease fire.

Ben S. Malcom and Ron Martz, *White Tigers: My Secret War in North Korea*. Washington, D.C.: Brassey's, 1996.

Operation Leopard   January 1951

The core of partisan operations in Korea, Operation Leopard, was central to the expanded use of those fleeing from North Korea. Thousands who were being driven out of the territory now held by the North Koreans and Chinese had moved out to the islands that dotted the western coastline. Seeing these as a potential military asset, small groups of partisans were organized in January 1951 as Attrition Sections under the Guerrilla Section, Eighth Army G-3 (Miscellaneous).

Force Able, a six man cadre, was created with the code name Operation Leopard. The leaders suggested that the group be named Leopard, explaining that the leopard hunts its prey with stealth, kills quickly, and makes a speedy exit. The small units, the teams that would carry on the individual missions, were called Donkeys. Here the idea was that donkeys are stubborn, tenacious, are able to carry large loads for long period of time, and they kick hard when they are harassed.

Leopard set up on the east coast island of Paengnyong-do. The partisans were to infiltrate, blow bridges, destroy roads and railways,

and ambush Chinese detachments. Leopard's seaborne and interior operations began to produce results as infiltration teams made contact with other partisan groups already operating within North Korean territory. While the extent of their success is hard to evaluate, there is certainly evidence that these operations made it necessary for the Communists to divert troops from badly needed front line commands to deal with the attacks. The unit expanded to more than 8,000 men and women by June 1951. In January 1952 **Operation Wolfpack** was formed out of the eastern part of Leopard's area. Later, on 11 November 1952, Operation Leopard along with Operation Wolfpack and Task Force Scannon (originally Kirkland) were redefined as U.S. Partisan Infantry Regiments, 8240 AU, Korea.

Ben S. Malcom and Ron Martz, *White Tigers: My Secret War in North Korea*. Washington, D.C.: Brassey's, 1996, pp. 125–129.

Operation Mustang I   July 1951

The Mustang operations were designed to send teams into occupied territory to rescue United Nations prisoners of war. Central to this planning was the desire to rescue General William Dean, U.S. 24th Infantry Division commander, who had been taken during the retreat from Taejon. Operation Mustang I planned to parachute in troops from Baker Section, take the camp where he was being held, free all the prisoners, and escape by means of a helicopter launched from a ship off shore. The original plan was cancelled in July 1951.

Ed Evanhoe, *Dark Moon: Eighth Army Special Operations in the Korean War*. Annapolis, MD: Naval Institute Press, 1995, pp. 117–23, 157–58.

Operation Mustang II
September 1951

Operation Mustang II was based on much the same plan as **Mustang I**, and was designed to rescue some prisoners of war, including General William Dean, commander, U.S. 24th Infantry Division. The plan, which had been approved by Far East Command Headquarters, was drawn up in early September. It was to be a parachute drop sending in troops who would take control of the camp where Dean was being held, free him and the other prisoners, and escape by helicopter launched from off shore. The mission was cancelled after persons who were aware of the preparations for the raid crashed in North Korean territory and it was assumed the mission had been compromised.

Ed Evanhoe, *Dark Moon: Eighth Army Special Operations in the Korean War.* Annapolis, MD: Naval Institute Press, 1995, pp. 117–23, 157–58.

Operation Mustang III
2 January 1952

Launched by Baker Section, Operation Mustang III was organized as a nineteen member Korean partisan operation. They were to contact a group that had been freelancing in northwest Korea (Donkey 15) in order to provide radio contact with **Operation Leopard** and to offer advanced training in sabotage. A part of their job was to contact prisoners of war and try and establish some escape and evasion routes from these camps. By this time, however, General William Dean had dropped from sight and was not heard from again until he was turned over during **Operation Big Switch**. The flight went down near Wonsan, North Korea, when the last man in the team threw a grenade into the C-47 as he exited. M/Sgt. Davis T. Harrison was badly wounded but he and Corporal George Tatarkis managed to jump. Both were captured. Harrison was released in 1953 but Tatarkis was not heard from again. Radio contact was lost with the group just a few days after the drop.

Ed Evanhoe, *Dark Moon: Eighth Army Special Operations in the Korean War.* Annapolis, MD: Naval Institute Press, 1995, pp. 117–23, 157–58.

Operation Mustang IV
16 March 1952

This operation was launched on 16 March 1952 in far northwestern North Korea. The sixteen man crew was sent with the same general mission as **Mustang III**, but placed in a somewhat different area. Their job was to cut the railway that was serving as the main enemy supply route, and as an added duty to gather information about American prisoners being held at Camp Two, just southwest of Chongsongjin. The team landed successfully and operated for six days before they were either killed or captured.

Ed Evanhoe, *Dark Moon: Eighth Army Special Operations in the Korean War.* Annapolis, MD: Naval Institute Press, 1995, pp. 117–23, 157–58.

Operation Mustang V   14 May 1952

This was launched with **Operation Mustang VI** but dropped into an area near the rail junction of Kanggye. The unit had the assignment of establishing escape and evasion routes for American prisoners of war. There was no contact with the party after it dropped.

Ed Evanhoe, *Dark Moon: Eighth Army Special Operations in the Korean War.* Annapolis, MD: Naval Institute Press, 1995, pp. 117–23, 157–58.

Operation Mustang VI   15 May 1952

In conjunction with **Mustang V**, men were dropped farther south, but the ten man crew had the same assignment: develop escape and evasion routes for prisoners of war. There was no contact with the party after it was dropped.

Ed Evanhoe, *Dark Moon: Eighth Army Special Operations in the Korean War.* Annapolis, MD: Naval Institute Press, 1995, pp. 117–23, 157–58.

Operation Mustang VII
24 October 1952

This five man crew was dropped in the vicinity of prisoner of war camps in far northern North Korea. There was some initial success for a few days and then headquarters lost all contact with the members of the group.

Ed Evanhoe, *Dark Moon: Eighth Army Special Operations in the Korean War.* Annapolis, MD: Naval Institute Press, 1995, pp. 117–23, 157–58.

Operation Mustang VIII
24 October 1952

In this case a six man crew was dropped near a rail junction located on the Chongchon River about twenty-five miles north of Anju. They successfully dropped, but then there were no more transmissions and it was reported that they had all been killed or captured.

Ed Evanhoe, *Dark Moon: Eighth Army Special Operations in the Korean War.* Annapolis, MD: Naval Institute Press, 1995, pp. 117–23, 157–58.

Operation Pappy   12 June 1953

The final cease-fire agreement, when signed, would return many of the occupied islands to the Communists. With the end of the conflict it was necessary to withdraw partisans who were stationed on them, and then proceed to demobilization. The effort to do this was called Operation Pappy. It called for CCRAK (Combined Command for Reconnaissance Activities, Korea) and the Guerrilla Division of the 8240th Army Unit to pull all partisans off the mainland and the islands north of the 38th parallel twenty-four hours before the truce was signed. The order went out and partisans began to withdraw only to be told the next day that they had to go back and retake the islands. The armistice agreement had not been signed as they had anticipated, and it was necessary to try and re-establish their positions. In most cases this was not successful and they suffered heavy causalities in the effort.

U.S. Navy helicopter delivering supplies to partisans on off-shore islands (Center for the Study of the Korean War).

Even when the armistice was signed it was very difficult to get the partisans to withdraw. More than a few wanted to stay and fight. The U.S. Army gave them a choice. They could withdraw and continue to receive support until they came under the jurisdiction of the ROK Army, or they could remain on the island without support, on their own, and most likely would become stateless refugees.

The evacuation of the partisans and their families was no small job; an estimated 10,000 partisans lived on the islands and more than 3,000 of them had their families with them. The withdrawal was set in stages, first from the smaller islands to consolidation points, then on to one of the five islands partisans were allowed to occupy according to the truce agreement: Paengnyong-do, Taechong-do, Sochong-do, Yangpyong-do, and U-do. The evacuation required dozens of vessels; LSTs, junks, and even minesweepers were involved. Tensions tended to run fairly high as the partisans were slowly disarmed and returned to South Korea. A significant number deserted rather than be drafted into the ROK Army. Some eventually returned to North Korea.

Michael Haas, *In the Devil's Shadow: U.N. Special Operations During the Korean War.* Annapolis, MD: Naval Institute Press, 2000, p. 61.

Ben S. Malcom and Ron Martz, *White Tigers: My Secret War with North Korea.* Washington, D.C: Brassey's, 1996, p. 188.

Operation Quicksilver   February 1954

Operation Quicksilver was a wrap-up operation designed as an orderly dismissal of the more than twenty-thousand partisans who fought with the United Nations against North Korea. The hope was that the majority could be integrated into units of the Republic of Korea Army. The operation was established for several highly significant reasons, not the least of which was, regardless of their service to the United Nations, the partisans were dan-

gerous individuals whose loyalty was never clearly known. While the government wanted to take full advantage of the special skills these men had learned, especially in unconventional warfare, to strengthen the Republic of Korea (ROK) forces, it was also important that the individuals be identified so that if they joined ROK units the commanders could avoid difficulties that might arise. ROK commanders were warned not to include more than seven of the partisans in any unit for fear that might "corrupt" the unit. They were also warned not to place them too near rear areas from which they might desert the group.

The heart of the operation was the orderly, and honorable discharge of any partisan who had given two or more years of service. In return for their service they were to be given a uniform, mess gear, four blankets, two hundred pounds of rice and transportation to any place they wished in South Korea. The U.S. Army released the men from service requiring only that they turn in their weapons and, for some reason never explained, their canteen cups.

The operation was finally completed in March 1954 during which time the number of partisans had dwindled with desertions, transfers, and discharges. Of the 22,000 men under arms, fewer than 10,000 actually entered the ROK Army.

Ben S. Malcom and Ron Martz, *White Tigers: My Secret War in North Korea.* Washington: Brassey's, 1996.

Operation Rabbit I   31 March 1953

The third largest parachute drop of the Korean War, and one of the final two partisan airborne missions behind enemy lines to take place during the war, was Operation Rabbit I. The rather ambitious operation was designed with two missions: first to conduct sabotage, and second to establish stay-behind units southwest of Wonsan and northeast of Pyonggang. The operation consisted of two groups of twenty partisans each. The first group was dropped about thirty miles west of Hungnam. The second group parachuted into the vicinity of Sogo-ri and near the Wonsan-Pyongyang railway. After the drop no one from the group was ever heard of again.

Ben S. Malcom and Ron Martz, *White Tigers: My Secret War in North Korea*. Washsington, D.C.: Brassey's, 1996, 136.

Operation Rabbit II   7 April 1953

This was a follow up on **Operation Rabbit I**, the largest of the partisan drops behind enemy lines to take place during the war. It was itself the final drop set up by the Combined Command Reconnaissance Activities, Korea, 8240th AU. Operation Rabbit II was a six man augmentation to Rabbit I and was dropped into a zone near the town of Kangdong. It had the same general mission — sabotage and stay-behind sites — but neither the members of this team, nor of Rabbit I, were ever heard from again.

Ben S. Malcom and Ron Martz, *White Tigers: My Secret War in North Korea*. Washington, D.C.: Brassey's, 1996, 136.

Operation Rabbits   Late 1950s

This is one of those historical occasions about which there is a lot of information but almost no verification. Because it keeps coming up in Korean War literature, Operation Rabbits is discussed here. The operation apparently was established in order to parachute South Korean actresses and models into North Korean territory. Their mission was to attach themselves as concubines to high ranking North Korean or Chinese officers, thereby to extract information from them. When successful they would return to UN lines, give the special password, and be taken for debriefing. The source of this information identifies a pilot named Heine Aderholt who claims that he dropped some of the "Rabbits"

and a Lieutenant Robert Brewers, a man understood to be their handler. Aderholt admits that there were no records of any kind kept during this operation. There is no doubt that Heine Aderholt, who later became a brigadier general, was an intriguing character and that he flew missions for Operation Aviary. Unfortunately he passed away before being able to clarify this information. There is no record of this operation in the works of two of the major historians of clandestine activities, Ed Evanhoe or Michael Haas.

Lance Zedric entry, *Korean War Educator*; www.koreanwar-educator.org/home.

Operation Red Frog   October 1952

Not all operations conducted were all that serious, of course, and one such operation emerged from the treacherous boredom that accompanied so many of the clandestine forces. It was a fact that when not engaged in convert action, or planning for it, there really was very little to do. One such action was Operation Red Frog. It emerged out of the October 1952 charge that had been leveled by the Communists that the United States was involved in germ warfare. They were, the Communists insisted, dropping lice and other bacteria related bugs. When Admiral C. Turner Joy, the U.S. delegate, asked the Communists for evidence, they very seriously displayed three frogs painted an international orange. The frogs were not afflicted with any dangerous disease, but it was true, they had been painted and dropped by the U.S.

A month or so before, several large wooden crates and eight small, fairly light boxes had been delivered by a C-46 that landed at K-16. It was addressed to the Aviary Officer. The boxes were delivered to the 8240th AU orderly room and the crates to the mess hall, where it was discovered they contained Kirn Beer. After enjoying some of the success of **Operation**

Vice Admiral C. Turner Joy, senior UN delegate to armistice negotiations (Joseph Adams Collection: Center for the Study of the Korean War).

Amber Liquid, the men turned their attention to the cardboard boxes, which, it was discovered, contained small cases attached to a small parachute with a frog in each one. The frogs contained within had all been painted orange, and sometime around midnight the first of the cases went out the door of a C-46 flying over Chinnampo. Other cases followed there, and then later over Pyongyang.

Ed Evanhoe, *Dark Moon: Eighth Army Special Operations in the Korean War*. Annapolis, MD: Naval Institute Press, 1995.

Operation Salamander   July 1950

Operation Salamander was the name given to overall covert seaborne operations set up for long-range insertion into North Korean territory. The operations, and even the success or failure of these missions, are even more obscure than those of **Operation Aviary**, with whom these missions worked. They were conducted by partisans supported by a minimum of U.S. and Air Force personnel. They operated among the thousands of miles of coast, particularly among the small uninhabited islands off North Korea's western coastline within easy distance of the mainland. The islands were far too many for the Communists to occupy and they became excellent platforms for the agents who were sent inland to conduct both reconnaissance and sabotage.

The operation was particularly useful during the desperate fighting around Pusan in July to September 1950, but were also active prior to and immediately after the Inchon invasion. Both then and later, the most difficult problem the Salamander operations faced was the scarcity of boats necessary to accomplish their missions. Admiral Sohn Won-yil, commander in chief of the South Korean Navy, reportedly loaned a single fishing boat so that reconnaissance work could be done during the fighting at Pusan, but Salamander, like Aviary, became more effective after the Inchon landing, where the North Korean geography proved to be more friend than enemy. It was not until later that U.S. Navy harbor patrol boats and some U.S. Air Force crash boats were made available for insertion and retrieval work. The key to their success, however, was the commitment of the handful of men and women who undertook such missions. Michael Haas makes this comment about them: "Venturing forth as spies with only the poorest of equipment and training provided by the Americans, they performed well beyond any standard that could possibly have been expected from those who sent them."

There were a couple of reasons for Salamander having a somewhat better experience than Operation Aviary. The first is that the operatives never ventured too far away from the United Nations controlled islands so that escape could be arranged when necessary. A second reason is that the Commonwealth warships, assigned to protect these off-shore activities, were extremely effective in getting in and out. Whatever was the reason, later reports conclude that the rate of Salamander agent returns "never dropped below 90 percent and the number and value of [Salamander] reports easily equaled those of Operation Aviary."

Michael E. Haas, *In the Devil's Shadow: UN Special Operations During the Korean War*. Annapolis, MD: Naval Institute Press, 2000, p. 31.

Operation Shining Moon
4 March 1951

Very little is available about this operation other than it was launched in support of **Operation Killer**. Partisans from William Able's Donkey 4 (later Leopard Base) were responsible for conducting Operation Shining Moon.

Clay Blair, *The Forgotten War: American in Korea 1950–1953*. New York: Times Books, 1987, pp. 228–229.

Operation Spitfire 18 June 1951

This was one of the few of Eighth Army's Baker Section airdrops to take place during 1951. Based on the same plan as **Operation Virginia I**, this one included American, British, and Korean participants. However, unlike Virginia, this was not a slash and burn mission, but rather an effort to establish a long-term guerrilla base deep in Communist territory in Central Korea. In Operation Spitfire, the Far East Command Liaison group parachuted on 18 June 1951, dropping an advanced pathfinder team consisting of two Americans, one British and two Koreans. They were joined a week later by nine additional Koreans, an American, and a British officer. The operation was commanded by Captain Ellery Anderson.

The assignment turned out to be far more difficult than anyone anticipated. In the first place, the Caucasians were not free to move about within the population and lacking lan-

guage skills were not able to help in securing food and supplies from the local citizens. Contrary to what the crew had been led to believe, there seemed to be no popular support for the raid at all. The team was decimated in less than a week and Operation Spitfire broke up.

Fearing exposure from local groups and already running out of supplies, the group called for a supply mission. When it came it proved their undoing. Searching for a spot to drop the supplies, the air crews alerted the Communists to the presence of the group. And then, when the planes dropped the supplies, they dropped them right on top of the camp, giving it away immediately. The agents were attacked at dawn the following day by a Chinese battalion. Some team members managed to get away as they scattered. A few managed to get back on 25 July to UN lines being held by the 25th Infantry Division. Six of the Koreans, one American — SFC William T. Miles — and one British team member were never heard from again.

The abortion of this operation, like Operation Virginia, led to a discussion within Miscellaneous Group regarding the viability of future parachute drop groups. Agreement was reached to continue the operation, but not to send either American or British members along.

Ed Evanhoe, *Dark Moon: Eighth Army Special Operations in the Korean War*. Annapolis, MD: Naval Institute Press, 1995, pp. 103–116.
Michael Haas, *In the Devil's Shadow: U.N. Special Operations During the Korean War*. Annapolis, MD: Naval Institute Press, 2000, p. 57–60.
Ben S. Malcom and Ron Martz, *White Tigers: My Secret War in North Korea*. Washington, D.C.: Brassey's, 1996.

Operation Stole January 1951

The Central Intelligence Agency received hard evidence that the Chinese Communists had chartered a Norwegian freighter and dispatched it to Bombay, India, where it took on a full cargo of medical supplies provided by the Indian government. Despite his loud claims of neutrality, Prime Minister Jawaharlal Nehru gave frequent verbal support to the Chinese, but now his actions were offering more material help. Norway, on the other hand, was a member of the United Nations, and while voicing its commitment to neutrality allowed its ships to be used in trade. The medical equipment was enough to outfit three hospitals complete with surgeons, physicians, nurses and other medical personnel and their gear. The supplies also included much needed medical and food stuffs.

The impact that such a boost might have on Chinese Communist morale, and the military effect of such an improved morale, were too much. It was believed that it might eventually cost thousands of American lives. Something had to be done, but what? The nations involved were neutral countries and whatever was done had to be free of any suspicion that America was involved. The U.S. had avoided declaring a blockade against China because of the British position, for they still traded with China as a means of protecting Hong Kong.

Both the Navy and the Air Force were ruled out because it would be far too easy to identify their involvement, though both participated in monitoring the movements of the cargo ship. If the ship entered a North Korean port then it could be bombed, but on the high seas there was little that could be legally done. The job, therefore, was given to the CIA, who gave it to Hans V. Tofte, a Danish-American with a remarkable history during World War II. He put together Operation TP Stole (TP was the CIA designation for Korean War Operations).

Tofte enlisted the aid of Generalissimo Chiang Kai-shek, with whom he had worked during World War II, and with the Chinese's help several CIA agents moved out to sea. With the Americans remaining below, Nationalist Chinese boarding parties took command of the freighter, transferred the cargo to their own ships, and the crew of the Norwegian freighter was allowed to sail their empty ship away. The medical staff was not heard from again. Operation Stole was a great success.

William B. Breuer, *Shadow Warriors: The Covert War in Korea*. New York: John Wiley and Sons, 1996, pp. 128–29.
Joseph C. Goulden, *Korea: The Untold Story of the War*. New York: Times Books, 1982.

Operation Storm Trooper

Guerrilla operations Commander Lieutenant Colonel J. D. Vanderpool discovered a supply of German World War II SS uniforms, including the rifles and pistols, in a supply room in Seoul, Korea. He had no idea where they came from, but at the same time had no intention of letting them go to waste. When he leaned of a raid being planned against the mainland to be led by Captain George Lamm, he suggested that they might arrive at their mission as a fully equipped SS Squad. Two weeks later, at dawn, a C-46 flew over Haeju, North Korea, and fourteen parachutists floated to the ground. Captain Lamm and his Wolfpack 6 reconnaissance force linked up with the bogus SS troopers some three hours later. For twelve hours the costumed men had moved about North Korea confusing many and taking twelve prisoners. The next night all the men linked up with waiting boats and made it back to their own lines. According to Ed Evanhoe, the Soviet ambassador handed a mystified West German ambassador a formal complaint charging German troops in Korea.

Ed Evanhoe, *Dark Moon: Eighth Army Special Operations in the Korean War*. Annapolis, MD: Naval Institute Press, 1995.

Operation Tropic   April 1952

A Central Intelligence Agency operation, this plan parachuted spies and guerrillas into Chinese Communist territory, mostly in Liaoning and Kirin, the Manchurian provinces through which the Communists were sending Chinese troops and supplies.

The agents worked for the Far East Development Company, a CIA front. Operation Tropic was the code name for CIA covert operations in which the Civil Air Transport (CAT) crews operated out of Atsug Naval Air Station in Japan. CAT was the CIA air transport service established in August 1950. They were trained for parachute jumps, instructed on radio and explosives, and taught the use of small arms, and then dropped into virgin territory to start guerrilla activities. The missions began in April 1952 and the first teams were dropped by C-47s, DC-4s, and B-17s into Manchuria. The efforts were not highly successful and many of the first units to land were caught, interrogated and imprisoned.

Two of those caught were men who occupied prime leadership positions, John T. Downey and Richard G. Fecteau. When captured they were tried by the Chinese and imprisoned. In December 1971 Fecteau was released after serving nineteen of his twenty year sentence. In 1972 when President Nixon made his trip to China he asked about Downey and admitted that he had been a CIA agent. Once the Americans had "admitted their crime," the Communists released Downey on 12 March 1973 after he had served twenty-one years of a life sentence.

William B. Breuer, *Shadow Warriors: The Covert War in Korea.* New York: John Wiley and Sons, 1996, pp. 215–218, 240.

William Leary, *Perilous Missions: Civil Air Transportation and CIA Covert Operations in Asia.* Washington, D.C.: Smithsonian Institution Press, 2002.

Operation Trudy Jackson

September 1950

Operation Trudy Jackson was one of the more remarkable stories to come out of the Korean War. A reconnaissance mission sponsored by the Central Intelligence Agency and the American Military Intelligence, it began a week prior to the attack on Inchon. Led by Navy Lieutenant Eugene Franklin Clark, a small group that included some Royal Marines, members of the South Korean police force, some South Korean naval personnel

under Lieutenant Youn Joung Ski, and partisans landed at Yonghung-do and Taemui-do. The ROK had put men ashore two weeks earlier and discovered that the island was undefended. Clark organized some of the Korean civilians into what he called the Young Men's Association. Both islands were located in Flying Fish Channel on the approach to Inchon.

Clark was an old "China Hand," an ex petty officer who was well versed in life in Korea. Once ashore, Clark and his band were able to collect information and relay it back to the forces preparing for the invasion. Using locals, he provided information about tides, mudflats, seawalls, and details on what enemy fortifications had been established. He and his crew ran daily mine patrols to be sure that the Communists were not mining Flying Fish Channel. Paramount to his investigation was the height of the tides and the extent of the mudflats. The maps of the area were not well done, and more exact readings were necessary if the invasion fleet was to land troops and still get back for the second round. Ironically, the best maps, he discovered, were those made by the Japanese.

When the North Koreans got wind of what was going on, they sent a small sixteen-man detachment to investigate the island. Clark's men mounted a .50 caliber machine gun on the bow of a motorized sampan and in a short battle were able to kill all the enemy soldiers. However, the intelligence was not without cost. The North Koreans were reported to have killed 50 civilians later because they were believed to have helped Clark.

Among other things, Clark discovered a lighthouse on Palmi-do which stood on top of a 219 foot peak that overlooked Inchon Harbor. He lit the beacon the night before the invasion fleet — the UN attack transports and their support — were making their way up Flying Fish Channel, thus giving them a beacon to aid in navigation. Lieutenant Clark received the Silver Star and the Legion of Merit for his contribution.

William B. Breuer, *Shadow Warriors: The Covert War in Korea.* New York: John Wiley and Sons, 1996, pp. 69, 77, 82–83.

Thomas Fleming, *Secrets of Inchon: The Untold Story of the Most Daring Covert Mission of the Korean War.* G.P. Putnam and Sons, 2002.

Operation Virginia I   15 March 1951

Four U.S. Army Rangers and twenty recruits from the Republic of Korean Army's officer candidate school launched Operation Virginia I on 15 March 1951. While there was a great deal of interest in harassing the Communist troops in the area, and in aiding the interdiction of supplies behind the lines, in this particular case the launch was neither well planned nor executed. Michael E. Haas describes it best: "Even with the benefit of a half century of hindsight, the Virginia I and Spitfire missions still appear to be a sorry spectacle of U.S. Army leadership at its worst."

The Korean segment of this group had only been with Baker Section for ten days, with no previous training, and for reasons of security it had been necessary to replace their more familiar leader, 1st Lieutenant Bob Brewer, who was considered to be in possession of too much sensitive information to be risked. To add to their troubles the leaderless team was dropped into an unmarked zone (later to be acknowledged as eight miles south of the correct zone) during the night and in fresh deep snow. After a long march they arrived at the location of the anticipated target, a North Korean railroad tunnel that ran inland from the coastline. It was supposed to be isolated and poorly guarded, but quick reconnaissance showed that the area was so heavily guarded that any attempt seemed unreasonable. Deciding not to complete the assignment, the group spent nearly two weeks trying to get back to the extraction point. Finally, on 30 March, helicopters sent by the U.S. Navy extracted three of the agents. In the process one of the helicopters was destroyed. The mission, having no radio with which to set up another extraction, was lost and within a week it was over.

Two of the men, Ranger Martin Watson and helicopter pilot Lieutenant (JG) John H. Thorton, were captured. Both survived the war and were released with other United Nations prisoners in **Operation Big Switch**.

Ed Evanhoe, *Dark Moon: Eighth Army Special Operations in the Korean War.* Annapolis, MD: Naval Institute Press, 1995, pp. 47–62.

Michael E. Haas, *In the Devil's Shadow: UN Special Operations During the Korean War.* Annapolis, MD: Naval Institute Press, 2000, pp. 56–57.

Operation Wolfpack   1 January 1952

Operation Wolfpack was the second formation of a partisan military group that would operate behind North Korean lines. As a result of thousands of refugees fleeing North Korea ahead of advancing Communist troops, many of them anxious to fight the invaders, the United States organized the Attrition Section under Guerrilla Section, Eighth Army G-3 (Miscellaneous) and a six-man core was established called **Operation Leopard**. When the number of partisans involved grew to more than 8,000 during May of 1951, Operation Wolfpack was formed. They were located first on the island of Yangpyong-do and then were moved to Kumhwa-do at the mouth of the Han River. This second group then took on the eastern part of Leopard's area of facility and ran operations in the section as far east as Sunui-do. They were also quickly involved in raids on the mainland, curtailing the movement of Chinese Communist Forces. Later, in early November 1952, Operation Leopard, Operation Wolfpack, and Task Force Scannon (originally Operation Kirkland) were redefined as United States Partisan Infantry Regiment, Korea 8240th AU.

Michael E. Haas, *In the Devil's Shadow: UN Special Operations during the Korean War.* Annapolis, MD: Naval Institute Press, 2000.

Conclusion

Having researched these operations, it seems only reasonable that I might have arrived at some conclusion about them. And yet, other than the fact they all involved men of great courage, the operations are both very much alike and share little in common. Perhaps that is the way of war, or perhaps only the burden of historians.

A significant number of the operations that are listed in this compilation were carried out successfully. Quite a number of the operations, well planned and anticipated, were cancelled even before they got started. Some few were postponed for a month or two and then re-established. Some operations conducted were nothing short of disastrous. The historian is hard put to try and evaluate them because the vast majority of them were a success, or a failure, in the context of the immediate situation. Making any "after-the-fact" analysis is difficult. Many were designed to take prisoners and in that regard were not all that successful, as prisoners became more difficult to find as the war went on. But at the same time they nevertheless successfully killed many of the enemy, destroyed some facilities, or furnished reconnaissance not previously available. To compare them is much like the much maligned comparison of oranges and apples.

Many of the ground operations were little less than campaigns and employed major numbers of troops. During much of the war the Marines fought as infantry and suffered the same shortages as did the rest of the ground forces. Generally speaking the larger of the operations were ground efforts and were carried out after considerable planning and even rehearsals, and were executed with flare and efficiency. Others, the smaller ones, were more focused and were more inclined to be activated on short notice and with under-prepared troops, and were not so successful.

During the war American air commanders tended to see victory in bombing the enemy into submission. In fact, Kathryn Weathersby, in a highly significant paper, "Ending the Korean War: Considerations on the Role of History," suggests that most of today's conflict with the North Koreans emerged from the saturation bombing conducted during the war. All in all the air operations were successful (and in effect destroyed much of North Korea) but they were not necessarily effective, limited in a good part by the UN rules forbidding attacks on targets in China. There is still much to be said for the fact that the North Korean capacity to survive was pretty much a match for the United Nations' ability to destroy.

The Air Force believed that it was operating with barebones facilities, limited personnel strength and obsolescent types of aircraft. But it was successful; that is, the goal identified by the operation was accomplished — railways were destroyed, tunnels demolished, buildings blown up, enemy ground troops attacked, Communist airplanes fought — but the long term justification for the mission was not often achieved. The interdiction did not stop

Communist supply, the raids of saturation did not bring the North Koreans to a standstill, and the scattered attacks on choke-points did not delay the movement of reinforcements. Many of the operations seemed to have been seen as a means to accomplish what was not being accomplished by routine services. Perhaps the next generation of historians will have more to work with and can answer some of these questions.

Naval operations were often very complex and were generally involved with some larger related mission. Certainly the UN naval forces were able to maintain their dominance on the seas, but just as surely were unable completely counteract shore and coastline defenses. In part this was true because of the lack of facilities. While the speed and size of reinforcements were impressive, base facilities in the Far East were marginal at best. The operational mission was to protect the seas, guard the coasts, deliver the goods, and reinforce the ground troops when needed, and naval forces completed all these missions. Smaller efforts, like tempting the enemy to come out and fight, were far less successful. The ease with which the naval forces were able to move up and down the coasts meant that they were great assets in support of Eighth Army and Tenth Corps. It is wise to remember the words of Malcolm Cagle, "Without command of the seas, between the Free World and Korea, and in the waters adjacent to that beleaguered peninsula, the Korean War, as fought, most certainly would have been lost both militarily and politically with a finality that would now be plain to every American" (Cagle and Manson).

A good number of the specialized operations were tight on focus and had a better record of successful completion. This is, of course, because many were functional rather than combat-related and success had to be determined in a different manner. **Operation Christmas Kiddie Lift**, under many names, had a significant humanitarian function but

was neither a complicated nor dangerous one. Many of the Marine helicopter experiments were extremely difficult and of significant service to the Marines at the time and the armed forces in general, and they were often dangerous, but they are difficult to compare to operations that were less experimental and more risky.

Recalling the services of American military and Central Intelligence Agency, as well as partisans who served in the many clandestine and covert actions in Korea, one must marvel at their courage and dedication. But despite this, any fair analysis of the total of their contribution must come up short. The most descriptive word to emerge from those few but excellent accounts of these services is *confusion*: confusion over organization, over mission, over training, and even over targets. There can be little doubt that the missions of interdiction and harassment must have caused the Communists some considerable difficulty, and perhaps even required them to station troops in areas that might otherwise have been more easily guarded. But in total one has to wonder if the gain was worth the risk. Michael Haas, historian and retired special operations officer, says it well. While the military had the resources, "its disdain for special operations and collective low opinion of unconventional warfare greatly diminished these inherent organizational strength." As far as the CIA efforts were concerned, Haas continued, "They fell into a counter-productive squabble from which only the Communists would benefit." Many things remain unexplained from that period, not the least of which is why military officers on special operations were not entitled to wear the Combat Infantryman's Badge or even a combat patch.

Although the Korean War was fought completely in Korea, the war was a global watershed. The United States, fearing that Korea was a potential first stage in World War III, increased its military budget massively, formed treaties with most of the Pacific nations, developed NATO, and committed to a separate nationalist government on Taiwan.

Michael E. Haas, *In the Devil's Shadow: U.N. Special Operations During the Korean War.* Annapolis, MD: Naval Institute Press, 2000, p. 211.

Malcolm W. Cagle and Frank A. Manson, *The Sea War in Korea.* Annapolis, MD: United States Naval Institute, 1957, p. 491.

Kathryn Weathersby, "Ending the Korean War: Considerations on the Role of History." Washington, D.C.: Working Paper Series: U.S.–Korea Institute at SAIS, 2008.

Appendix 1. United Nations Command Participants

Ground Forces

Country	1951	1952	1953
Australia	912	1,844	2,282
Belgium Volunteer	558	579	900
Canada	5,403	5,155	6,146
Columbia	1,050	1,007	1,068
Ethiopia	1,153	1,094	1,271
French Battalion	738	1,185	1,119
Greece Expeditionary Force	1,027	899	1,263
India (non-combatants)	333	276	70
Italy (non-combatants)	0	66	72
Luxembourg	44	44	44
Netherlands Detachment	725	565	819
New Zealand	797	1,111	1,389
Norway (non-combatants)	79	109	105
Philippine Expeditionary Forces	1,143	1,494	1,496
Sweden (non-combatants)	162	148	154
Republic of Korea	273,266	376,418	590,911
Royal Thai Forces	1,057	2,274	1,294
Turkish Brigade	4,602	4,878	5,455
United Kingdom	8,278	13,043	14,198
United States (all ground)	253,266	265,864	302,483

Naval Forces (Ships)

	1951	1952	1953
Republic of Korea	34	67	76
United States	186	195	261

As of October 1952

Australia	4
Canada	3
Colombia	1
Denmark	1
Netherlands	1
New Zealand	2
Thailand	2
United Kingdom	22

Air Forces by Squadron

Country	1951	1952	1953
Australia	1	1	1
Canada	1	1	1
South Africa	1	1	1
United States	58	67	66

Commanding General Eighth United States Army

Lieutenant General Walton H. Walker	3 September to 23 December 1950
Lieutenant General Matthew B. Ridgway	26 December 1950 to 13 April 1951
Lieutenant General James A. Van Fleet	14 April 1951 to 10 February 1953
Lieutenant General Maxwell D. Taylor	11 February 1953

Appendix 2. United States Ground Troops in Korea

Divisions

1st Cavalry Division ("The First Team")
2nd Infantry Division ("Indian Head Division")
3rd Infantry Division ("Marne Division")
7th Infantry Division ("Bayonet Division")
24th Infantry Division ("Victory Division")
25th Infantry Division ("Tropic Lightning Division")
40th Infantry Division ("Grizzly Division")
45th Infantry Division ("Thunderbird Division")
1st Marine Division

Separate Infantry Regiments

5th Regimental Combat Team
29th Infantry Regiment ("The Two Niner")
65th Regimental Combat Team ("Borinqueneers")
187th Airborne Regimental Combat Team ("The Rakkasans")

Appendix 3.
Communist Forces Involved

Chinese Communist:
Military Leaders at the Time
of China's Entry into the War

Commander-in Chief, PLA • Marshal Zhu De (Chu The)
Commander-in Chief, CPV • Marshall Peng Te'Huai (Peng Dehuai)
Commander, Northeast Defense Army • General Lin Piao
Commander, 9th Group Army • General Song Fang
Commander, 13th Group Army • General Li Tianyu

People's Liberation Army and Chinese Volunteer Army

The Chinese used deceptive designations to deceive UN Command as to the size and disposition of their troops. The following are those listed as committed to North Korea in November 1950. They were in two Army Groups, the 9th and 13th. In most cases an Army unit consisted of three infantry divisions.

9th Group Army

20th Army
26th Army
27th Army

13 Group Army

38th Army
39th Army
40th Army
50th Army
66th Army
42nd Army
1, 2nd, 8th Motorized Artillery Divisions

Democratic People's Republic of Korea:
Military Leaders at the Beginning of the War

KPA Front Headquarters • General Kim Chaek
I KPA Corps, Western • Lt. General Kim Ung
II KPA Corps, Eastern • Lt. General Kim Mu Chong
III KPA Corps, Reserves • Lt. General Yu Jyong Su
IV to VIII Corps were activated after China's entry.

Army as of July 1951

I KPA Corps — 8th, 9th, 47th KPA Divisions
II KPA Corps — 2nd, 13th and 27th KPA Divisions
III KPA Corps — 1st, 15th, and 45th KPA Divisions
IV KPA Corps — 4th, 5th, 26th Brigade
V KPA Corps — 6th, 12th, 32nd Division
VI KPA Corps — 9th 17th, 18, 23rd Division
VII KPS Corps — 3rd KPA Guards Division, 24th, 37th, 46th, 63rd Brigade

Air Force as of July 1951

1st Assault Aviation Regiment — 93 fighters
1st Fighter Aviation Regiment — 70 attack aircraft
1st Combined Regiment — 40–50 trainers

Navy as of July 1951

30 Japanese-made patrol boats and smaller craft
35 Soviet-provided medium patrol boats, torpedo boats and sweepers
1,000 ton Japanese-made troop transports
Approximately 14,000 personnel
A full strength infantry division of 11,000 to 12,000 men.
The minister of internal affairs held a 19,000 to 20,000 man border constabulary for coastal defense.

Appendix 4.
Korean War Campaigns

Army and Air Force Campaign Designation and Dates

UN Defensive	27 June to September 1950
UN Offensive	16 September to 1 November 1950
CCF Intervention	3 November 1950 to 24 January 1951
First UN Counteroffensive	25 January to 21 April 1951
CCF Spring Offensive	22 April to 8 July 1951
UN Summer–Fall Offensive	9 July to 27 November 1951
Second Korean Winter	1 May to 30 November 1952
Third Korean Winter	1 December 1952 to 30 April 1953
Korean Summer–Fall	1 May to 31 July 1953

Navy and Marine Campaign Designation and Dates

North Korean Aggression	27 June to 2 November 1950
Communist Chinese Aggression	3 November 1950 to 24 January 1951
Inchon Landing	13–17 September 1950
First UN Counteroffensive	25 January to 21 April 1951
CCF Spring Offensive	22 April to 8 July 1951
UN Summer–Fall Offensive	9 July to 27 November 1951
Second Korean Winter	28 November 1952 to 30 April 1952
Korean Defense Summer–Fall	1 May to 30 November 1952
Third Korean Winter	1 December 1952 to 30 April 1953
Korean Summer–Fall	1 May to 27 July 1953

United States Air Force Air Phases

Phase I	July 1950 to 25 November 1950
Air Phase II	25 November 1950 to 10 July 1951
Operation Strangle	Junet to August 1951
Air Phase III	10 July 1951 to 27 July 1953

Bibliography

No sources were discovered in which one can locate a listing of all the varied operations conducted during the Korean War. A good many of the operations are only briefly mentioned in the narrative histories and often ignored in the more specialized works. Some operations are discussed, or at least mentioned, in after-action reports, but these are fewer than expected. Additional information can be located from any of the works included in the bibliography; all were used in one fashion or another to locate materials for inclusion, or are excellent general references.

Primary Collections

Army Plans and Operations Division, Record Group 319, National Archives, Suitland, Maryland
Center for the Study of the Korean War, Graceland University, Independence, Missouri
Charles Givens, Papers and Memoirs
Norman O. Nelson Collection
Laurence Oglethorpe, Memoirs
Paul Wolfgeher Collection
Central Plains Region, National Archives and Records Administration, Kansas City, Missouri
Eisenhower Presidential Library and Museum, Abilene, Kansas
Modern Military Records Branch, National Archives, Washington, D.C.
Truman Presidential Museum and Library, Independence, Missouri
United States Military History Institute, Carlisle Barracks, Pennsylvania
United States Marine Corps History (Division) Navy Yard, Washington, D.C.

Electronic

The Canadian Army, Korea. http://wiki.galbijm.com/index

The Chosin Few. http://home.hawaii.rr.com.chosin/main.html
The Korean War. http://www.korean-war.com
Korean War Information. http://www.koreanwar.org
Korean War Net. http://www.koreanwar.net
Korean War Roundup. http://www.2id/org/volume 3/htm
Korean War Site. http://www.korean-war.com
Situation Maps. http://www.Kwanan.com//v//019.htm
Veterans History. http://www.theforgottenvictory.org

Secondary

Alexander, Bevin. *Korea: The First War We Lost.* New York: Hippocrene Books, 1986.
Alexander, Joseph H., and Merrill L. Bartlett. *Sea Soldiers in the Cold War: Amphibious Warfare 1945–1991.* Annapolis, MD: Naval Institute Press, 1995.
Appleman, Roy E. *Disaster in Korea.* College Station: Texas A&M University Press, 1989.
_____. *East of the Chosin: Entrapment and Breakout in Korea, 1950.* College Station: Texas A&M University Press, 1987.
_____. *Ridgway Duels for Korea.* College Station: Texas A&M University Press, 1990.
_____. *South to the Naktong, North to the Yalu.* U.S. Army in the Korean War Series, Washington, D.C.: U.S. Government Printing Office, 1961.
Ballenger, Lee. *The Outpost War: U.S. Marines in Korea.* Dulles, VA: Brassey's, 2000, 2001.
Bartlett, Merrill. *Assault from the Sea.* Annapolis, MD: Naval Institute Press, 1983.
Barlett, Norman. *With the Australians in Korea.* Canberra: Australian War Memorial, 1954.
Berebitsky, William. *A Very Long Weekend: The Army National Guard in Korea, 1950–1953.* Shippensburg, PA: White Mane, 1966.
Black, Robert W. *Rangers in Korea.* New York: Ivy Books, 1989.
Blair, Clay. *The Korean War: America in Korea 1950–1953.* New York: Times Books, 1987.
Breuer, William. *Shadow Warriors: The Covert Wars in Korea.* New York: John Wiley, 1996.
Brune, Lester, ed. *The Korean War: Handbook of the*

Literature and Research. Westport, CT: Greenwood Press, 1996.

Cagle, Malcolm W., and Frank A. Manson. *The Sea War in Korea.* Annapolis, MD: Naval Institute Press, 1957.

Carew, Tim. *Korea: The Commonwealth at War.* London: Cassell, 1967.

Catchpole, Brian. *The Korean War.* New York: Carroll and Graf, 2000.

Cho, Grace. *Haunting the Korean Diaspora: Shame, Secrecy, and the Forgotten War.* Minneapolis: University of Minnesota Press, 2008.

Clark, Eugene F. *The Secrets of Inchon: The Untold Story of the Most Daring Covert Mission of the Korean War.* New York: G.P. Putnam's Sons, 2002.

Coleman, Bradley Lynn. "The Colombian Army in Korea 1950–1954." *Journal of Military History,* Vol. 69, No. 4, October 2005, p. 1137.

_____. "Recovering the Korean War Dead, 1950–1958: Graves Registration, Forensic Anthropology, and Wartime Memorialization." *Journal of Military History,* Vol. 72, No. 1, 2007, p. 179.

Cunningham-Boothe, Ashley, and Peter N. Farrar. *British Forces in the Korean War.* Leamington Spa, England: British Korean Veterans Association, 1989.

Dailey, Edward L. *MacArthur's X Corps in Korea: Inchon to the Yalu, 1950.* Paducah, KY: Turner, 1999.

Darragh, Shawn M. "Hwanghae-do: The War of the Donkeys." *Army,* 34: 11 (November 1989), pp. 66–75.

Daskalopoulos, Ioannis. *The Greeks in Korea.* Washington, D.C.: Department of the Army, Office of the Assistant Chief of Staff for Intelligence, 1988.

Day, James Sanders. "Partisan Operations of the Korean War." Master's thesis, University of Georgia, 1989.

Doll, Thomas. *USN/USMC Over Korea: U.S. Navy/Marine Corps Air Operations Over Korea 1950–1953.* Carrollton, TX: Squadron/Signal Press, 1980.

Donnelly, William M. "Coalition Combat: Supporting South Korean Forces." *Joint Forces Quarterly* 28 (Spring-Summer) 2001, pp. 71–77.

Drury, Robert, and Tom Calvin. *The Last Stand of Fox Company: A True Story of the U.S. Marines in Combat.* New York: Grove/Atlantic, 2009.

Edwards, Paul M. *The Hill Wars of the Korean Conflict.* Jefferson, NC: McFarland, 2006.

_____. *Korean War Almanac.* New York: Facts on File, 2006.

Evanhoe, Ed. *Dark Moon: Eighth Army Special Operations in the Korean War.* Annapolis, MD: Naval Institute Press, 1995.

_____. "The Search for General Dean: CIA/Eighth Army Plan Dramatic Rescue of American General." *Behind the Lines* (September-October 1994), p. 22.

Farrar-Hockley, Anthony. *The British Part in the Korean War: A Distant Obligation.* London: hmso, 1990.

Field, James A., Jr. *History of United States Naval Operations: Korea.* Washington, D.C.: Director of Naval History, 1962.

Fleming, Thomas. "MacArthur's Pirates," *Military History Quarterly,* Summer 2000.

_____. *Secrets of Inchon: The Untold Story of the Most Daring Covert Mission of the Korean War.* G.P. Putnam's Sons, 2002.

Futrell, Robert Frank. *The United States Air Force in Korea 1950–1953.* Washington, D.C.: Office of Air Force History, 1981.

Goulden, Joseph C. *Korea: the Untold Story of the War.* New York: Times Books, 1982.

Grey, Jeffrey. *The Commonwealth Armies and the Korean War: An Alliance Study.* New York: Manchester University Press, 1988.

Gugeler, Russell A. *Combat Actions in Korea.* Washington, D.C.: Combat Forces Press, 1954.

Haas, Michael E. *In the Devil's Shadow: U.N. Special Operations in the Korean War.* Annapolis, MD: Naval Institute Press, 2000.

Hallion, Richard P. *The Naval Air War in Korea.* Baltimore, MD: Nautical and Aviation Publishing, 1986.

Hannings, Bud. *The Korean War: An Exhaustive Chronology,* 3 vols. McFarland, 2007.

Herman, Jan K. *Frozen in Memory: U.S. Navy Medicine in the Korean War.* Booklocker.com, 2006.

Hermes, Walter G. *Truce Tent and Fighting Front: United States Army in the Korean War.* Washington, D.C.: U.S. Army Center of Military History, 1966.

Holly, David C. "The ROK Navy: Reorganization After World War II with U.S. Aid: Its Record During the Korean Conflict." *Naval Institute Proceedings,* 78 (November 1952), pp. 1218–25.

Holober, Frank. *Raiders of the China Coast: CIA Covert Operations During the Korean War.* Annapolis, MD: Naval Institute Press, 1999.

Hughes, Charles. *Accordion War, Korea 1951: The Life and Death of a Marine Rifle Company.* South Carolina: Charles Hughes, 2006.

Huston, James A. *Guns and Butter, Powder and Rice: U.S. Army Logistics of the Korean War.* Selinsgrove, PA: Susquehanna University Press, 1989.

Johnston, William. *A War of Patrols: Canadian Army Operations in Korea.* Vancouver, B.C.: UBC Press, 2003.

Karig, Walter, Malcolm Cagle, and Frank A. Manson. *Battle Report: The War in Korea.* New York: Rinehart, 1952.

Kemp, Robert F. *Combined Operations in the Korean War.* Carlisle Barracks, PA: U.S. Army War College, 1989.

Kim Chum-kon. *The Korean War.* Seoul, Korea: Kwangnyong, 1973.

Knott, Richard C. *Attack From the Sky: Naval Air Operations in the Korean War.* Washington, D.C.: Naval Historical Center, 2004.

Kreisher, Otto. "The Rise of the Helicopter During the Korean War." *Aviation History,* January 2007.

Kublion, H. "The ROK Navy," *Naval Institute Proceedings* (October 1953): 1,134–135.

Lansdown, John R.P. *With the Carriers in Korea.* Winslow, England: Crecy, 1997.

Levine, Alan J. *Stalin's Last War: Korea and the Approach to World War III.* Jefferson, NC: McFarland, 2005.

Malcom, Ben S., and Ron Martz. *White Tiger: My Secret War in North Korea.* Washington, D.C.: Brassey's, 1996.

Marion, Forest L. "Air Force Special Operations Korean War Chronology." Hurlburt Field, Fla.: Air Force Special Operations Command/History Office, 1998.

Marshall, S.L.A. *Operation Punch and the Capture of Hill 440: Suwon, Korea, February 1951.* Chevy Chase, MD: Johns Hopkins University Press, 1952.

Matray, James I., ed. *Historical Dictionary of the Korean War.* Westport, CT: Greenwood Press, 1991.

McFarland, Keith. *The Korean War: An Annotated Bibliography.* Westport, CT: Greenwood Press, 2009.

McGibbon, Ira. *New Zealand and the Korean War, Volume II, Combat Operations.* Melbourne: Oxford University Press, 1996.

McManus, John C. *The 7th Regiment: Combat in an Age of Terror, The Korean War Through the Present.* New York: Macmillan Forge Books, 2008.

Meid, Pat, et al. *United States Marine Corps Operations in Korea, 1950–1953,* Vol. 5. Washington, D.C.: Headquarters, United States Marine Corps, 1972.

Meyers, Edward C. *Thunder in the Morning Calm: The Royal Canadian Navy in Korea, 1950–1953.* St. Catherines, Ontario: Vanwell, 1991.

Millett, Allan R. *The Korean War.* Washington, D.C.: Potomac, 2007.

_____. *This War for Korea: American, Asian, and European Combatants and Civilians, 1945–1953.* Washington, D.C.: Brassey's, 2002.

Miralda, Edward (ed). *The U.S. Navy in the Korean War.* Annapolis, MD: Naval Institute Press, 2007.

Montross, Lynn. *Cavalry of the Sky: The Story of the U.S. Marine Combat Helicopters.* New York: Harper and Brothers, 1954.

_____, Hubard D. Kuokka, and Norman W. Hicks. *U.S. Marine Operations in Korea 1950–1953,* 5 vols. Washington, D.C.: Headquarters, U.S. Marine Corps, 1962.

Mossman, Billy C. *U.S. Army in the Korean War: Ebb and Flow.* Washington, D.C.: Office of the Chief of Military History, 1990.

Nalty, Bernard C. *Outpost War: U.S. Marines from the Nevada Battles to the Armistice.* Washington, D.C.: Commemorative Series, U.S. Marine Corps Historical Center, 2001.

_____. *Stalemate: U.S. Marines from Bunker Hill to the Hook.* Washington, D.C.: Commemorative Series, U.S. Marine Corps Historical Center, 2001.

Nelson, Norman O. "Battles, Operations, and Outposts Found in the Korean War." Independence, MO: Graceland University, Center for the Study of the Korean War.

Neufeld, Jacob, and George W. Watson, Jr. (ed). *Coalition Warfare in the Korean War 1950–1953.* Washington, D.C.: United States Air Force History Museum, 2005.

O'Dowd, Ben. *In Valiant Company: Diggers in Battle— Korea, 1950–51.* Australia: University of Queensland Press, 2000.

Paik Sun Yup. *From Pusan to Panmunjom.* Dulles, VA: Brassey's, 1992.

Paschall, Rod. "Special Operations in Korea." *Conflict,* Vol. 7, No. 2, Washington, D.C.: Government Printing Office, nd.

Peate, Les. *The War That Wasn't: Canadians in the Korean War.* Ottawa, Canada: Esprit de Corps, 2005.

Price, Scott T. *The Forgotten Service in the Forgotten War: The U.S. Coast Guard's Role in the Korean Conflict.* Annapolis, MD: Naval Institute Press, 2000.

Rottman, Gordon L. *Korean War Order of Battle: United States, United Nations, and Communist Ground, Naval, and Air Forces, 1950–1953.* Westport, CT: Praeger, 2002.

Russell, William C. *Stalemate and Standoff: The Bloody Outpost War.* DeLeon Springs, FL: William Russell, 1993.

Sandler, Stanley. *The Korean War: An Encyclopedia.* New York: Garland, 1995.

Schnabel, James F. *Policy and Direction: The First Year.* Washington, D.C.: Office of the Chief of Military History, 1972.

Smith, W. Thomas, Jr. *Alpha Bravo Delta Guide to the Korean Conflict.* New York: Alpha Books, 2004.

Stanton, Shelby. *America's Tenth Legion: X Corps in Korea.* Novato, CA: Presidio Press, 1989.

Sullivan, John A. *Toy Soldiers: Memoirs of a Combat Platoon Leader in Korea.* Jefferson, NC: McFarland, 1991.

Summers, Harry G., Jr. *Korean War Almanac.* New York: Facts on File, 1990.

Toland, John. *In Mortal Combat: Korea, 1950–1953.* New York: William Morrow, 1991.

Tucker, Spencer, ed. *Encyclopedia of the Korean War,* 3 vols. Santa Barbara, CA: abc-clio, 2000.

Wang Xuedug, Richard Peters, and Xiaobing Li (eds.). "The Chosin Reservoir: A Chinese Captain's Story." *Voices from the Korean War: Personal Stories of American, Korean, and Chinese Soldiers.* Lexington: University of Kentucky Press, 2004.

Watson, Brent Bryon. *Far Eastern Tour: The Canadian Infantry in Korea 1950–1953.* Montreal: McGill-Queen's University Press, 2002.

Weathersby, Kathryn. "Ending the Korean War: Considerations on the Role of History." Working Paper Series. Washington, D.C.: U.S.–Korea Institute at SAIS, 2008.

Whelan, Richard. *Drawing the Line: The Korean War, 1950–1953.* Boston: Little Brown, 1990.

Wolfhgeher, Paul. "The Battle Hills, Outposts, Operations, and Battle Lines of the Korean War." Unpublished manuscript. Independence, MO: Graceland University, Center for the Study of the Korean War.

Xi Zhang. "China's Entry into the Korean War." *Chinese Historians* 6 (Spring 1993) pp. 1–30.

Index

Numbers in ***bold italics*** indicate pages with illustrations.